A Great American Philosopher

William James, brother of the famous novelist
Henry James, was born in New York City in
1842 and died in 1910. After graduating from
Harvard Medical School, he taught physiology.
Later his interests turned to psychology and,
finally, philosophy. Writing in a vivid and lucid
style, James won world-wide recognition for
his realistic philosophy. He and John Dewey
are considered the two most important minds
in American Philosophy.

Joseph L. Blau, Ph.D., author of the Introduction, is an Associate Professor of the Philosophy of Religion at Columbia University and
Director of the Institute for Ethical Studies,
New York Society for Ethical Culture. He has
published numerous books and articles in the
fields of philosophy and the history of ideas,
and is one of the founders of the Metropolitan
New York American Studies Association as
well as of the American Society for the Study
of Religion.

WILLIAM JAMES

PRAGMATISM AND OTHER ESSAYS

Introduction by Joseph L. Blau

WASHINGTON SQUARE PRESS
PUBLISHED BY POCKET BOOKS NEW YORK

A Washington Square Press Publication of
POCKET BOOKS, a Simon & Schuster division of
GULF & WESTERN CORPORATION
1230 Avenue of the Americas, New York, N.Y. 10020

ISBN: 0-671-46629-1

First Washington Square Press printing September, 1963

15 14 13 12 11 10 9 8 7

WASHINGTON SQUARE PRESS, WSP and colophon are
registered trademarks of Simon & Schuster.

Printed in the U.S.A.

CONTENTS

INTRODUCTION

The mind of the thoughtful man, in the latter part of the nineteenth century, was divided against itself. Intellectually, it was dominated by the scientific world view. Its physical concepts were those of a universe of atomic particles in determinate motion—what is frequently referred to as the "billiard ball universe" of nineteenth-century physics. Its views of life and of the biological sciences were driven in a similar direction by the impact of evolutionary thought, culminating in the theory of Darwin. Emotionally, however, it was still living in a pre-scientific universe, in which man was a special creation of a beneficent deity whose care and concern for his creatures was such that, when necessary, he performed miracles, setting aside the laws of nature on behalf of his favorites. The hard-headed insisted that human beings lived in a world in which consequences followed their antecedents with inexorable regularity, regardless of human wishes, hopes or ideals. The soft-hearted insisted that human desires and human efforts could make a difference to the course of events.

The distinction of William James (1842–1910) as a philosopher for the people during this period is that he presented with grace and clarity and with considerable learning a view that could reconcile hard-headedness and soft-heartedness. Professional philosophers have always distrusted James. He wrote too well; he expressed himself too clearly to be regarded as profound; however tortured may have been his own course in the reaching of a position, his style never betrayed him by being tortuous. He made philosophic thought seem too easy, within the reach of everyone. The questions that obsessed him were those that possessed the minds of his contemporaries, rather than the special technical questions of the philosophic fraternity. Throughout his later years, he was forever promising himself to write an exposition of his philosophic position in a technical fashion for the benefit of his professional brothers, but he died leaving only fragments of this statement. Yet among American philosophers no other except Ralph Waldo Emerson has been so widely read both at home and in Europe, and no other has been so heartily welcomed as a spokesman for a characteristically American attitude of mind.

Although the works for which William James is chiefly remembered as philosopher were written during the last decade of his life, his introduction to philosophy came early. His father, the elder Henry James, was a man of independent means who devoted the greater part of his life to developing a profound but eccentric philosophic theology. At the James's dinner table, it was an everyday affair for the conversation to center on some philosophic issue; the father apparently enjoyed getting the discussion started and then sitting back and listening to his children's efforts to resolve problems that had troubled the world's outstanding thinkers for generations, if not centuries. From this time on, William James had a lasting interest in philosophy and joined enthusiastically with his friends in informal discussions of "metaphysical" questions. Indeed, the view for which he was later to become celebrated was formed in one such discussion group, dominated by Charles Sanders Peirce, in about 1870. William James wrote, during the 1870's and 1880's, a few papers of philosophic content, in which the seeds of his later position were sowed. But it was not until 1897 that he turned his professional interest to philosophy.

James and his brothers were educated in a most irregular fashion. Their father was as much at home in Europe as in America, and his mobility became the pattern of life for the whole family. William could not make up his mind what career he wanted to follow. He thought he might become an artist, but he also was drawn to a career in science. Characteristically, his father gave him the opportunity to explore both possibilities. Ultimately, he became a doctor, and was appointed to Harvard College to teach physiology in 1872. Four years later, he was responsible for the establishment of a small, and admittedly inadequate psychological laboratory at Harvard; he had been impressed by the new discipline of physiological psychology that was being brought to birth in the psychological laboratories of the German universities, and he hoped to bring about a similar study in America. Characteristically, James himself used the laboratory very little; there is a record of his experimental studies of dizziness carried on there, but James was not particularly a laboratory scientist. The importance of the Harvard laboratory is that, despite its limitations, some of the students who trained there were led to go further in their later studies.

James was, by this time, more interested in the general field of psychology than in the special area where psychology and physiology overlap. He moved into the department of philosophy, in the first instance, in order to teach his version of psychology. He was widely read in French and British as well as German writers on psychology, so that his course and his system came to include a selection of themes from the typical emphases of the European systems. Because of this breadth of approach, he was able to break through the type of psychology, based largely on British models, that was then dominant in the American colleges. For more than a century, British psychology had been locked in an embrace of death with a theory of knowledge based upon a strict dualism of mind and matter and insisting that the mind was the passive recipient of simple impressions from an external world. These simple impressions were not themselves impressions of objects, but of unrelated qualities. In order to form ideas of objects, the hitherto passive mind had to bring constellations of qualities into relations with each other. The way in which the mind did this was by association of like impressions. For this "associational" psychology James substituted an analysis of mind as a sort of behavior with relation to the external world. Mind, to him, was an activity, a dynamic process; he regarded it, somewhat in the light of evolutionary biology, as one of the processes by means of which the human organism adjusted to and integrated with its environment.

In 1890, after some eleven years of work, James published a remarkable two-volume treatise on *The Principles of Psychology*. Most reviewers immediately recognized the book for the important work that it was; a few were less kind to it. One of the complaints was that the book was too well written; this was a major element in the review by James Sully in *Mind*. Another, more justified criticism was that the organization of James's book was too unsystematic, too personal in tone. Perhaps the review of the *Principles* by James's old friend, G. Stanley Hall, best illustrates this criticism: "Passing now to *the work as a whole,* the author might be described as an *impressionist* in psychology. His portfolio contains sketches old and new, ethical, literary, scientific and metaphysical, some exquisite and charming in detail and even color, others rough charcoal outlines, but all together stimulating and suggestive, and showing great industry and versatility. . . . The author is a veritable storm-bird, fascinated by problems most impossible of solution, and surest where specialists and experts in his own field are most in doubt, and finding it very hard to get up interest in the most important matters, if settled and agreed to, even to state them well." Hall defended the principle of association and other more traditional doctrines of the psychology of the period against James's attacks, yet in the end he was perceptive enough to say: "It is on the whole and after all the best work in any language, and we earnestly advise anyone with the least interest in psychology to own and study it."

Discounting the stylistic criticism—for, after all, it is not necessary for a good book to be dull—the most remarkable feature of James's *Principles* is its anticipation of the directions in which twentieth-century psychology was to move. Probably few of its specific statements on points of detail would be accepted today, but its general approach is far more suggestive of that of the psychoanalysts and of the *Gestalt* school than of either the traditional empirical psychology of the British or the metaphysical psychology of the Germans (prior to the development of experimentalism). Perhaps the most startlingly "modern" aspect of James's psychology was his inclusion of non-intellectual factors in his analysis. For him, the emotions and the sub- and unconscious processes were every bit as important as and much more interesting than the conscious processes. His most influential discussion, concerned with the "stream of consciousness," flowed from his novel functional and behavioral interpretation of psychology and had important consequences for his philosophy as well as for twentieth-century literature.

Prior to James, consciousness had been treated, in the tradition of British empiricism, as a succession of separate, unrelated mental impressions. Sometimes, said James, in order to improve our "conceptual handling" of experience, it may be useful to talk as if there were these separate perceptions and conceptions in it. But in actuality there are no such distinct divisions. We must not assume that the arbitrary separation that we introduce for our own convenience describes the reality of consciousness. Instead, he insisted, consciousness is a steady flow, a stream of ideas, perceptions and relations. Some of this flow is at the center of our attention at any one time; but even when our concern is focused on the center, there is an awareness of a penumbra of sensations and fleeting impressions. Furthermore, James thought, "No one ever had a simple sensation by itself. Consciousness, from our natal day, is of a teeming multiplicity of objects and relations, and what we call simple sensations are results of discriminative attention, pushed often to a very high degree." As a consequence of this emphasis, every thought, since it marks off a part of the on-going stream of consciousness by selective attention, "tends to be part of a personal consciousness" within which the selection goes on. To put this point more sharply, awareness of self is a consequence of the focusing of attention on momentary states of the stream of consciousness.

Viewed from the perspective of his later philosophy, which he called "radical empiricism," the most significant aspect of his psychological discussion of the stream of consciousness was his insistence that consciousness of relations is part of the stream, not a construction of the mind superimposed upon atoms of sensation. "If there be such things as feelings at all, *then so surely as relations between objects exist in rerum natura, so surely, and more surely, do feelings exist to which these relations are known.*" When James translated this statement into the language of his philosophy, it became the factual proposition that "the relations between things, conjunctive as well as disjunctive, are just as much matters of direct particular experience, neither more so nor less so, than the things themselves." Coupled with the postulate that the proper material for philosophic debate "shall be things definable in terms drawn from experience," his proposition concerning relations led to a "generalized conclusion . . . that therefore the parts of experience hold together from next to next by relations that are themselves parts of experience." We do not need to import, either from the realm of the supernatural or from the transcendent nature of the mind itself, an explanation of the connectedness of the universe of our experience. "The directly apprehended universe . . . possesses in its own right a concatenated or continuous structure." Relations are objectively present in the universe; they are subjectively present in our experience of the universe.

In general, James's psychology and his philosophy were very closely interlinked. In the preface to his *Principles of Psychology* he claimed to have excluded metaphysical speculation from that work; his reviewers did not agree that he had done so successfully. In his philosophical writings, and notably in those collected in this volume, his psychological orientation led him to an absorbing interest in the subjective conditions of belief rather than to a concern for the objective evidences of truth. This is the basic difference between James and his friend, Charles Sanders Peirce, who invented the term "pragmatism" which James popularized. For Peirce, pragmatism was a theory of meaning, akin to the procedures of the laboratory scientist. The meaning of any statement, for Peirce, is determined by the sum of its verifiable consequences. Another way of saying this is that there is a series of propositions deducible from any statement; some of these propositions can be tested by laboratory procedures or their equivalent, while some can not be so tested. The meaning of the original statement can be given by an exhaustive listing of the testable propositions that follow from it. The truth of the statement is something else again; for Peirce it is the correspondence of the assertion in the statement with the consensus that would be reached by an infinite assemblage of qualified and objective investigators if their investigations were carried out far enough. Peirce's definitions of both truth and meaning depended upon public procedures. James's definitions of both truth and meaning were far more subjective and personal.

Like Peirce, James thought of meaning in terms of the consequences of a statement, for in all forms of pragmatism meaning and truth are located in the future rather than in the past. But the consequences to which James turned in the search for meaning were personal rather than social, private rather than public. The meaning of a statement to me is to be found in its particular consequences in my future practical experience even as its meaning for you will emerge in your future experience. One might translate James here by saying that the meaning is to be found in the continuing flow of one's stream of consciousness. The meaning of a statement is the use to which I can put it. Similarly, he personalized his theory of truth; a true statement is one that leads me to achieve, in my future experience, the results I anticipate and thus satisfy my expectations while a false statement does not lead to the results I anticipate. In investigating the truth or falsity of a statement, the question we are asking, said James, is "what concrete difference will its being true make in any one's actual life?" If this is what truth means, then it is clear that a statement is not to be called true at the moment when it is made; we can call it true only after its particular consequences in someone's future experience have occurred. This is what we must understand by James's insistence that "the truth of an idea is not a stagnant property inherent in it. Truth *happens* to an idea. It *becomes* true, is *made* true by events." Truth is, then, a process of discovery.

As far as scientific ideas are concerned, there would be no significant difference between Peirce and James, since for James one of the criteria of true statements as satisfactory guides was social. "True ideas," he said, "lead to consistency, stability, and flowing human intercourse. They lead away from excentricity and isolation, from foiled and barren thinking." The difference appears only when one comes to consider the sort of statement which does not have directly verifiable consequences of a public nature. With respect to such statements, James was prepared to examine the consequences of *belief* in the statement instead of the consequences of the statement itself. If belief in the statement makes a difference in the life experiences of those who believe, James was willing to grant the statement what he called "truth value." The psychologist in James even went so far as to take note that there are some instances "where faith in a fact can help create the fact." In those cases, James said in his famous essay entitled "The Will to Believe," in which there is no valid intellectual reason for choosing between conflicting propositions, we have a right to believe in that alternative which will have the most satisfactory consequences as a result of our belief, in the long run, and insofar as we can foresee the consequences. Truth and usefulness have become completely fused in James's theory. Thus, while James's view of truth developed out of a scientific approach that would completely satisfy the hard-headed of his time, by introducing the "will to believe," he had made a place for the needs of the soft-hearted.

In his final summation of the "notion of truth," James said that " 'the true,' to put it very briefly, is only the expedient in the way of our thinking, just as 'the right' is only the expedient in the way of our behaving." This denial of absolute truth did not sit well with James's younger colleague in the Harvard department of philosophy, Josiah Royce, who wondered whether James would be satisfied to put a witness on the stand in court and have him swear to tell "the expedient, the whole expedient, and nothing but the expedient, so help him future experience." And certainly even those members of the clergy who appreciated the help that James's "will to believe" gave the doctrine of the existence of God were unhappy about James's treatment of "the right" as merely expedient behavior rather than conformity to an absolute ethical standard. James himself never denied that there might be an ethical standard; but he found that all attempts to state such a standard lacked universal applicability. He found in them all, however, a common feature, namely, that all are attempts to satisfy the demands of some conscious being, and he formulated as his moral standard the satisfaction of demands. Ideally, all the demands of everyone concerned might theoretically be satisfied by the same action; in practice, however, demands are always in conflict. In resolving this difficulty, James was led to a virtual restatement of the "greatest happiness" principle of the Utilitarians; that course is good, or is to be chosen, that will satisfy the greatest number of demands of the greatest number of people. It is, in short, "the expedient in the way of our behaving."

Many philosophers have been deeply impressed by the unity that they found in the world (or imposed upon it). James was most deeply impressed by its variety, its pluralism. "The word 'or,' " he once wrote, "names a genuine reality." He thought of his "pluralistic universe" somewhat after the model of the "stream of consciousness." The ultimate constitution of reality is neither simple unity nor disjointed multiplicity but a "strung-along" connectedness. "Every part, tho it may not be in actual or immediate connexion, is nevertheless in some possible or mediated connexion, with every other part however remote, through the fact that each part hangs together with its very next neighbors in inextricable interfusion." He recognized that this account of the universe depended upon his prior discussions "of the confluence of every passing moment of concretely felt experience with its immediately next neighbors." His pluralistic view was opposed, on the one hand, to that of the idealists, like Royce, for whom all diversity was swallowed up by the Absolute, and, on the other hand, to the piecemeal universe of the usual version of empiricism, with its "chopping up experience into atomistic sensations, incapable of union with one another until a purely intellectual principle has swooped down upon them from on high and folded them in its own conjunctive categories."

Differences of world view such as these he ascribed to differences of temperament. "A philosophy is the expression of a man's intimate character, and all definitions of the universe are but deliberately adopted reactions of human characters upon it." We are, therefore, entitled to look to James's own philosophy for evidence as to what kind of man he was, for although a philosopher gives impersonal reasons for his conclusions, "his temperament really gives him a stronger bias than any of his more strictly objective premises."

What kind of man was William James? He was a man whose training in the hard-headedness of science never completely subdued his soft-hearted belief that men are not merely automata, strictly determined in a mechanical world, but are, at least to some degree, the makers and shapers of their world. He was a man whose soft-heartedness never led him to the absurdity of arguing counter to the evidence, for he insisted, hard-headedly, that there are fields in which exact scientific knowledge is possible. Withal, he was a man who was eternally ready to lend a sympathetic ear to the wildest of theories because he could not be convinced that all wisdom was of the academy or that there was only one clearly marked road to truth. He was interested in the new, rather than the old; the might-be-true, rather than the has-been-true; the future rather than the past. The universe in which he lived was open on every hand. Perhaps his most characteristic utterance was one of delight in his summer home, with fourteen doors, all opening outward. For, as Jerome Nathanson has so well said, "The doors of his soul as well opened out to the multifarious experiences of a moving world, in which nothing was settled and so much remained to be done."

JOSEPH L. BLAU

BIBLIOGRAPHY

1. WORKS OF WILLIAM JAMES (chronologically arranged)

The Literary Remains of the Late Henry James, William James, ed., Boston, J. R. V. Osgood, 1885.

Principles of Psychology, New York, Henry Holt & Co., 1890, 2 vols.

Psychology, Briefer Course, New York, Henry Holt & Co., 1892.

The Will to Believe, and Other Essays in Popular Philosophy, New York, Longmans, Green & Co., 1897.

Human Immortality: Two Supposed Objections to the Doctrine, Boston, Houghton, Mifflin & Co., 1898.

Talks to Teachers on Psychology: and to Students on Some of Life's Ideals, New York, Henry Holt & Co., 1900.

The Varieties of Religious Experience: A Study in Human Nature, New York, Longmans, Green & Co., 1902.

Pragmatism: A New Name for Some Old Ways of Thinking, New York, Longmans, Green & Co., 1907.

The Meaning of Truth, A Sequel to "Pragmatism," New York, Longmans, Green & Co., 1909.

A Pluralistic Universe: Hibbert Lectures on the Present Situation in Philosophy, New York, Longmans, Green & Co., 1909.

Some Problems of Philosophy: A Beginning of an Introduction to Philosophy, New York, Longmans, Green & Co., 1911. (posthumous)

Memories and Studies, New York, Longmans, Green & Co., 1911. (posthumous)

Essays in Radical Empiricism, New York, Longmans, Green & Co., 1912. (posthumous)

Collected Essays and Reviews, New York, Longmans, Green & Co., 1920. (posthumous)

Letters of William James, edited by his son, Henry James, Boston, The Atlantic Monthly Press, 1920.

II. WORKS ABOUT WILLIAM JAMES

Blau, Joseph L., "Pragmatic Perspectives," in *Men and Movements in American Philosophy,* New York, Prentice Hall, 1952, Chap. 7.

Nathanson, Jerome, "William James: The Possibilities of Effort," in *Forerunners of Freedom,* Washington, American Council on Public Affairs, 1941, Chap. 3.

Otto, M.C. et. al. *In Commemoration of William James, 1842–1892,* Madison, Wisconsin, The University of Madison, 1942.

Perry, Ralph Barton, *The Thought and Character of William James,* Boston, Little Brown & Co., 1935. 2 vols. (also abridged in one vol.)

Schneider, Herbert W., "Radical Empiricism," in *A History of American Philosophy,* New York, Columbia University Press, 1946. Part VIII.

William James, the Man and the Thinker, New York, Columbia University Press, 1942.

PRAGMATISM

AUTHOR'S PREFACE TO
PRAGMATISM

The lectures that follow were delivered at the Lowell Institute in Boston in November and December, 1906, and in January, 1907, at Columbia University, in New York. They are printed as delivered, without developments or notes. The pragmatic movement, so-called—I do not like the name, but apparently it is too late to change it—seems to have rather suddenly precipitated itself out of the air. A number of tendencies that have always existed in philosophy have all at once become conscious of themselves collectively, and of their combined mission; and this has occurred in so many countries, and from so many different points of view, that much unconcerted statement has resulted. I have sought to unify the picture as it presents itself to my own eyes, dealing in broad strokes, and avoiding minute controversy. Much futile controversy might have been avoided, I believe, if our critics had been willing to wait until we got our message fairly out.

If my lectures interest any reader in the general subject, he will doubtless wish to read farther. I therefore give him a few references.

In America, John Dewey's *Studies in Logical Theory* are the foundation. Read also by Dewey the articles in the *Philosophical Review*, vol. xv, pp. 113 and 465, in *Mind*, vol. xv, p. 293, and in the *Journal of Philosophy*, vol. iv, p. 197.

Probably the best statements to begin with, however, are F. C. S. Schiller's in his *Studies in Humanism*, especially the essays numbered i, v, vi, vii, xviii and xix. His previous essays and in general the polemic literature of the subject are fully referred to in his footnotes.

Furthermore, see J. Milhaud: *le Rationnel*, 1898, and the fine articles by Le Roy in the *Revue de Métaphysique*, vols.

3

7, 8 and 9. Also articles by Blondel and De Sailly in the *Annales de Philosophie Chrétienne*, 4me Série, vols. 2 and 3. Papini announces a book on Pragmatism, in the French language, to be published very soon.

To avoid one misunderstanding at least, let me say that there is no logical connexion between pragmatism, as I understand it, and a doctrine which I have recently set forth as "radical empiricism." The latter stands on its own feet. One may entirely reject it and still be a pragmatist.

HARVARD UNIVERSITY, April, 1907.

THE PRESENT DILEMMA
IN PHILOSOPHY

In the preface to that admirable collection of essays of his called *Heretics*, Mr. Chesterton writes these words: "There are some people—and I am one of them—who think that the most practical and important thing about a man is still his view of the universe. We think that for a landlady considering a lodger it is important to know his income, but still more important to know his philosophy. We think that for a general about to fight an enemy it is important to know the enemy's numbers, but still more important to know the enemy's philosophy. We think the question is not whether the theory of the cosmos affects matters, but whether in the long run anything else affects them."

I think with Mr. Chesterton in this matter. I know that you, ladies and gentlemen, have a philosophy, each and all of you, and that the most interesting and important thing about you is the way in which it determines the perspective in your several worlds. You know the same of me. And yet I confess to a certain tremor at the audacity of the enterprise which I am about to begin. For the philosophy which is so important in each of us is not a technical matter; it is our more or less dumb sense of what life honestly and deeply means. It is only partly got from books; it is our individual way of just seeing and feeling the total push and pressure of the cosmos. I have no right to assume that many of you are students of the cosmos in the classroom sense, yet here I stand desirous of interesting you in a philosophy which to no small extent has to be technically treated. I wish to fill you with sympathy with a contemporaneous tendency in which I profoundly believe, and yet I have to talk like a professor to you who are not students. Whatever universe a professor believes in must at any rate be

5

a universe that lends itself to lengthy discourse. A universe
definable in two sentences is something for which the profes-
sorial intellect has no use. No faith in anything of that cheap
kind! I have heard friends and colleagues try to popularize
philosophy in this very hall, but they soon grew dry, and then
technical, and the results were only partially encouraging. So
my enterprise is a bold one. The founder of pragmatism himself recently gave a course of lectures at the Lowell Institute
with that very word in its title—flashes of brilliant light re-
lieved against Cimmerian darkness! None of us, I fancy, understood *all* that he said—yet here I stand, making a very
similar venture.

I risk it because the very lectures I speak of *drew*—they
brought good audiences. There is, it must be confessed, a curious fascination in hearing deep things talked about, even
though neither we nor the disputants understand them. We
get the problematic thrill, we feel the presence of the vastness.
Let a controversy begin in a smoking-room anywhere, about
free-will or God's omniscience, or good and evil, and see how
every one in the place pricks up his ears. Philosophy's results
concern us all most vitally, and philosophy's queerest arguments tickle agreeably our sense of subtlety and ingenuity.

Believing in philosophy myself devoutly, and believing also
that a kind of new dawn is breaking upon us philosophers, I
feel impelled, *per fas aut nefas,* to try to impart to you some
news of the situation.

Philosophy is at once the most sublime and the most trivial
of human pursuits. It works in the minutest crannies and it
opens out the widest vistas. It "bakes no bread," as has been
said, but it can inspire our souls with courage; and repugnant
as its manners, its doubting and challenging, its quibbling and
dialectics, often are to common people, no one of us can get
along without the far-flashing beams of light it sends over the
world's perspectives. These illuminations at least, and the con-
trast-effects of darkness and mystery that accompany them,
give to what it says an interest that is much more than professional.

The history of philosophy is to a great extent that of a certain clash of human temperaments. Undignified as such a
treatment may seem to some of my colleagues, I shall have to
take account of this clash and explain a good many of the di-
vergencies of philosophers by it. Of whatever temperament a

professional philosopher is, he tries, when philosophizing, to sink the fact of his temperament. Temperament is no conventionally recognized reason, so he urges impersonal reasons only for his conclusions. Yet his temperament really gives him a stronger bias than any of his more strictly objective premises. It loads the evidence for him one way or the other, making for a more sentimental or a more hard-hearted view of the universe, just as this fact or that principle would. He trusts his temperament. Wanting a universe that suits it, he believes in any representation of the universe that does suit it. He feels men of opposite temper to be out of key with the world's character, and in his heart considers them incompetent and "not in it," in the philosophic business, even though they may far excel him in dialectical ability.

Yet in the forum he can make no claim, on the bare ground of his temperament, to superior discernment or authority. There arises thus a certain insincerity in our philosophic discussions: the potentest of all our premises is never mentioned. I am sure it would contribute to clearness if in these lectures we should break this rule and mention it, and I accordingly feel free to do so.

Of course I am talking here of very positively marked men, men of radical idiosyncracy, who have set their stamp and likeness on philosophy and figure in its history. Plato, Locke, Hegel, Spencer, are such temperamental thinkers. Most of us have, of course, no very definite intellectual temperament, we are a mixture of opposite ingredients, each one present very moderately. We hardly know our own preferences in abstract matters; some of us are easily talked out of them, and end by following the fashion or taking up with the beliefs of the most impressive philosopher in our neighborhood, whoever he may be. But the one thing that has *counted* so far in philosophy is that a man should *see* things, see them straight in his own peculiar way, and be dissatisfied with any opposite way of seeing them. There is no reason to suppose that this strong temperamental vision is from now onward to count no longer in the history of man's beliefs.

Now the particular difference of temperament that I have in mind in making these remarks is one that has counted in literature, art, government, and manners as well as in philosophy. In manners we find formalists and free-and-easy persons. In government, authoritarians and anarchists. In literature,

purists or academicals, and realists. In art, classics and roman-
tics. You recognize these contrasts as familiar; well, in philosophy we have a very similar contrast expressed in the pair
of terms "rationalist" and "empiricist," "empiricist" meaning
your lover of facts in all their crude variety, "rationalist"
meaning your devotee to abstract and eternal principles. No
one can live an hour without both facts and principles, so it
is a difference rather of emphasis; yet it breeds antipathies of
the most pungent character between those who lay the emphasis differently; and we shall find it extraordinarily convenient to express a certain contrast in men's ways of taking
their universe, by talking of the "empiricist" and of the "rationalist" temper. These terms make the contrast simple and
massive.

More simple and massive than are usually the men of
whom the terms are predicated. For every sort of permu-
tation and combination is possible in human nature; and
if I now proceed to define more fully what I have in mind
when I speak of rationalists and empiricists, by adding to
each of those titles some secondary qualifying characteristics,
I beg you to regard my conduct as to a certain extent arbitrary.
I select types of combination that nature offers very frequently, but by no means uniformly, and I select them
solely for their convenience in helping me to my ulterior
purpose of characterizing pragmatism. Historically we find
the terms "intellectualism" and "sensationalism" used as syn-
onyms of "rationalism" and "empiricism." Well, nature seems
to combine most frequently with intellectualism an idealistic
and optimistic tendency. Empiricists on the other hand are
not uncommonly materialistic, and their optimism is apt to
be decidedly conditional and tremulous. Rationalism is always
monistic. It starts from wholes and universals, and makes
much of the unity of things. Empiricism starts from the parts,
and makes of the whole a collection—is not averse therefore
to calling itself pluralistic. Rationalism usually considers itself
more religious than empiricism, but there is much to say
about this claim, so I merely mention it. It is a true claim
when the individual rationalist is what is called a man of
feeling, and when the individual empiricist prides himself on
being hard-headed. In that case the rationalist will usually also
be in favor of what is called free-will, and the empiricist will
be a fatalist—I use the terms most popularly current. The

rationalist finally will be of dogmatic temper in his affirmations, while the empiricist may be more sceptical and open to discussion.

I will write these traits down in two columns. I think you will practically recognize the two types of mental make-up that I mean if I head the columns by the titles "tender-minded" and "tough-minded" respectively.

THE TENDER-MINDED.	THE TOUGH-MINDED.
Rationalistic (going by "principles")	Empiricist (going by "facts")
Intellectualistic	Sensationalistic
Idealistic	Materialistic
Optimistic	Pessimistic
Religious	Irreligious
Free-willist	Fatalistic
Monistic	Pluralistic
Dogmatical	Sceptical

Pray postpone for a moment the question whether the two contrasted mixtures which I have written down are each inwardly coherent and self-consistent or not—I shall very soon have a good deal to say on that point. It suffices for our immediate purpose that tender-minded and tough-minded people, characterized as I have written them down, do both exist. Each of you probably knows some well-marked example of each type, and you know what each example thinks of the example on the other side of the line. They have a low opinion of each other. Their antagonism, whenever as individuals their temperaments have been intense, has formed in all ages a part of the philosophic atmosphere of the time. It forms a part of the philosophic atmosphere to-day. The tough think of the tender as sentimentalists and soft-heads. The tender feel the tough to be unrefined, callous, or brutal. Their mutual reaction is very much like that that takes place when Bostonian tourists mingle with a population like that of Cripple Creek. Each type believes the other to be inferior to itself; but disdain in the one case is mingled with amusement, in the other it has a dash of fear.

Now, as I have already insisted, few of us are tenderfoot Bostonians pure and simple, and few are typical Rocky Mountain toughs, in philosophy. Most of us have a hankering for the good things on both sides of the line. Facts are good, of course—give us lots of facts. Principles are good—give us plenty of principles. The world is indubitably one if you look at it in one way, but as indubitably is it many, if you look at it in another. It is both one and many—let us adopt a sort of pluralistic monism. Everything of course is necessarily determined, and yet of course our wills are free: a sort of free-will determinism is the true philosophy. The evil of the parts in undeniable, but the whole can't be evil: so practical pessimism may be combined with metaphysical optimism. And so forth—your ordinary philosophic layman never being a radical, never straightening out his system, but living vaguely in one plausible compartment of it or another to suit the temptations of successive hours.

But some of us are more than mere laymen in philosophy. We are worthy of the name of amateur athletes, and are vexed by too much inconsistency and vacillation in our creed. We cannot preserve a good intellectual conscience so long as we keep mixing incompatibles from opposite sides of the line.

And now I come to the first positively important point which I wish to make. Never were as many men of a decidedly empiricist proclivity in existence as there are at the present day. Our children, one may say, are almost born scientific. But our esteem for facts has not neutralized in us all religiousness. It is itself almost religious. Our scientific temper is devout. Now take a man of this type, and let him be also a philosophic amateur, unwilling to mix a hodgepodge system after the fashion of a common layman, and what does he find his situation to be, in this blessed year of our Lord 1906? He wants facts; he wants science; but he also wants a religion. And being an amateur and not an independent originator in philosophy he naturally looks for guidance to the experts and professionals whom he finds already in the field. A very large number of you here present, possibly a majority of you, are amateurs of just this sort.

Now what kinds of philosophy do you find actually offered to meet your need? You find an empirical philosophy that is not religious enough, and a religious philosophy that is not empirical enough for your purpose. If you look to the quarter where facts are most considered you find the whole tough-minded program in operation, and the "conflict between science and religion" in full blast. Either it is that Rocky

Mountain tough of a Haeckel with his materialistic monism, his ether-god and his jest at your God as a "gaseous verte-brate"; or it is Spencer treating the world's history as a redistribution of matter and motion solely, and bowing religion politely out at the front door—she may indeed continue to exist, but she must never show her face inside the temple.

For a hundred and fifty years past the progress of science has seemed to mean the enlargement of the material universe and the diminution of man's importance. The result is what one may call the growth of naturalistic or positivistic feeling. Man is no lawgiver to nature, he is an absorber. She it is who stands firm; he it is who must accommodate himself. Let him record truth, inhuman though it be, and submit to it! The romantic spontaneity and courage are gone, the vision is materialistic and depressing. Ideals appear as inert by-products of physiology; what is higher is explained by what is lower and treated forever as a case of "nothing but"—nothing but something else of a quite inferior sort. You get, in short, a materialistic universe, in which only the tough-minded find themselves congenially at home.

If now, on the other hand, you turn to the religious quarter of consolation, and take counsel of the tender-minded philosophies, what do you find?

Religious philosophy in our day and generation is, among us English-reading people, of two main types. One of these is more radical and aggressive, the other has more the air of fighting a slow retreat. By the more radical wing of religious philosophy I mean the so-called transcendental idealism of the Anglo-Hegelian school, the philosophy of such men as Green, the Cairds, Bosanquet, and Royce. This philosophy has greatly influenced the more studious members of our protestant minis-try. It is pantheistic, and undoubtedly it has already blunted the edge of the traditional theism in protestantism at large.

That theism remains, however. It is the lineal descendant, through one stage of concession after another, of the dogmatic scholastic theism still taught rigorously in the seminaries of the catholic church. For a long time it used to be called among us the philosophy of the Scottish school. It is what I meant by the philosophy that has the air of fighting a slow retreat. Between the encroachments of the hegelians and other philosophers of the "Absolute," on the one hand, and those of the scientific evolutionists and agnostics, on the other, the men that give us this kind of a philosophy, James Martineau, Professor Bowne, Professor Ladd and others, must feel themselves rather tightly squeezed. Fair-minded and candid as you like, this philosophy is not radical in temper. It is eclectic, a thing of compromises, that seeks a *modus vivendi* above all things. It accepts the facts of darwinism, the facts of cerebral physiology, but it does nothing active or enthusiastic with them. It lacks the victorious and aggressive note. It lacks *prestige* in consequence; whereas absolutism has a certain *prestige* due to the more radical style of it.

These two systems are what you have to choose between if you turn to the tender-minded school. And if you are the lovers of facts I have supposed you to be, you find the trail of the serpent of rationalism, of intellectualism, over everything that lies on that side of the line. You escape indeed the materialism that goes with the reigning empiricism; but you pay for your escape by losing contact with the concrete parts of life. The more absolutistic philosophers dwell on so high a level of abstraction that they never even try to come down. The absolute mind which they offer us, the mind that makes our universe by thinking it, might, for aught they show us to the contrary, have made any one of a million other universes just as well as this. You can deduce no single actual particular from the notion of it. It is compatible with any state of things whatever being true here below. And the theistic God is almost as sterile a principle. You have to go to the world which he has created to get any inkling of his actual character: he is the kind of god that has once for all made that kind of a world. The God of the theistic writers lives on as purely abstract heights as does the Absolute. Absolutism has a certain sweep and dash about it, while the usual theism is more insipid, but both are equally remote and vacuous. What *you* want is a philosophy that will not only exercise your powers of intellectual abstraction, but that will make some positive connexion with this actual world of finite human lives.

You want a system that will combine both things, the scientific loyalty to facts and willingness to take account of them, the spirit of adaptation and accommodation, in short, but also the old confidence in human values and the resultant spontaneity, whether of the religious or of the romantic type. And this is then your dilemma: you find the two parts of your *quaesitum* hopelessly separated. You find empiricism with inhumanism and irreligion; or else you find a rationalistic philosophy that indeed may call itself religious, but that keeps out of all definite touch with concrete facts and joys and sorrows.

I am not sure how many of you live close enough to philosophy to realize fully what I mean by this last reproach, so I will dwell a little longer on that unreality in all rationalistic systems by which your serious believer in facts is so apt to feel repelled.

I wish that I had saved the first couple of pages of a thesis which a student handed me a year or two ago. They illustrated my point so clearly that I am sorry I can not read them to you now. This young man, who was a graduate of some Western college, began by saying that he had always taken for granted that when you entered a philosophic classroom you had to open relations with a universe entirely distinct from the one you left behind you in the street. The two were supposed, he said, to have so little to do with each other, that you could not possibly occupy your mind with them at the same time. The world of concrete personal experiences to which the street belongs is multitudinous beyond imagination, tangled, muddy, painful and perplexed. The world to which your philosophy-professor introduces you is simple, clean and noble. The contradictions of real life are absent from it. Its architecture is classic. Principles of reason trace its outlines, logical necessities cement its parts. Purity and dignity are what it most expresses. It is a kind of marble temple shining on a hill.

In point of fact it is far less an account of this actual world than a clear addition built upon it, a classic sanctuary in which the rationalist fancy may take refuge from the intolerably confused and gothic character which mere facts present. It is no *explanation* of our concrete universe, it is another thing altogether, a substitute for it, a remedy, a way of escape.

Its temperament, if I may use the word temperament here, is utterly alien to the temperament of existence in the concrete. *Refinement* is what characterizes our intellectualist philosophies. They exquisitely satisfy that craving for a refined object of contemplation which is so powerful an appetite of the mind. But I ask you in all seriousness to look abroad on this colossal universe of concrete facts, on their awful bewilderments, their surprises and cruelties, on the wilderness which they show, and then to tell me whether "refined" is the one inevitable descriptive adjective that springs to your lips.

Refinement has its place in things, true enough. But a philosophy that breathes out nothing but refinement will never satisfy the empiricist temper of mind. It will seem rather a monument of artificiality. So we find men of science preferring to turn their backs on metaphysics as on something altogether cloistered and spectral, and practical men shaking philosophy's dust off their feet and following the call of the wild.

Truly there is something a little ghastly in the satisfaction with which a pure but unreal system will fill a rationalist mind. Leibnitz was a rationalist mind, with infinitely more interest in facts than most rationalist minds can show. Yet if you wish for superficiality incarnate, you have only to read that charmingly written *Théodicée* of his, in which he sought to justify the ways of God to man, and to prove that the world we live in is the best of possible worlds. Let me quote a specimen of what I mean.

Among other obstacles to his optimistic philosophy, it falls to Leibnitz to consider the number of the eternally damned. That it is infinitely greater, in our human case, than that of those saved, he assumes as a premise from the theologians, and then proceeds to argue in this way. Even then, he says:

"The evil will appear as almost nothing in comparison with the good, if we once consider the real magnitude of the City of God. Coelius Secundus Curio has written a little book, *De Amplitudine Regni Coelestis*, which was reprinted not long ago. But he failed to compass the extent of the kingdom of the heavens. The ancients had small ideas of the works of God. . . . It seemed to them that only our earth had inhabitants, and even the notion of our antipodes gave them pause. The rest of the world for them consisted of some shining globes and a few crystalline spheres. But today, whatever be the limits that we may grant or refuse to the Universe we must recognize in it a countless number of globes, as big as ours or bigger, which have just as much right as it has to support rational inhabitants, tho it does not follow that these need all be men. Our earth is only one among the six principal satellites of our sun. As all the fixed stars are suns, one sees how small a place among visible things our earth takes up, since it is only a satellite of one among them. Now all these suns *may* be inhabited by none but happy creatures; and nothing obliges us to believe that the number of damned persons is very great; for *a very few instances and samples suffice for the utility which good draws from evil.* Moreover, since there is no reason to suppose that there are stars everywhere, may there not be a great space beyond the region of the stars? And this immense space, surrounding all this region, . . . may be replete with happiness and glory. . . . What now becomes of the consideration of our Earth and of its denizens? Does it not dwindle to something incomparably less than a physical point, since our Earth is but a point compared with the distance of the fixed stars. Thus the part of the Universe which we know, being almost lost in nothingness compared with that which is unknown to us, but which we are yet obliged to admit; and all the evils that we know lying in this almost-nothing; it follows that the evils may be almost-nothing in comparison with the goods that the Universe contains."

Leibnitz continues elsewhere:

"There is a kind of justice which aims neither at the amendment of the criminal, nor at furnishing an example to others, nor at the reparation of the injury. This justice is founded in pure fitness, which finds a certain satisfaction in the expiation of a wicked deed. The Socinians and Hobbes objected to this punitive justice, which is properly vindictive justice, and which God has reserved for himself at many junctures. . . . It is always founded in the fitness of things, and satisfies not only the offended party, but all wise lookers-on, even as beautiful music or a fine piece of architecture satisfies a well-constituted mind. It is thus that the torments of the damned continue, even tho they serve no longer to turn any one away from sin, and that the rewards of the blest continue, even tho they confirm no one in good ways. The damned draw to themselves ever new penalties by their continuing sins, and the blest attract ever fresh joys by their unceasing progress in good. Both facts are founded on the principle of fitness, . . . for God has made all things harmonious in perfection as I have already said."

Leibnitz's feeble grasp of reality is too obvious to need comment from me. It is evident that no realistic image of the experience of a damned soul had ever approached the portals of his mind. Nor had it occurred to him that the smaller is the number of "samples" of the genus "lost-soul" whom God throws as a sop to the eternal fitness, the more unequitably grounded is the glory of the blest. What he gives us is a cold literary exercise, whose cheerful substance even hell-fire does not warm.

And do not tell me that to show the shallowness of rationalist philosophizing I have had to go back to a shallow wigpated age. The optimism of present-day rationalism sounds just as shallow to the fact-loving mind. The actual universe is a thing wide open, but rationalism makes systems, and systems must be closed. For men in practical life perfection is something far off and still in process of achievement. This for rationalism is but the illusion of the finite and relative: the absolute ground of things is a perfection eternally complete.

I find a fine example of revolt against the airy and shallow optimism of current religious philosophy in a publication of that valiant anarchistic writer Morrison I. Swift. Mr. Swift's anarchism goes a little farther than mine does, but I confess that I sympathize a good deal, and some of you, I know, will sympathize heartily with his dissatisfaction with the idealistic optimisms now in vogue. He begins his pamphlet on *Human Submission* with a series of city reporter's items from newspapers (suicides, deaths from starvation, and the like) as specimens of our civilized régime. For instance:

"After trudging through the snow from one end of the city to the other in the vain hope of securing employment, and with his wife and six children without food and ordered to leave their home in an upper east-side tenement-house because of non-payment of rent, John Corcoran, a clerk, today ended his life by drinking carbolic acid. Corcoran lost his position three weeks ago through illness, and during the period of idleness his scanty savings disappeared. Yesterday he obtained work with a gang of city snow-shovelers, but he was too weak from illness, and was forced to quit after an hour's trial with the shovel. Then the weary task of looking for employment was again resumed. Thoroughly discouraged, Corcoran returned to his home last night to find his wife and children without food and the notice of dispossession on the door. On the following morning he drank the poison.

"The records of many more such cases lie before me [Mr. Swift goes on]; an encyclopedia might easily be filled with their kind. These few I cite as an interpretation of the Universe. 'We are aware of the presence of God in his world,' says a writer in a recent English review. [The very presence of ill in the temporal order is the condition of the perfection of the eternal order, writes Professor Royce (*The World and the Individual*, II, 385).] 'The Absolute is the richer for every discord and for all the diversity which it embraces,' says F. H. Bradley (*Appearance and Reality*, 204). He means that these slain men make the universe richer, and that is philosophy. But while Professors Royce and Bradley and a whole host of guileless thoroughfed thinkers are unveiling Reality and the Absolute and explaining away evil and pain, this is the condition of the only beings known to us anywhere in the universe with a developed consciousness of what the universe is. What these people experience *is* Reality. It gives us an absolute phase of the universe. It is the personal experience of those best qualified in our circle of knowledge to *have* experience, to tell us *what is*. Now what does *thinking about* the experience of these persons come to, compared to directly and personally feeling it as they feel it? The philosophers are dealing in shades, while those who live and feel know truth. And the mind of mankind—not yet the mind of philosophers and of the proprietary class—but of the great mass of the silently thinking men and feeling men, is coming to this view. They are judging the universe as they have hitherto permitted the hierophants of religion and learning to judge *them*. . . .

"This Cleveland workingman, killing his children and himself [another of the cited cases] is one of the elemental stupendous facts of this modern world and of this universe. It cannot be glozed over or minimized away by all the treatises on God, and Love, and Being, helplessly existing in their monumental vacuity. This is one of the simple irreducible elements of this world's life, after millions of years of opportunity and twenty centuries of Christ. It is in the mental world what atoms or sub-atoms are in the physical, primary, indestructible. And what it blazons to man is the imposture of all philosophy which does not see in such events the consummate factor of all conscious experience. These facts invincibly prove religion a nullity. Man will not give religion two thousand centuries or twenty centuries more to try itself and waste human time. Its time is up; its probation is ended; its own record ends it. Mankind has not æons and eternities to spare for trying out discredited systems." [1]

Such is the reaction of an empiricist mind upon the rationalist bill of fare. It is an absolute "No, I thank you." "Religion," says Mr. Swift, "is like a sleep-walker to whom actual things are blank." And such, tho possibly less tensely charged with feeling, is the verdict of every seriously inquiring amateur in philosophy today who turns to the philosophy-professors for the wherewithal to satisfy the fulness of his nature's needs. Empiricist writers give him a materialism, rationalists give him something religious, but to that religion "actual things are blank." He becomes thus the judge of us philosophers. Tender or tough, he finds us wanting. None of us may treat his verdicts disdainfully, for after all, his is the typically perfect mind, the mind the sum of whose demands is greatest, the mind whose criticisms and dissatisfactions are fatal in the long run.

It is at this point that my own solution begins to appear. I offer the oddly-named thing pragmatism as a philosophy that can satisfy both kinds of demands. It can remain religious like the rationalisms, but at the same time, like the empiricisms, it can preserve the richest intimacy with facts. I hope I may be able to leave many of you with as favorable an opinion of it as I preserve myself. Yet, as I am near the end of my hour, I will not introduce pragmatism bodily now. I will begin with it on the stroke of the clock next time. I prefer at the present moment to return a little on what I have said.

If any of you here are professional philosophers, and some of you I know to be such, you will doubtless have felt my discourse so far to have been crude in an unpardonable, nay, in an almost incredible degree. Tender-minded and tough-minded, what a barbaric disjunction! And, in general, when philosophy is all compacted of delicate intellectualities and subtleties and scrupulosities, and when every possible sort of combination and transition obtains within its bounds, what a brutal caricature and reduction of highest things to the lowest possible expression is it to represent its field of conflict as a sort of rough-and-tumble fight between two hostile temperaments! What a childishly external view! And again, how stupid it is to treat the abstractness of rationalist systems as a crime, and to damn them because they offer themselves as sanctuaries and places of escape, rather than as prolongations of the world of facts. Are not all our theories just remedies and places of escape? And, if philosophy is to be religious, how can she be anything else than a place of escape from the crassness of reality's surface? What better thing can she do than raise us out of our animal senses and show us another and a nobler home for our minds in that great framework of ideal principles subtending all reality, which the intellect divines? How can principles and general views ever be anything but abstract outlines? Was Cologne cathedral built without an architect's plan on paper? Is refinement in itself an abomination? Is concrete rudeness the only thing that's true?

Believe me, I feel the full force of the indictment. The picture I have given is indeed monstrously over-simplified and rude. But like all abstractions, it will prove to have its use. If philosophers can treat the life of the universe abstractly, they must not complain of an abstract treatment of the life of philosophy itself. In point of fact the picture I have given is, however coarse and sketchy, literally true. Temperaments with their cravings and refusals do determine men in their philosophies, and always will. The details of systems may be reasoned out piece-meal, and when the student is working at a system, he may often forget the forest for the single tree. But when the labor is accomplished, the mind always performs its big summarizing act, and the system forthwith stands over against one like a living thing, with that strange simple note of individuality which haunts our memory, like the wraith of the man, when a friend or enemy of ours is dead.

Not only Walt Whitman could write "who touches this book touches a man." The books of all the great philosophers are like so many men. Our sense of an essential personal flavor in each one of them, typical but indescribable, is the finest fruit of our own accomplished philosophic education. What the system pretends to be is a picture of the great universe of God. What it is—and oh so flagrantly!—is the revelation of how intensely odd the personal flavor of some fellow creature is. Once reduced to these terms (and all our philosophies get reduced to them in minds made critical by learning) our commerce with the systems reverts to the informal, to the instinctive human reaction of satisfaction or dislike. We grow as peremptory in our rejection or admission, as when a person presents himself as a candidate for our favor; our verdicts are couched in as simple adjectives of praise or dispraise. We measure the total character of the universe as we feel it, against the flavor of the philosophy proffered us and one word is enough.

"Statt de lebendigen Natur," we say, "da Gott die Menschen schuf hinein"—that nebulous concoction, that wooden, that straight-laced thing, that crabbed artificiality, that musty schoolroom product, that sick man's dream! Away with it. Away with all of them! Impossible! Impossible!

Our work over the details of his system is indeed what gives us our resultant impression of the philosopher, but it is on the resultant impression itself that we react. Expertness in philosophy is measured by the definiteness of our summarizing reactions, by the immediate perceptive epithet with which the expert hits such complex objects off. But great expertness is not necessary for the epithet to come. Few people have definitely articulated philosophies of their own. But almost every one has his own peculiar sense of a certain total character in the universe, and of the inadequacy fully to match it of the peculiar systems that he knows. They don't just cover *his* world. One will be too dapper, another too pedantic, a third too much of a job-lot of opinions, a fourth too morbid, and a fifth too artificial, or what not. At any rate he and we know off-hand that such philosophies are out of plumb and out of key and out of "whack," and have no business to speak up in the universe's name. Plato, Locke, Spinoza, Mill, Caird, Hegel—I prudently avoid names nearer home!—I am sure that to many of you, my hearers, these names are little more than reminders of as many curious personal ways of falling short. It would be an obvious absurdity if such ways of taking the universe were actually true.

We philosophers have to reckon with such feelings on your part. In the last resort, I repeat, it will be by them that all our philosophies shall ultimately be judged. The finally victorious way of looking at things will be the most completely *impressive* way to the normal run of minds.

One word more—namely about philosophies necessarily being abstract outlines. There are outlines and outlines, outlines of buildings that are *fat*, conceived in the cube by their planner, and outlines of buildings invented flat on paper, with the aid of ruler and compass. These remain skinny and emaciated even when set up in stone and mortar, and the outline already suggests that result. An outline in itself is meagre, truly, but it does not necessarily suggest a meagre thing. It is the essential meagreness of *what is suggested* by the usual rationalistic philosophies that moves empiricists to their gesture of rejection. The case of Herbert Spencer's system is much to the point here. Rationalists feel his fearful array of insufficiencies. His dry schoolmaster temperament, the hurdy-gurdy monotony of him, his preference for cheap makeshifts in argument, his lack of education even in mechanical principles, and in general the vagueness of all his fundamental ideas, his whole system wooden, as if knocked together out of cracked hemlock boards—and yet the half of England wants to bury him in Westminster Abbey.

Why? Why does Spencer call out so much reverence in spite of his weakness in rationalistic eyes? Why should so many educated men who feel that weakness, you and I perhaps, wish to see him in the Abbey notwithstanding? Simply because we feel his heart to be *in the right place* philosophically. His principles may be all skin and bone, but at any rate his books try to mould themselves upon the particular shape of this particular world's carcass. The noise of facts resounds through all his chapters, the citations of fact never cease, he emphasizes facts, turns his face towards their quarter; and that is enough. It means the right *kind* of thing for the empiricist mind.

The pragmatistic philosophy of which I hope to begin talking in my next lecture preserves as cordial a relation with facts, and, unlike Spencer's philosophy, it neither begins nor ends by turning positive religious constructions out of doors—it treats them cordially as well.

I hope I may lead you to find it just the mediating way of thinking that you require.

WHAT PRAGMATISM MEANS

Some years ago, being with a camping party in the mountains, I returned from a solitary ramble to find every one engaged in a ferocious metaphysical dispute. The *corpus* of the dispute was a squirrel—a live squirrel supposed to be clinging to one side of a tree-trunk; while over against the tree's opposite side a human being was imagined to stand. This human witness tries to get sight of the squirrel by moving rapidly round the tree, but no matter how fast he goes, the squirrel moves as fast in the opposite direction, and always keeps the tree between himself and the man, so that never a glimpse of him is caught. The resultant metaphysical problem now is this: *Does the man go round the squirrel or not?* He goes round the tree, sure enough, and the squirrel is on the tree; but does he go round the squirrel? In the unlimited leisure of the wilderness, discussion had been worn threadbare. Everyone had taken sides, and was obstinate; and the numbers on both sides were even. Each side, when I appeared therefore appealed to me to make it a majority. Mindful of the scholastic adage that whenever you meet a contradiction you must make a distinction, I immediately sought and found one, as follows: "Which party is right," I said, "depends on what you *practically mean* by 'going round' the squirrel. If you mean passing from the north of him to the east, then to the south, then to the west, and then to the north of him again, obviously the man does go round him, for he occupies these successive positions. But if on the contrary you mean being first in front of him, then on the right of him, then behind him, then on his left, and finally in front again, it is quite as obvious that the man fails to go round him, for by the compensating movements the squirrel makes, he keeps his belly turned towards the man all the time, and his back turned away. Make the distinction, and there is no occasion for any farther dispute. You are both right and both wrong according as you conceive the verb 'to go round' in one practical fashion or the other."

Although one or two of the hotter disputants called my speech a shuffling evasion, saying they wanted no quibbling or scholastic hair-splitting, but meant just plain honest English "round," the majority seemed to think that the distinction had assuaged the dispute.

I tell this trivial anecdote because it is a peculiarly simple example of what I wish now to speak of as *the pragmatic method*. The pragmatic method is primarily a method of settling metaphysical disputes that otherwise might be interminable. Is the world one or many?—fated or free?—material or spiritual?—here are notions either of which may or may not hold good of the world; and disputes over such notions are unending. The pragmatic method in such cases is to try to interpret each notion by tracing its respective practical consequences. What difference would it practically make to any one if this notion rather than that notion were true? If no practical difference whatever can be traced, then the alternatives mean practically the same thing, and all dispute is idle. Whenever a dispute is serious, we ought to be able to show some practical difference that must follow from one side or the other's being right.

A glance at the history of the idea will show you still better what pragmatism means. The term is derived from the same Greek word πράγμα, meaning action, from which our words "practice" and "practical" come. It was first introduced into philosophy by Mr. Charles Peirce in 1878. In an article entitled "How to Make Our Ideas Clear," in the *Popular Science Monthly* for January of that year,[1] Mr. Peirce, after pointing out that our beliefs are really rules for action, said that, to develop a thought's meaning, we need only determine what conduct it is fitted to produce: that conduct is for us its sole significance. And the tangible fact at the root of all our thought-distinctions, however subtle, is that there is no one of them so fine as to consist in anything but a possible difference of practice. To attain perfect clearness in our thoughts of an object, then, we need only consider what conceivable effects of a practical kind the object may involve

—what sensations we are to expect from it, and what reactions we must prepare. Our conception of these effects, whether immediate or remote, is then for us the whole of our conception of the object, so far as that conception has positive significance at all.

This is the principle of Peirce, the principle of pragmatism. It lay entirely unnoticed by any one for twenty years, until I, in an address before Professor Howison's philosophical union at the University of California, brought it forward again and made a special application of it to religion. By that date (1898) the times seemed ripe for its reception. The word "pragmatism" spread, and at present it fairly spots the pages of the philosophic journals. On all hands we find the "pragmatic movement" spoken of, sometimes with respect, sometimes with contumely, seldom with clear understanding. It is evident that the term applies itself conveniently to a number of tendencies that hitherto have lacked a collective name, and that it has "come to stay."

To take in the importance of Peirce's principle, one must get accustomed to applying it to concrete cases. I found a few years ago that Ostwald, the illustrious Leipzig chemist, had been making perfectly distinct use of the principle of pragmatism in his lectures on the philosophy of science, though he had not called it by that name.

"All realities influence our practice," he wrote me, "and that influence is their meaning for us. I am accustomed to put questions to my classes in this way: In what respects would the world be different if this alternative or that were true? If I can find nothing that would become different, then the alternative has no sense."

That is, the rival views mean practically the same thing, and meaning, other than practical, there is for us none. Ostwald in a published lecture gives this example of what he means. Chemists have long wrangled over the inner constitution of certain bodies called "tautomerous." Their properties seemed equally consistent with the notion that an instable hydrogen atom oscillates inside of them, or that they are instable mixtures of two bodies. Controversy raged, but never was decided. "It would never have begun," says Ostwald, "if the combatants had asked themselves what particular experimental fact could have been made different by one or the other view being correct. For it would then have appeared that no difference of fact could possibly ensue; and the quarrel was as unreal as if, theorizing in primitive times about the raising of dough by yeast, one party should have invoked a 'brownie,' while another insisted on an 'elf' as the true cause of the phenomenon." [2]

It is astonishing to see how many philosophical disputes collapse into insignificance the moment you subject them to this simple test of tracing a concrete consequence. There can *be* no difference anywhere that doesn't *make* a difference elsewhere—no difference in abstract truth that doesn't express itself in a difference in concrete fact and in conduct consequent upon that fact, imposed on somebody, somehow, somewhere, and somewhen. The whole function of philosophy ought to be to find out what definite difference it will make to you and me, at definite instants of our life, if this world-formula or that world-formula be the true one.

There is absolutely nothing new in the pragmatic method. Socrates was an adept at it. Aristotle used it methodically. Locke, Berkeley, and Hume made momentous contributions to truth by its means. Shadworth Hodgson keeps insisting that realities are only what they are "known as." But these forerunners of pragmatism used it in fragments: they were preluders only. Not until in our time has it generalized itself, become conscious of a universal mission, pretended to a conquering destiny. I believe in that destiny, and I hope I may end by inspiring you with my belief.

Pragmatism represents a perfectly familiar attitude in philosophy, the empiricist attitude, but it represents it, as it seems to me, both in a more radical and in a less objectionable form than it has ever yet assumed. A pragmatist turns his back resolutely and once for all upon a lot of inveterate habits dear to professional philosophers. He turns away from abstraction and insufficiency, from verbal solutions, from bad *a priori* reasons, from fixed principles, closed systems, and pretended absolutes and origins. He turns towards concreteness and adequacy, towards facts, towards action and towards power. That means the empiricist temper regnant and the rationalist temper sincerely given up. It means the open air and possibilities of nature, as against dogma, artificiality, and the pretence of finality in truth.

At the same time it does not stand for any special results. It is a method only. But the general triumph of that method would mean an enormous change in what I called in my last lecture the "temperament" of philosophy. Teachers of the ultra-rationalistic type would be frozen out, much as the courtier type is frozen out in republics, as the ultramontane type of priest is frozen out in protestant lands. Science and metaphysics would come much nearer together, would in fact work absolutely hand in hand.

Metaphysics has usually followed a very primitive kind of quest. You know how men have always hankered after unlawful magic, and you know what a great part in magic *words* have always played. If you have his name, or the formula of incantation that binds him, you can control the spirit, genie, afrite, or whatever the power may be. Solomon knew the names of all the spirits, and having their names, he held them subject to his will. So the universe has always appeared to the natural mind as a kind of enigma, of which the key must be sought in the shape of some illuminating or power-bringing word or name. That word names the universe's *principle*, and to possess it is after a fashion to possess the universe itself. "God," "Matter," "Reason," "the Absolute," "Energy," are so many solving names. You can rest when you have them. You are at the end of your metaphysical quest.

But if you follow the pragmatic method, you cannot look on any such word as closing your quest. You must bring out of each word its practical cash-value, set it at work within the stream of your experience. It appears less as a solution, then, than as a program for more work, and more particularly as an indication of the ways in which existing realities may be *changed*.

Theories thus become instruments, not answers to enigmas, in which we can rest. We don't lie back upon them, we move forward, and, on occasion, make nature over again by their aid. Pragmatism unstiffens all our theories, limbers them up and sets each one at work. Being nothing essentially new, it harmonizes with many ancient philosophic tendencies. It agrees with nominalism for instance, in always appealing to particulars; with utilitarianism in emphasizing practical aspects; with positivism in its disdain for verbal solutions, useless questions and metaphysical abstractions.

All these, you see, are *anti-intellectualist* tendencies. Against rationalism as a pretension and a method pragmatism is fully armed and militant. But, at the outset, at least, it stands for no particular results. It has no dogmas, and no doctrines save its method. As the young Italian pragmatist Papini has well said, it lies in the midst of our theories, like a corridor in a hotel. Innumerable chambers open out of it. In one you may find a man writing an atheistic volume; in the next some one on his knees praying for faith and strength; in a third a chemist investigating a body's properties. In a fourth a system of idealistic metaphysics is being excogitated; in a fifth the impossibility of metaphysics is being shown. But they all own the corridor, and all must pass through it if they want a practicable way of getting into or out of their respective rooms.

No particular results then, so far, but only an attitude of orientation, is what the pragmatic method means. *The attitude of looking away from first things, principles, "categories," supposed necessities; and of looking towards last things, fruits, consequences, facts.*

So much for the pragmatic method! You may say that I have been praising it rather than explaining it to you, but I shall presently explain it abundantly enough by showing how it works on some familiar problems. Meanwhile the word pragmatism has come to be used in a still wider sense, as meaning also a certain *theory of truth.* I mean to give a whole lecture to the statement of that theory, after first paving the way, so I can be very brief now. But brevity is hard to follow, so I ask for your redoubled attention for a quarter of an hour. If much remains obscure, I hope to make it clearer in the later lectures.

One of the most successfully cultivated branches of philosophy in our time is what is called inductive logic, the study of the conditions under which our sciences have evolved. Writers on this subject have begun to show a singular unanimity as to what the laws of nature and elements of fact mean, when formulated by mathematicians, physicists and chemists. When the first mathematical, logical, and natural uniformities, the first *laws,* were discovered, men were so carried away by the clearness, beauty and simplification that resulted, that they believed themselves to have deciphered authentically the eternal thoughts of the Almighty. His mind also thundered and reverberated in syllogisms. He also thought in conic sections, squares and roots and ratios, and geometrized like Euclid. He made Kepler's laws for the planets to follow; he made velocity increase proportionally to the time in falling bodies; he made the law of the sines for light to obey when refracted; he established the classes, orders, families and genera of plants and animals, and fixed the distances between them. He thought the archetypes of all things, and devised their variations; and when we rediscover any one of these his wondrous institutions, we seize his mind in its very literal intention.

But as the sciences have developed farther the notion has gained ground that most, perhaps all, of our laws are only approximations. The laws themselves, moreover, have grown so numerous that there is no counting them; and so many rival formulations are proposed in all the branches of science that investigators have become accustomed to the notion that no theory is absolutely a transcript of reality, but that any one of them may from some point of view be useful. Their great use is to summarize old facts and to lead to new ones. They are only a man-made language, a conceptual shorthand, as some one calls them, in which we write our reports of nature; and languages, as is well known, tolerate much choice of expression and many dialects.

Thus human arbitrariness has driven divine necessity from scientific logic. If I mention the names of Sigwart, Mach, Ostwald, Pearson, Milhaud, Poincaré, Duhem, Ruyssen, those of you who are students will easily identify the tendency I speak of, and will think of additional names.

Riding now on the front of this wave of scientific logic Messrs. Schiller and Dewey appear with their pragmatistic account of what truth everywhere signifies. Everywhere, these teachers say, "truth" in our ideas and beliefs means the same thing that it means in science. It means, they say, nothing but this, *that ideas (which themselves are but parts of our experience) become true just in so far as they help us to get into satisfactory relations with other parts of our experience,* to summarize them and get about among them by conceptual short-cuts instead of following the interminable succession of particular phenomena. Any idea upon which we can ride, so to speak; any idea that will carry us prosperously from any one part of our experience to any other part, linking things satisfactorily, working securely, simplifying, saving labor; is true for just so much, true in so far forth, true *instrumentally*. This is the "instrumental" view of truth taught so successfully at Chicago, the view that truth in our ideas means their power to "work," promulgated so brilliantly at Oxford.

Messrs. Dewey, Schiller and their allies, in reaching this general conception of all truth, have only followed the example of geologists, biologists and philologists. In the establishment of these other sciences, the successful stroke was always to take some simple process actually observable in operation—as denudation by weather, say, or variation from parental type, or change of dialect by incorporation of new words and pronunciations—and then to generalize it, making it apply to all times, and produce great results by summating its effects through the ages.

The observable process which Schiller and Dewey particularly singled out for generalization is the familiar one by which any individual settles into *new opinions*. The process here is always the same. The individual has a stock of old opinions already, but he meets a new experience that puts them to a strain. Somebody contradicts them; or in a reflective moment he discovers that they contradict each other; or he hears of facts with which they are incompatible; or desires arise in him which they cease to satisfy. The result is an inward trouble to which his mind till then had been a stranger, and from which he seeks to escape by modifying his previous mass of opinions. He saves as much of it as he can, for in this matter of belief we are all extreme conservatives. So he tries to change first this opinion, and then that (for they resist change very variously), until at last some new idea comes up which he can graft upon the ancient stock with a minimum of disturbance of the latter, some idea that mediates between the stock and the new experience and runs them into one another most felicitously and expediently.

This new idea is then adopted as the true one. It preserves the older stock of truths with a minimum of modification, stretching them just enough to make them admit the novelty, but conceiving that in ways as familiar as the case leaves possible. An *outrée* explanation, violating all our preconceptions, would never pass for a true account of a novelty. We should scratch round industriously till we found something less eccentric. The most violent revolutions in an individual's beliefs leaves most of his old order standing. Time and space, cause and effect, nature and history, and one's own biography remain untouched. New truth is always a go-between, a smoother-over of transitions. It marries old opinion to new fact so as ever to show a minimum of jolt, a maximum of continuity. We hold a theory true just in proportion to its success in solving this "problem of maxima and minima." But success in solving this problem is eminently a matter of approximation. We say this theory solves it on the whole more satisfactorily than that theory; but that means more satisfactorily to ourselves, and individuals will emphasize their points of satisfaction differently. To a certain degree, therefore, everything here is plastic.

The point I now urge you to observe particularly is the part played by the older truths. Failure to take account of it is the source of much of the unjust criticism levelled against pragmatism. Their influence is absolutely controlling. Loyalty to them is the first principle—in most cases it is the only principle; for by far the most usual way of handling phenomena so novel that they would make for a serious re-arrangement of our preconception is to ignore them altogether, or to abuse those who bear witness for them.

You doubtless wish examples of this process of truth's growth, and the only trouble is their superabundance. The simplest case of new truth is of course the mere numerical addition of new kinds of facts, or of new single facts of old kinds, to our experience—an addition that involves no alteration in the old beliefs. Day follows day, and its contents are simply added. The new contents themselves are not true, they simply *come* and *are*. Truth is *what we say about* them, and when we say that they have come, truth is satisfied by the plain additive formula.

But often the day's contents oblige a re-arrangement. If I should now utter piercing shrieks and act like a maniac on this platform, it would make many of you revise your ideas as to the probable worth of my philosophy. "Radium" came the other day as part of the day's content, and seemed for a moment to contradict our ideas of the whole order of nature, that order having come to be identified with what is called the conservation of energy. The mere sight of radium paying heat away indefinitely out of its own pocket seemed to violate that conservation. What to think? If the radiations from it were nothing but an escape of unsuspected "potential" energy, pre-existent inside of the atoms, the principle of conservation would be saved. The discovery of "helium" as the radiation's outcome, opened a way to this belief. So Ramsay's view is generally held to be true, because, although it extends our old ideas of energy, it causes a minimum of alteration in their nature.

I need not multiply instances. A new opinion counts as "true" just in proportion as it gratifies the individual's desire to assimilate the novel in his experience to his beliefs in stock. It must both lean on old truth and grasp new fact; and its success (as I said a moment ago) in doing this, is a matter for the individual's appreciation. When old truth grows, then, by new truth's addition, it is for subjective reasons. We are in the process and obey the reasons. That new idea is truest which performs most felicitously its function of satisfying our double urgency. It makes itself true, gets itself classed as true, by the way it works; grafting itself then upon the ancient body of truth, which thus grows much as a tree grows by the activity of a new layer of cambium.

Now Dewey and Schiller proceed to generalize this observation and to apply it to the most ancient parts of truth. They also once were plastic. They also were called true for human reasons. They also mediated between still earlier truths and what in those days were novel observations. Purely objective truth, truth in whose establishment the function of giving human satisfaction in marrying previous parts of experience with newer parts played no rôle whatever, is nowhere to be found. The reasons why we call things true is the reason why they *are* true, for "to be true" *means* only to perform this marriage-function.

The trail of the human serpent is thus over everything. Truth independent; truth that we *find* merely; truth no longer malleable to human need; truth incorrigible, in a word; such truth exists indeed superabundantly—or is supposed to exist by rationalistically minded thinkers; but then it means only the dead heart of the living tree, and its being there means only that truth also has its paleontology, and its "prescription," and may grow stiff with years of veteran service and petrified in men's regard by sheer antiquity. But how plastic even the oldest truths nevertheless really are has been vividly shown in our day by the transformation of logical and mathematical ideas, a transformation which seems even to be invading physics. The ancient formulas are reinterpreted as special expressions of much wider principles, principles that our ors never got a glimpse of in their present shape and formulation.

Mr. Schiller still gives to all this view of truth the name of "Humanism," but, for this doctrine too, the name of pragmatism seems fairly to be in the ascendent, so I will treat it under the name of pragmatism in these lectures.

Such then would be the scope of pragmatism—first, a method; and second, a genetic theory of what is meant by truth. And these two things must be our future topics.

What I have said of the theory of truth will, I am sure, have appeared obscure and unsatisfactory to most of you by reason of its brevity. I shall make amends for that hereafter. In a lecture on "common sense" I shall try to show what I mean by truths grown petrified by antiquity. In another lecture I shall expatiate on the idea that our thoughts become true in proportion as they successfully exert their go-between function. In a third I shall show how hard it is to discriminate subjective from objective factors in Truth's development. You may not follow me wholly in these lectures; and if you do, you may not wholly agree with me. But you will, I know, regard me at least as serious, and treat my effort with respectful consideration.

You will probably be surprised to learn, then, that Messrs. Schiller's and Dewey's theories have suffered a hailstorm of contempt and ridicule. All rationalism has risen against them. In influential quarters Mr. Schiller, in particular, has been treated like an impudent schoolboy who deserves a spanking. I should not mention this, but for the fact that it throws so much sidelight upon that rationalistic temper to which I have opposed the temper of pragmatism. Pragmatism is uncomfortable away from facts. Rationalism is comfortable only in the presence of abstractions. This pragmatist talk about truths in the plural, about their utility and satisfactoriness, about the success with which they "work," etc., suggests to the typical intellectualist mind a sort of coarse lame second-rate makeshift article of truth. Such truths are not real truth. Such tests are merely subjective. Against this, objective truth must be something non-utilitarian, haughty, refined, remote, august, exalted. It must be an absolute correspondence of our thoughts with an equally absolute reality. It must be what we *ought* to think unconditionally. The conditioned ways in which we *do* think are so much irrelevance and matter for psychology.

Down with psychology, up with logic, in all this question! See the exquisite contrast of the types of mind! The pragmatist clings to facts and concreteness, observes truth at its work in particular cases, and generalizes. Truth, for him, becomes a class-name for all sorts of definite working-values in experience. For the rationalist it remains a pure abstraction, to the bare name of which we must defer. When the pragmatist undertakes to show in detail just *why* we must defer, the rationalist is unable to recognize the concretes from which his own abstraction is taken. He accuses us of *denying* truth; whereas we have only sought to trace exactly why people follow it and always ought to follow it. Your typical ultra-abstractionist fairly shudders at concreteness: other things equal, he positively prefers the pale and spectral. If the two universes were offered, he would always choose the skinny outline rather than the rich thicket of reality. It is so much purer, clearer, nobler.

I hope that as these lectures go on, the concreteness and closeness to facts of the pragmatism which they advocate may be what approves itself to you as its most satisfactory peculiarity. It only follows here the example of the sister-sciences, interpreting the unobserved by the observed. It brings old and new harmoniously together. It converts the absolutely empty notion of a static relation of "correspondence" (what that may mean we must ask later) between our minds and reality, into that of a rich and active commerce (that any one may follow in detail and understand) between particular thoughts of ours, and the great universe of other experiences in which they play their parts and have their uses.

But enough of this at present? The justification of what I say must be postponed. I wish now to add a word in further explanation of the claim I made at our last meeting, that pragmatism may be a happy harmonizer of empiricist ways of thinking with the more religious demands of human beings.

Men who are strongly of the fact-loving temperament, you may remember me to have said, are liable to be kept at a distance by the small sympathy with facts which that philosophy from the present-day fashion of idealism offers them. It is far too intellectualistic. Old-fashioned theism was bad enough, with its notion of God as an exalted monarch, made up of a lot of unintelligible or preposterous "attributes"; but, so long as it held strongly by the argument from design, it kept some touch with concrete realities. Since, however, darwinism has once for all displaced design from the minds of the "scientific," theism has lost that foothold; and some kind of an immanent or pantheistic deity working *in* things rather than above them is, if any, the kind recommended to our contemporary imagination. Aspirants to a philosophic religion turn, as a rule, more hopefully nowadays towards idealistic pantheism than towards the older dualistic theism, in spite of the fact that the latter still counts able defenders.

But, as I said in my first lecture, the brand of pantheism offered is hard for them to assimilate if they are lovers of facts, or empirically minded. It is the absolutistic brand, spurning the dust and reared upon pure logic. It keeps no connexion whatever with concreteness. Affirming the Absolute Mind, which is its substitute for God, to be the rational presupposition of all particulars of fact, whatever they may be, it remains supremely indifferent to what the particular facts in our world actually are. Be they what they may, the Absolute will father them. Like the sick lion in Esop's fable, all footprints lead into his den, but *nulla vestigia retrorsum.* You cannot redescend into the world of particulars by the Absolute's aid, or deduce any necessary consequences of detail important for your life from your idea of his nature. He gives you indeed the assurance that all is well with *Him,* and for his eternal way of thinking; but thereupon he leaves you to be finitely saved by your own temporal devices.

Far be it from me to deny the majesty of this conception, or its capacity to yield religious comfort to a most respectable class of minds. But from the human point of view, no one can pretend that it doesn't suffer from the faults of remoteness and abstractness. It is eminently a product of what I have ventured to call the rationalistic temper. It disdains empiricism's needs. It substitutes a pallid outline for the real world's richness. It is dapper, it is noble in the bad sense, in the sense in which to be noble is to be inapt for humble service. In this real world of sweat and dirt, it seems to me that when a view of things is "noble," that ought to count as a presumption against its truth, and as a philosophic disqualification. The prince of darkness may be a gentleman, as we are told he is, but whatever the God of earth and heaven is, he can surely be no gentleman. His menial services are needed in the dust of our human trails, even more than his dignity is needed in the empyrean.

Now pragmatism, devoted though she be to facts, has no such materialistic bias as ordinary empiricism labors under. Moreover, she has no objection whatever to the realizing of abstractions, so long as you get about among particulars with their aid and they actually carry you somewhere. Interested in no conclusions but those which our minds and our experiences work out together, she has no *a priori* prejudices against theology. *If theological ideas prove to have a value for concrete life, they will be true, for pragmatism, in the sense of being good for so much. For how much more they are true, will depend entirely on their relations to the other truths that also have to be acknowledged.*

What I said just now about the Absolute, of transcendental idealism, is a case in point. First, I called it majestic and said it yielded religious comfort to a class of minds, and then I accused it of remoteness and sterility. But so far as it affords such comfort, it surely is not sterile; it has that amount of value; it performs a concrete function. As a good pragmatist, I myself ought to call the Absolute true "in so far forth," then; and I unhesitatingly now do so.

But what does *true in so far forth* mean in this case? To answer, we need only apply the pragmatic method. What do believers in the Absolute mean by saying that their belief affords them comfort? They mean that since, in the Absolute finite evil is "overruled" already, we may, therefore, whenever we wish, treat the temporal as if it were potentially the eternal, be sure that we can trust its outcome, and, without sin, dismiss our fear and drop the worry of our finite responsibility. In short, they mean that we have a right ever and anon to take a moral holiday, to let the world wag in its own way, feeling that its issues are in better hands than ours and are none of our business.

The universe is a system of which the individual members may relax their anxieties occasionally, in which the don't-care mood is also right for men, and moral holidays in order —that, if I mistake not, is part, at least, of what the Absolute is "known-as," that is the great difference in our particular experiences which his being true makes, for us, that is his cash-value when he is pragmatically interpreted. Farther than that the ordinary lay-reader in philosophy who thinks favorably of absolute idealism does not venture to sharpen his conceptions. He can use the Absolute for so much, and so much is very precious. He is pained at hearing you speak incredulously of the Absolute, therefore, and disregards your criticisms because they deal with aspects of the conception that he fails to follow.

If the Absolute means this, and means no more than this, who can possibly deny the truth of it? To deny it would be to insist that men should never relax, and that holidays are never in order.

I am well aware how odd it must seem to some of you to hear me say that an idea is "true" so long as to believe it is profitable to our lives. That it is *good,* for as much as it profits, you will gladly admit. If what we do by its aid is good, you will allow the idea itself to be good in so far forth, for we are the better for possessing it. But is it not a strange misuse of the word "truth," you will say, to call ideas also "true" for this reason?

To answer this difficulty fully is impossible at this stage of my account. You touch here upon the very central point of Messrs. Schiller's, Dewey's and my own doctrine of truth, which I can not discuss with detail until my sixth lecture. Let me now say only this, that truth is *one species of good,* and not, as is usually supposed, a category distinct from good, and co-ordinate with it. *The true is the name of whatever proves itself to be good in the way of belief, and good, too, for definite, assignable reasons.* Surely you must admit this, that if there were *no* good for life in true ideas, or if the knowledge of them were positively disadvantageous and false ideas the only useful ones, then the current notion that truth is divine and precious, and its pursuit a duty, could never have grown up or become a dogma. In a world like that, our duty would be to *shun* truth, rather. But in this world, just as certain foods are not only agreeable to our taste, but good for our teeth, our stomach, and our tissues; so certain ideas are not only agreeable to think about, or agreeable as supporting other ideas that we are fond of, but they are also helpful in life's practical struggles. If there be any life that it is really better we should lead, and if there be any idea which, if believed in, would help us to lead that life, then it would be really *better for us* to believe in that idea, *unless, indeed, belief in it incidentally clashed with other greater vital benefits.*

"What would be better for us to believe!" This sounds very like a definition of truth. It comes very near to saying "what we *ought* to believe:" and in *that* definition none of you would find any oddity. Ought we ever not to believe what it is *better for us* to believe? And can we then keep the notion of what is better for us, and what is true for us, permanently apart?

Pragmatism says no, and I fully agree with her. Probably you also agree, so far as the abstract statement goes, but with a suspicion that if we practically did believe everything that made for good in our own personal lives, we should be found indulging all kinds of fancies about this world's affairs, and all kinds of sentimental superstitions about a world hereafter. Your suspicion here is undoubtedly well founded, and it is evident that something happens when you pass from the abstract to the concrete that complicates the situation.

I said just now that what is better for us to believe is true *unless the belief incidentally clashes with some other vital benefit.* Now in real life what vital benefits is any particular belief of ours most liable to clash with? What indeed except the vital benefits yielded by *other beliefs* when these prove incompatible with the first ones? In other words, the greatest enemy of any one of our truths may be the rest of our truths. Truths have once for all this desperate instinct of self-preservation and of desire to extinguish whatever contradicts them. My belief in the Absolute, based on the good it does me, must run the gauntlet of all my other beliefs. Grant that it may be true in giving me a moral holiday. Nevertheless, as I conceive it—and let me speak now confidentially, as it were, and merely in my own private person—it clashes with other truths of mine whose benefits I hate to give up on its account. It happens to be associated with a kind of logic of which I am the enemy, I find that it entangles me in metaphysical paradoxes that are inacceptable, etc., etc. But as I have enough trouble in life already without adding the trouble of carrying these intellectual inconsistencies, I personally just give up the Absolute. I just *take* my moral holidays; or else as a professional philosopher, I try to justify them by some other principle.

If I could restrict my notion of the Absolute to its bare

holiday-giving value, it wouldn't clash with any other truths. But we can not easily thus restrict our hypotheses. They carry supernumerary features, and these it is that clash so. My disbelief in the Absolute means then disbelief in those other supernumerary features, for I fully believe in the legitimacy of taking moral holidays.

You see by this what I meant when I called pragmatism a mediator and reconciler and said, borrowing the word from Papini, that she "unstiffens" our theories. She has in fact no prejudices whatever, no obstructive dogmas, no rigid canons of what shall count as proof. She is completely genial. She will entertain any hypothesis, she will consider any evidence. It follows that in the religious field she is at a great advantage both over positivistic empiricism, with its anti-theological bias, and over religious rationalism, with its exclusive interest in the remote, the noble, the simple, and the abstract in the way of conception.

In short, she widens the field of search for God. Rationalism sticks to logic and the empyrean. Empiricism sticks to the external senses. Pragmatism is willing to take anything, to follow either logic or the senses and to count the humblest and most personal experiences. She will count mystical experiences if they have practical consequences. She will take a God who lives in the very dirt of private fact—if that should seem a likely place to find him.

Her only test of probable truth is what works best in the way of leading us, what fits every part of life best and combines with the collectivity of experience's demands, nothing being omitted. If theological ideas should do this, if the notion of God, in particular, should prove to do it, how could pragmatism possibly deny God's existence? She could see no meaning in treating as "not true" a notion that was pragmatically so successful. What other kind of truth could there be, for her, than all this agreement with concrete reality?

In my last lecture I shall return again to the relations of pragmatism with religion. But you see already how democratic she is. Her manners are as various and flexible, her resources as rich and endless, and her conclusions as friendly as those of mother nature.

SOME METAPHYSICAL PROBLEMS
PRAGMATICALLY CONSIDERED

I am now to make the pragmatic method more familiar by giving you some illustrations of its application to particular problems. I will begin with what is driest, and the first thing I shall take will be the problem of *Substance*. Every one uses the old distinction between substance and attribute, enshrined as it is in the very structure of human language, in the difference between grammatical subject and predicate. Here is a bit of blackboard crayon. Its modes, attributes, properties, accidents, or affections—use which term you will—are whiteness, friability, cylindrical shape, insolubility in water, etc., etc. But the bearer of these attributes is so much *chalk,* which thereupon is called the substance in which they inhere. So the attributes of this desk inhere in the substance "wood," those of my coat in the substance "wool," and so forth. Chalk, wood, and wool, show again, in spite of their differences, common properties, and in so far forth they are themselves counted as modes of a still more primal substance, *matter,* the attributes of which are space-occupancy and impenetrability. Similarly our thoughts and feelings are affections or properties of our several *souls,* which are substances, but again not wholly in their own right, for they are modes of the still deeper substance "spirit."

Now it was very early seen that all *we know* of the chalk is the whiteness, friability, etc., all *we know* of the wood is the combustibility and fibrous structure. A group of attributes is what each substance here is known-as, they form its sole cash-value for our actual experience. The substance is in every case revealed through *them;* if we were cut off from *them* we should never suspect its existence; and if God should keep sending them to us in an unchanged order, miraculously

annihilating at a certain moment the substance that supported
them, we never could detect the moment, for our experiences
themselves would be unaltered. Nominalists accordingly adopt
the opinion that substance is a spurious idea due to our
inveterate human trick of turning names into things. Phenomena come in groups—the chalk-group, the wood-group, etc.
—and each group gets its name. The name we then treat as
in a way supporting the group of phenomena. The low thermometer today, for instance, is supposed to come from something called the "climate." Climate is really only the name
for a certain group of days, but it is treated as if it lay *behind*
the day, and in general we place the name, as if it were a
being, behind the facts it is the name of. But the phenomenal
properties of things, nominalists say, surely do not really inhere in names, and if not in names then they do not inhere
in anything. They *ad*here, or *co*here, rather, *with each other,*
and the notion of a substance inaccessible to us, which we
think accounts for such cohesion by supporting it, as cement might support pieces of mosaic, must be abandoned.
The fact of the bare cohesion itself is all that the notion of the
substance signifies. Behind that fact is nothing.

Scholasticism has taken the notion of substance from common sense and made it very technical and articulate. Few
things would seem to have fewer pragmatic consequences for
us than substances, cut off as we are from every contact with
them. Yet in one case scholasticism has proved the importance
of the substance-idea by treating it pragmatically. I refer to
certain disputes about the mystery of the Eucharist. Substance here would appear to have momentous pragmatic value.
Since the accidents of the wafer don't change in the Lord's
supper, and yet it has become the very body of Christ, it must
be that the change is in the substance solely. The bread-
substance must have been withdrawn, and the divine substance substituted miraculously without altering the immediate sensible properties. But tho these don't alter, a tremendous difference has been made, no less a one than this, that
we who take the sacrament, now feed upon the very substance
of divinity. The substance-notion breaks into life, then, with
tremendous effect, if once you allow that substances can
separate from their accidents, and exchange these latter.

This is the only pragmatic application of the substance-
idea with which I am acquainted; and it is obvious that it

will only be treated seriously by those who already believe in the "real presence" on independent grounds.

Material substance was criticised by Berkeley with such telling effect that his name has reverberated through all subsequent philosophy. Berkeley's treatment of the notion of matter is so well known as to need hardly more than a mention. So far from denying the external world which we know, Berkeley corroborated it. It was the scholastic notion of a material substance unapproachable by us, *behind* the external world, deeper and more real than it, and needed to support it, which Berkeley maintained to be the most effective of all reducers of the external world to unreality. Abolish that substance, he said, believe that God, whom you can understand and approach, sends you the sensible world directly, and you confirm the latter and back it up by his divine authority. Berkeley's criticism of "matter" was consequently absolutely pragmatistic. Matter is known as our sensations of colour, figure, hardness and the like. They are the cash-value of the term. The difference matter makes to us by truly being is that we then get such sensations; by not being, is that we lack them. These sensations then are its sole meaning. Berkeley doesn't deny matter, then; he simply tells us what it consists of. It is a true name for just so much in the way of sensations.

Locke, and later Hume, applied a similar pragmatic criticism to the notion of *spiritual substance*. I will only mention Locke's treatment of our "personal identity." He immediately reduces this notion to its pragmatic value in terms of experience. It means, he says, so much "consciousness," namely the fact that at one moment of life we remember other moments, and feel them all as parts of one and the same personal history. Rationalism had explained this practical continuity in our life by the unity of our soul-substance. But Locke says: suppose that God should take away the consciousness, should *we* be any the better for having still the soul-principle? Suppose he annexed the same consciousness to different souls, should *we*, as we realize *ourselves*, be any the worse for that fact? In Locke's day the soul was chiefly a thing to be rewarded or punished. See how Locke, discussing it from this point of view, keeps the question pragmatic:

"Suppose," he says, "one to think himself to be the same *soul* that once was Nestor or Thersites. Can he think their actions his own any more than the actions of any other man that ever existed? But let him once find himself *conscious* of any of the actions of Nestor, he then finds himself the same person with Nestor. . . . In this personal identity is founded all the right and justice of reward and punishment. It may be reasonable to think, no one shall be made to answer for what he knows nothing of, but shall receive his doom, his consciousness accusing or excusing. Supposing a man punished now for what he had done in another life, whereof he could be made to have no consciousness at all, what difference is there between that punishment and being created miserable?"

Our personal identity, then, consists, for Locke, solely in pragmatically definable particulars. Whether, apart from these verifiable facts, it also inheres in a spiritual principle, is a merely curious speculation. Locke, compromiser that he was, passively tolerated the belief in a substantial soul behind our consciousness. But his successor Hume, and most empirical psychologists after him, have denied the soul, save as the name for verifiable cohesions in our inner life. They redescend into the stream of experience with it, and cash it into so much small-change value in the way of "ideas" and their peculiar connexions with each other. As I said of Berkeley's matter, the soul is good or "true" for just *so much,* but no more.

The mention of material substance naturally suggests the doctrine of "materialism," but philosophical materialism is not necessarily knit up with belief in "matter," as a metaphysical principle. One may deny matter in that sense, as strongly as Berkeley did, one may be a phenomenalist like Huxley, and yet one may still be a materialist in the wider sense, of explaining higher phenomena by lower ones, and leaving the destinies of the world at the mercy of its blinder parts and forces. It is in this wider sense of the word that materialism is opposed to spiritualism or theism. The laws of physical nature are what run things, materialism says. The highest productions of human genius might be ciphered by one who had complete acquaintance with the facts, out of their physiological conditions, regardless whether nature be there only for our minds, as idealists contend, or not. Our minds in any case would have to record the kind of nature it is, and write it down as operating through blind laws of physics. This is the complexion of present day materialism, which may better be called naturalism. Over against it stands "theism," or what in a wide sense may be termed "spiritualism." Spiritualism says that mind not only witnesses and records things, but also runs and operates them: the world being thus guided, not by its lower, but by its higher element.

Treated as it often is, this question becomes little more than a conflict between aesthetic preferences. Matter is gross, coarse, crass, muddy; spirit is pure, elevated, noble; and since it is more consonant with the dignity of the universe to give the primacy in it to what appears superior, spirit must be affirmed as the ruling principle. To treat abstract principles as finalities, before which our intellects may come to rest in a state of admiring contemplation, is the great rationalist failing. Spiritualism, as often held, may be simply a state of admiration for one kind, and of dislike for another kind, of abstraction. I remember a worthy spiritualist professor who always referred to materialism as the "mud-philosophy," and deemed it thereby refuted.

To such spiritualism as this there is an easy answer, and Mr. Spencer makes it effectively. In some well-written pages at the end of the first volume of his Psychology he shows us that a "matter" so infinitely subtle, and performing motions as inconceivably quick and fine as those which modern science postulates in her explanations, has no trace of grossness left. He shows that the conception of spirit, as we mortals hitherto have framed it, is itself too gross to cover the exquisite tenuity of nature's facts. Both terms, he says, are but symbols, pointing to that one unknowable reality in which their oppositions cease.

To an abstract objection an abstract rejoinder suffices; and so far as one's opposition to materialism springs from one's disdain of matter as something "crass," Mr. Spencer cuts the ground from under one. Matter is indeed infinitely and incredibly refined. To any one who has ever looked on the face of a dead child or parent the mere fact that matter *could* have taken for a time that precious form, ought to make matter sacred ever after. It makes no difference what the *principle* of life may be, material or immaterial, matter at any rate cooperates, lends itself to all life's purposes. That beloved incarnation was among matter's possibilities.

But now, instead of resting in principles, after this stagnant intellectualist fashion, let us apply the pragmatic method to the question. What do we *mean* by matter? What practical difference can it make *now* that the world should be run by matter or by spirit? I think we find that the problem takes with this a rather different character.

And first of all I call your attention to a curious fact. It makes not a single jot of difference so far as the *past* of the world goes, whether we deem it to have been the work of matter or whether we think a divine spirit was its author.

Imagine, in fact, the entire contents of the world to be once for all irrevocably given. Imagine it to end this very moment, and to have no future; and then let a theist and a materialist apply their rival explanations to its history. The theist shows how a God made it; the materialist shows, and we will suppose with equal success, how it resulted from blind physical forces. Then let the pragmatist be asked to choose between their theories. How can he apply his test if a world is already completed? Concepts for him are things to come back into experience with, things to make us look for differences. But by hypothesis there is to be no more experience and no possible differences can now be looked for. Both theories have shown all their consequences and, by the hypothesis we are adopting, these are identical. The pragmatist must consequently say that the two theories, in spite of their different-sounding names, mean exactly the same thing, and that the dispute is purely verbal. [I am supposing, of course, that the theories *have* been equally successful in their explanations of what is.]

For just consider the case sincerely, and say what would be the *worth* of a God if he *were* there, with his work accomplished and his world run down. He would be worth no more than just that world was worth. To that amount of result, with its mixed merits and defects, his creative power could attain but go no farther. And since there is to be no future; since the whole value and meaning of the world has been already paid in and actualized in the feelings that went with it in the passing, and now go with it in the ending; since it draws no supplemental significance (such as our real world draws) from its function of preparing something yet to come; why then, by it we take God's measure, as it were. He is the Being who could once for all do *that;* and for that much we are thankful to him, but for nothing more. But now, on the contrary hypothesis, namely, that the bits of matter following their laws could make that world and do no less, should we

not be just as thankful to them? Wherein should we suffer
loss, then, if we dropped God as an hypothesis and made the
matter alone responsible? Where would any special deadness, or crassness, come in? And how, experience being what
is once for all, would God's presence in it make it any more
living or richer?

Candidly, it is impossible to give any answer to this question. The actually experienced world is supposed to be the
same in its details on either hypothesis, "the same, for our
praise or blame," as Browning says. It stands there indefea-
sibly: a gift which can't be taken back. Calling matter the
cause of it retracts no single one of the items that have made
it up, nor does calling God the cause augment them. They
are the God or the atoms, respectively, of just that and no
other world. The God, if there, has been doing just what
atoms could do—appearing in the character of atoms, so to
speak—and earning such gratitude as is due to atoms, and
no more. If his presence lends no different turn or issue to the
performance, it surely can lend it no increase of dignity. Nor
would indignity come to it were he absent, and did the atoms
remain only actors on the stage. When a play is once over,
and the curtain down, you really make it no better by claiming an illustrious genius for its author, just as you make it no
worse by calling him a common hack.

Thus if no future detail of experience or conduct is to be
deduced from our hypothesis, the debate between materialism
and theism becomes quite idle and insignificant. Matter and
God in that event mean exactly the same thing—the power,
namely, neither more nor less, that could make just this
completed world—and the wise man is he who in such a case
would turn his back on such a supererogatory discussion. Accordingly, most men instinctively, and positivists and scientists
deliberately, do turn their backs on philosophical disputes
from which nothing in the line of definite future consequences
can be seen to follow. The verbal and empty character of
philosophy is surely a reproach with which we are but too
familiar. If pragmatism be true, it is a perfectly sound reproach unless the theories under fire can be shown to have
alternative practical outcomes, however delicate and distant
these may be. The common man and the scientist say they
discover no such outcomes, and if the metaphysician can discern none either, the others certainly are in the right of it,

as against him. His science is then but pompous trifling; and the endowment of a professorship for such a being would be silly.

Accordingly, in every genuine metaphysical debate some practical issue, however conjectural and remote, is involved. To realize this, revert with me to our question, and place yourselves this time in the world we live in, in the world that *has* a future, that is yet uncompleted whilst we speak. In this unfinished world the alternative of "materialism or theism?" is intensely practical; and it is worth while for us to spend some minutes of our hour in seeing that it is so.

How, indeed, does the program differ for us, according as we consider that the facts of experience up to date are purposeless configurations of blind atoms moving according to eternal laws, or that on the other hand they are due to the providence of God? As far as the past facts go, indeed, there is no difference. Those facts are in, are bagged, are captured; and the good that's in them is gained, be the atoms or be the God their cause. There are accordingly many materialists about us today who, ignoring altogether the future and practical aspects of the question, seek to eliminate the odium attaching to the word materialism, and even to eliminate the word itself, by showing that, if matter could give birth to all these gains, why then matter, functionally considered, is just as divine an entity as God, in fact coalesces with God, is what you mean by God. Cease, these persons advise us, to use either of these terms, with their outgrown opposition. Use a term free of the clerical connotations, on the one hand; of the suggestion of grossness, coarseness, ignobility, on the other. Talk of the primal mystery, of the unknowable energy, of the one and only power, instead of saying either God or matter. This is the course to which Mr. Spencer urges us; and if philosophy were purely retrospective, he would thereby proclaim himself an excellent pragmatist.

But philosophy is prospective also, and, after finding what the world has been and done, and yielded, still asks the further question "what does the world *promise?*" Give us a matter that promises *success*, that is bound by its laws to lead our world ever nearer to perfection, and any rational man will worship that matter as readily as Mr. Spencer worships his own so-called unknowable power. It not only has made for righteousness up to date, but it will make for

righteousness forever; and that is all we need. Doing practically all that a God can do, it is equivalent to God, its function
is a God's function, and in a world in which a God would be
superfluous; from such a world a God could never lawfully be
missed. "Cosmic emotion" would here be the right name for
religion.

But *is* the matter by which Mr. Spencer's process of cosmic
evolution is carried on any such principle of never-ending
perfection as this? Indeed it is not, for the future end of every
cosmically evolved thing or system of things is foretold by
science to be death tragedy; and Mr. Spencer, in confining
himself to the aesthetic and ignoring the practical side of the
controversy, has really contributed nothing serious to its
relief. But apply now our principle of practical results, and
see what a vital significance the question of materialism or
theism immediately acquires.

Theism and materialism, so indifferent when taken retrospectively, point, when we take them prospectively, to wholly
different outlooks of experience. For, according to the theory
of mechanical evolution, the laws of redistribution of matter
and motion, though they are certainly to thank for all the good
hours which our organisms have ever yielded us and for all
the ideals which our minds now frame, are yet fatally certain
to undo their work again, and to redissolve everything that
they have once evolved. You all know the picture of the last
state of the universe, which evolutionary science foresees.
I can not state it better than in Mr. Balfour's words: "The
energies of our system will decay, the glory of the sun will
be dimmed, and the earth, tideless and inert, will no longer
tolerate the race which has for a moment disturbed its
solitude. Man will go down into the pit, and all his thoughts
will perish. The uneasy consciousness which in this obscure
corner has for a brief space broken the contented silence of
the universe, will be at rest. Matter will know itself no longer.
'Imperishable monuments' and 'immortal deeds,' death itself,
and love stronger than death, will be as if they had not been.
Nor will anything that is, be better or worse for all that the
labor, genius, devotion, and suffering of man have striven
through countless ages to effect." [1]

That is the sting of it, that in the vast driftings of the
cosmic weather, though many a jewelled shore appears, and
many an enchanted cloud-bank floats away, long lingering ere

it be dissolved—even as our world now lingers, for our joy—
yet when these transient products are gone, nothing, absolutely
nothing remains, to represent those particular qualities, those
elements of preciousness which they may have enshrined.
Dead and gone are they, gone utterly from the very sphere
and room of being. Without an echo; without a memory;
without an influence on aught that may come after, to make
it care for similar ideals. This utter final wreck and tragedy
is of the essence of scientific materialism as at present understood. The lower and not the higher forces are the eternal
forces, or the last surviving forces within the only cycle of
evolution which we can definitely see. Mr. Spencer believes
this as much as any one; so why should he argue with us as
if we were making silly aesthetic objections to the "grossness"
of "matter and motion," the principles of his philosophy, when
what really dismays us is the disconsolateness of its ulterior
practical results?

No, the true objection to materialism is not positive but
negative. It would be farcical at this day to make complaint
of it for what it *is*, for "grossness." Grossness is what grossness
does—we now know *that*. We make complaint of it, on the
contrary, for what it is *not*—not a permanent warrant for our
more ideal interests, not a fulfiller of our remotest hopes.

The notion of God, on the other hand, however inferior it
may be in clearness to those mathematical notions so current
in mechanical philosophy, has at least this practical superiority
over them, that it guarantees an ideal order that shall be
permanently preserved. A world with a God in it to say the
last word, may indeed burn up or freeze, but we then think
of him as still mindful of the old ideals and sure to bring them
elsewhere to fruition; so that, where he is, tragedy is only
provisional and partial, and shipwreck and dissolution not the
absolutely final things. This need of an eternal moral order
is one of the deepest needs of our breast. And those poets,
like Dante and Wordsworth, who live on the conviction of
such an order, owe to that fact the extraordinary tonic and
consoling power of their verse. Here then, in these different
emotional and practical appeals, in these adjustments of our
concrete attitudes of hope and expectation, and all the delicate
consequences which their differences entail, lie the real meanings of materialism and spiritualism—not in hair-splitting
abstractions about matter's inner essence, or about the meta-

physical attributes of God. Materialism means simply the denial that the moral order is eternal, and the cutting off of ultimate hopes; spiritualism means the affirmation of an eternal moral order and the letting loose of hope. Surely here is an issue genuine enough, for any one who feels it; and, as long as men are men, it will yield matter for a serious philosophic debate.

But possibly some of you may still rally to their defence. Even whilst admitting that spiritualism and materialism make different prophecies of the world's future, you may yourselves pooh-pooh the difference as something so infinitely remote as to mean nothing for a sane mind. The essence of a sane mind, you may say, is to take shorter views, and to feel no concern about such chimeras as the latter end of the world. Well, I can only say that if you say this, you do injustice to human nature. Religious melancholy is not disposed of by a simple flourish of the word insanity. The absolute things, the last things, the overlapping things, are the truly philosophic concerns; all superior minds feel seriously about them, and the mind with the shortest views is simply the mind of the more shallow man.

The issues of fact at stake in the debate are of course vaguely enough conceived by us at present. But spiritualistic faith in all its forms deals with a world of *promise,* while materialism's sun sets in a sea of disappointment. Remember what I said of the Absolute: it grants us moral holidays. Any religious view does this. It not only incites our more strenuous moments, but it also takes our joyous, careless, trustful moments, and it justifies them. It paints the grounds of justification vaguely enough, to be sure. The exact features of the saving future facts that our belief in God insures, will have to be ciphered out by the interminable methods of science: we can *study* our God only by studying his Creation. But we can *enjoy* our God, if we have one, in advance of all that labor. I myself believe that the evidence for God lies primarily in inner personal experiences. When they have once given you your God, his name means at least the benefit of the holiday. You remember what I said yesterday about the way in which truths clash and try to "down" each other. The truth of "God" has to run the gauntlet of all our other truths. It is on trial by them and they on trial by it. Our *final* opinion about God can be settled only after all the truths have straightened themselves out together. Let us hope that they shall find a *modus vivendi!*

Let me pass to a very cognate philosophic problem, the *question of design in nature.* God's existence has from time immemorial been held to be proved by certain natural facts. Many facts appear as if expressly designed in view of one another. Thus the woodpecker's bill, tongue, feet, tail, etc., fit him wondrously for a world of trees, with grubs hid in their bark to feed upon. The parts of our eye fit the laws of light to perfection, leading its rays to a sharp picture on our retina. Such mutual fitting of things diverse in origin argued design, it was held; and the designer was always treated as a man-loving deity.

The first step in these arguments was to prove that the design *existed.* Nature was ransacked for results obtained through separate things being co-adapted. Our eyes, for instance, originate in intra-uterine darkness, and the light originates in the sun, yet see how they fit each other. They are evidently made *for* each other. Vision is the end designed, light and eyes the separate means devised for its attainment.

It is strange, considering how unanimously our ancestors felt the force of this argument, to see how little it counts for since the triumph of the darwinian theory. Darwin opened our minds to the power of chance-happenings to bring forth "fit" results if only they have time to add themselves together. He showed the enormous waste of nature in producing results that get destroyed because of their unfitness. He also emphasized the number of adaptations which, if designed, would argue an evil rather than a good designer. *Here,* all depends upon the point of view. To the grub under the bark the exquisite fitness of the woodpecker's organism to extract him would certainly argue a diabolical designer.

Theologians have by this time stretched their minds so as to embrace the darwinian facts, and yet to interpret them as still showing divine purpose. It used to be a question of purpose against mechanism, of one *or* the other. It was as if one should say "My shoes are evidently designed to fit my feet, hence it is impossible that they should have been produced by machinery." We know that they are both: they are made by a machinery itself designed to fit the feet with shoes. Theology need only stretch similarly the designs of God. As the aim of a football-team is not merely to get the ball to a certain goal (if that were so, they would simply get up on some dark night and place it there), but to get it there by a fixed *machinery of conditions*—the game's rules and the opposing players; so the aim of God is not merely, let us say, to make men and to save them, but rather to get this done through the sole agency of nature's vast machinery. Without nature's stupendous laws and counter-forces, man's creation and perfection, we might suppose, would be too insipid achievements for God to have proposed them.

This saves the form of the design-argument at the expense of its old easy human content. The designer is no longer the old man-like deity. His designs have grown so vast as to be incomprehensible to us humans. The *what* of them so overwhelms us that to establish the mere *that* of a designer for them becomes of very little consequence in comparison. We can with difficulty comprehend the *character* of a cosmic mind whose purposes are fully revealed by the strange mixture of goods and evils that we find in this actual world's particulars. Or rather we cannot by any possibility comprehend it. The mere word "design" by itself has no consequences and explains nothing. It is the most barren of principles. The old question of *whether* there is design is idle. The real question is what *is* the world, whether or not it have a designer— and that can be revealed only by the study of all nature's particulars.

Remember that *no matter what* nature may have produced or may be producing, the means must necessarily have been adequate, must have been *fitted to that production*. The argument from fitness to design would consequently always apply, whatever were the product's character. The recent Mont-Pelée eruption, for example, required all previous history to produce that exact combination of ruined houses, human and animal corpses, sunken ships, volcanic ashes, etc., in just that one hideous configuration of positions. France had to be a nation and colonize Martinique. Our country had to exist and send our ships there. *If* God aimed at just that result, the means by which the centuries bent their influences towards it, showed exquisite intelligence. And so of any state of things whatever, either in nature or in history, which we find actually realized. For the parts of things must always make *some* definite resultant, be it chaotic or harmonious. When we look at what has actually come, the conditions must always appear perfectly designed to ensure it. We can always say, therefore, in any conceivable world, of any conceivable character, that the whole cosmic machinery *may* have been designed to produce it.

Pragmatically, then, the abstract word "design" is a blank cartridge. It carries no consequences, it does no execution. *What* design? and *what* designer? are the only serious questions, and the study of facts is the only way of getting even approximate answers. Meanwhile, pending the slow answer from facts, any one who insists that there *is* a designer and who is sure he is a divine one, gets a certain pragmatic benefit from the term—the same, in fact, which we saw that the terms God, Spirit, or the Absolute, yield us. "Design," worthless tho it be as a mere rationalistic principle set above or behind things for our admiration, becomes, if our faith concretes it into something theistic, a term of *promise*. Returning with it into experience, we gain a more confiding outlook on the future. If not a blind force but a seeing force runs things, we may reasonably expect better issues. This vague confidence in the future is the sole pragmatic meaning at present discernible in the terms design and designer. But if cosmic confidence is right not wrong, better not worse, that is a most important meaning. That much at least of possible "truth" the terms will then have in them.

Let me take up another well-worn controversy, *the free-will problem*. Most persons who believe in what is called their free-will do so after the rationalistic fashion. It is a principle, a positive faculty or virtue added to man, by which his dignity is enigmatically augmented. He ought to believe it for this reason. Determinists, who deny it, who say that individual men originate nothing, but merely transmit to the future the whole push of the past cosmos of which they are so small an expression, diminish man. He is less admirable, stripped of this creative principle. I imagine that more than half of you share our instinctive belief in free-will, and that admiration of it as a principle of dignity has much to do with your fidelity.

But free-will has also been discussed pragmatically, and, strangely enough, the same pragmatic interpretation has been put upon it by both disputants. You know how large a part questions of *accountability* have played in ethical controversy.

To hear some persons, one would suppose that all that ethics aims at is a code of merits and demerits. Thus does the old legal and theological leaven, the interest in crime and sin and punishment abide with us. "Who's to blame? whom can we punish? whom will God punish?"—these preoccupations hang like a bad dream over man's religious history.

So both free-will and determinism have been inveighed against and called absurd, because each, in the eyes of its enemies, has seemed to prevent the "imputability" of good or bad deeds to their authors. Queer antinomy this! Free-will means novelty, the grafting on to the past of something not involved therein. If our acts were predetermined, if we merely transmitted the push of the whole past, the free-willists say, how could we be praised or blamed for anything? We should be "agents" only, not "principals," and where then would be our precious imputability and responsibility?

But where would it be if we *had* free-will? rejoin the determinists. If a "free" act be a sheer novelty, that comes not *from* me, the previous me, but *ex nihilo*, and simply tacks itself on to me, how can I, the previous I, be responsible? How can I have any permanent *character* that will stand still long enough for praise or blame to be awarded? The chaplet of my days tumbles into a cast of disconnected beads as soon as the thread of inner necessity is drawn out by the preposterous indeterminist doctrine. Messrs. Fullerton and McTaggart have recently laid about them doughtily with this argument.

It may be good *ad hominem*, but otherwise it is pitiful. For I ask you, quite apart from other reasons, whether any man, woman or child, with a sense for realities, ought not to be ashamed to plead such principles as either dignity or imputability. Instinct and utility between them can safely be trusted to carry on the social business of punishment and praise. If a man does good acts we shall praise him, if he does bad acts we shall punish him—anyhow, and quite apart from theories as to whether the acts result from what was previous in him or are novelties in a strict sense. To make our human ethics revolve about the question of "merit" is a piteous unreality—God alone can know our merits, if we have any. The real ground for supposing free-will is indeed pragmatic, but it has nothing to do with this contemptible right to punish which has made such a noise in past discussions of the subject.

Free-will pragmatically means *novelties in the world*, the right to expect that in its deepest elements as well as in its surface phenomena, the future may not identically repeat and imitate the past. That imitation *en masse* is there, who can deny? The general "uniformity of nature" is presupposed by every lesser law. But nature may be only approximately uniform; and persons in whom knowledge of the world's past has bred pessimism (or doubts as to the world's good character, which become certainties if that character be supposed eternally fixed) may naturally welcome free-will as a *melioristic* doctrine. It holds up improvement as at least possible; whereas determinism assures us that our whole notion of possibility is born of human ignorance, and that necessity and impossibility between them rule the destinies of the world.

Free-will is thus a general cosmological theory of *promise*, just like the Absolute, God, Spirit or Design. Taken abstractly, no one of these terms has any inner content, none of them gives us any picture, and no one of them would retain the least pragmatic value in a world whose character was obviously perfect from the start. Elation at mere existence, pure cosmic emotion and delight, would, it seems to me, quench all interest in those speculations, if the world were nothing but a lubberland of happiness already. Our interest in religious metaphysics arises in the fact that our empirical future feels to us unsafe, and needs some higher guarantee. If the past and present were purely good, who could wish that the future might possibly not resemble them? Who could desire free-will? Who would not say, with Huxley, "let me be wound up every day like a watch, to go right fatally, and I ask no better freedom." "Freedom" in a world already perfect could only mean freedom to *be worse*, and who could be so insane as to wish that? To be necessarily what it is, to be impossibly aught else, would put the last touch of perfection upon optimism's universe. Surely the only *possibility* that one can rationally claim is the possibility that things may be *better*. That possibility, I need hardly say, is one that, as the actual world goes, we have ample grounds for desiderating.

Free-will thus has no meaning unless it be a doctrine of *relief*. As such, it takes its place with other religious doctrines. Between them, they build up the old wastes and repair the former desolations. Our spirit, shut within this courtyard of sense-experience, is always saying to the intellect upon the tower: "Watchman, tell us of the night, if it aught of promise bear," and the intellect gives it then these terms of promise.

Other than this practical significance, the words God, free-will, design, etc., have none. Yet dark tho they be in themselves, or intellectualistically taken, when we bear them into life's thicket with us the darkness *there* grows light about us. If you stop, in dealing with such words, with their definition, thinking that to be an intellectual finality, where are you? Stupidly staring at a pretentious sham! "Deus est Ens, a se, extra et supra omne genus, necessarium, unum, infinite perfectum, simplex, immutabile, immensum, aeternum, intelligens," etc.—wherein is such a definition really instructive? It means less than nothing, in its pompous robe of adjectives. Pragmatism alone can read a positive meaning into it, and for that she turns her back upon the intellectualist point of view altogether. "God's in his heaven; all's right with the world!" *That's* the real heart of your theology, and for that you need no rationalist definitions.

Why shouldn't all of us, rationalists as well as pragmatists, confess this? Pragmatism, so far from keeping her eyes bent on the immediate practical foreground, as she is accused of doing, dwells just as much upon the world's remotest perspectives.

See then how all these ultimate questions turn, as it were, upon their hinges; and from looking backwards upon principles, upon an *erkenntnisstheoretische Ich,* a God, a *Kausalitätsprinzip,* a Design, a Free-will, taken in themselves, as something august and exalted above facts—see, I say, how pragmatism shifts the emphasis and looks forward into facts themselves. The really vital question for us all is, What is this world going to be? What is life eventually to make of itself? The centre of gravity of philosophy must therefore alter its place. The earth of things, long thrown into shadow by the glories of the upper ether, must resume its rights. To shift the emphasis in this way means that philosophic questions will fail to be treated by minds of a less abstractionist type than heretofore, minds more scientific and individualistic in their tone yet not irreligious either. It will be an alteration in "the seat of authority" that reminds one almost of the protestant reformation. And as, to papal minds, protestantism has often seemed a mere mess of anarchy and confusion, such, no doubt, will pragmatism often seem to ultra-rationalist minds in philosophy. It will seem so much sheer trash, philosophically. But life wags on, all the same, and compasses its ends, in protestant countries. I venture to think that philosophic protestantism will compass a not dissimilar prosperity.

THE ONE AND THE MANY

We saw in the last lecture that the pragmatic method, in its dealings with certain concepts, instead of ending with admiring contemplation, plunges forward into the river of experience with them and prolongs the perspective by their means. Design, free-will, the absolute mind, spirit instead of matter, have for their sole meaning a better promise as to this world's outcome. Be they false or be they true, the meaning of them is this meliorism. I have sometimes thought of the phenomenon called "total reflexion" in Optics as a good symbol of the relation between abstract ideas and concrete realities, as pragmatism conceives it. Hold a tumbler of water a little above your eyes and look up through the water at its surface —or better still look similarly through the flat wall of an aquarium. You will then see an extraordinarily brilliant reflected image say of a candle-flame, or any other clear object, situated on the opposite side of the vessel. No ray, under these circumstances, gets beyond the water's surface: every ray is totally reflected back into the depths again. Now let the water represent the world of sensible facts, and let the air above it represent the world of abstract ideas. Both worlds are real, of course, and interact; but they interact only at their boundary, and the *locus* of everything that lives, and happens to us, so far as full experience goes, is the water. We are like fishes swimming in the sea of sense, bounded above by the superior element, but unable to breathe it pure or penetrate it. We get our oxygen from it, however, we touch it incessantly, now in this part, now in that, and every time we touch it, we turn back into the water with our course re-determined and re-energized. The abstract ideas of which the air consists are indispensable for life, but irrespirable by themselves, as it were,

57

and only active in their re-directing function. All similes are halting, but this one rather takes my fancy. It shows how something, not sufficient for life in itself, may nevertheless be an effective determinant of life elsewhere.

In this present hour I wish to illustrate the pragmatic method by one more application. I wish to turn its light upon the ancient problem of "the one and the many." I suspect that in but few of you has this problem occasioned sleepless nights, and I should not be astonished if some of you told me it had never vexed you at all. I myself have come, by long brooding over it, to consider it the most central of all philosophic problems, central because so pregnant. I mean by this that if you know whether a man is a decided monist or a decided pluralist, you perhaps know more about the rest of his opinions than if you give him any other name ending in *ist*. To believe in the one or in the many, that is the classification with the maximum number of consequences. So bear with me for an hour while I try to inspire you with my own interest in this problem.

Philosophy has often been defined as the quest or the vision of the world's unity. Few persons ever challenge this definition, which is true as far as it goes, for philosophy has indeed manifested above all things its interest in unity. But how about the *variety* in things? Is that such an irrelevant matter? If instead of using the term philosophy, we talk in general of our intellect and its needs, we quickly see that unity is only one of them. Acquaintance with the details of fact is always reckoned, along with their reduction to system, as an indispensable mark of mental greatness. Your "scholarly" mind, of encyclopedic, philological type, your man essentially of *learning*, has never lacked for praise along with your philosopher. What our intellect really aims at is neither variety nor unity taken singly, but *totality.'* In this, acquaintance with reality's diversities is as important as understanding their connection. Curiosity goes *pari passu* with the systematizing passion.

In spite of this obvious fact the unity of things has always been considered more *illustrious*, as it were, than their variety. When a young man first conceives the notion that the whole world forms one great fact, with all its parts moving abreast, as it were, and interlocked, he feels as if he were enjoying a great insight, and looks superciliously on all who still fall short of this sublime conception. Taken thus abstractly as it first comes to one, the monistic insight is so vague as hardly to seem worth defending intellectually. Yet probably every one in this audience in some way cherishes it. A certain abstract monism, a certain emotional response to the character of oneness, as if it were a feature of the world not coordinate with its manyness, but vastly more excellent and eminent, is so prevalent in educated circles that we might almost call it a part of philosophic common sense. Of *course* the world is One, we say. How else could it be a world at all? Empiricists as a rule are as stout monists of this abstract kind as rationalists are.

The difference is that the empiricists are less dazzled. Unity doesn't blind them to everything else, doesn't quench their curiosity for special facts, whereas there is a kind of rationalist who is sure to interpret abstract unity mystically and to forget everything else, to treat it as a principle; to admire and worship it; and thereupon to come to a full stop intellectually.

"The world is One!"—the formula may become a sort of number-worship. "Three" and "seven" have, it is true, been reckoned sacred numbers; but, abstractly taken, why is "one" more excellent than "forty-three," or than "two million and ten"? In this first vague conviction of the world's unity, there is so little to take hold of that we hardly know what we mean by it.

The only way to get forward with our notion is to treat it pragmatically. Granting the oneness to exist, what facts will be different in consequence? What will the unity be known as? The world is One—yes, but *how* one? What is the practical value of the oneness for *us?*

Asking such questions, we pass from the vague to the definite, from the abstract to the concrete. Many distinct ways in which a oneness predicated of the universe might make a difference, come to view. I will note successively the more obvious of these ways.

1. First, the world is at least *one subject of discourse*. If its manyness were so irremediable as to permit *no* union whatever of its parts, not even our minds could "mean" the whole of it at once: they would be like eyes trying to look in opposite directions. But in point of fact we mean to cover the whole of it by our abstract term "world" or "universe," which expressly intends that no part shall be left out. Such unity of discourse carries obviously no farther monistic

specifications. A "chaos," once so named, has as much unity of discourse as a cosmos. It is an odd fact that many monists consider a great victory scored for their side when pluralists say "the universe is many." " 'The Universe'!" they chuckle— "his speech bewrayeth him. He stands confessed of monism out of his own mouth." Well, let things be one in so far forth! You can then fling such a word as universe at the whole collection of them, but what matters it? It still remains to be ascertained whether they are one in any further or more valuable sense.

2. Are they, for example, *continuous?* Can you pass from one to another, keeping always in your one universe without any danger of falling out? In other words, do the parts of our universe *hang together*, instead of being like detached grains of sand?

Even grains of sand hang together through the space in which they are embedded, and if you can in any way move through such space, you can pass continuously from number one of them to number two. Space and time are thus vehicles of continuity by which the world's parts hang together. The practical difference to us, resultant from these forms of union, is immense. Our whole motor life is based upon them.

3. There are innumerable other paths of practical continuity among things. Lines of *influence* can be traced by which they hang together. Following any such line you pass from one thing to another till you may have covered a good part of the universe's extent. Gravity and heat-conduction are such all-uniting influences, so far as the physical world goes. Electric, luminous and chemical influences follow similar lines of influence. But opaque and inert bodies interrupt the continuity here, so that you have to step round them, or change your mode of progress if you wish to get farther on that day. Practically, you have then lost your universe's unity, *so far as it was constituted by those first lines of influence*.

There are innumerable kinds of connection that special things have with other special things; and the *ensemble* of any one of these connections forms one sort of *system* by which things are conjoined. Thus men are conjoined in a vast network of *acquaintanceship*. Brown knows Jones, Jones knows Robinson, etc.; and *by choosing your farther intermediaries rightly* you may carry a message from Jones to the Empress of China, or the Chief of the African Pigmies, or to any one

else in the inhabited world. But you are stopped short, as by
a non-conductor, when you choose one man wrong in this
experiment. What may be called love-systems are grafted
on the acquaintance-system. A loves (or hates) B; B loves (or
hates) C, etc. But these systems are smaller than the great
acquaintance-system that they presuppose.

Human efforts are daily unifying the world more and
more in definite systematic ways. We found colonial, postal,
consular, commercial systems, all the parts of which obey
definite influences that propagate themselves within the system but not to facts outside of it. The result is innumerable
little hangings-together of the world's parts within the larger
hangings-together, little worlds, not only of discourse but of
operation, within the wider universe. Each system exemplifies
one type or grade of union, its parts being strung on that
peculiar kind of relation, and the same part may figure in
many different systems, as a man may hold various offices and
belong to several clubs. From this "systematic" point of view,
therefore, the pragmatic value of the world's unity is that all
these definite networks actually and practically exist. Some
are more enveloping and extensive, some less so; they are
superposed upon each other; and between them all they let
no individual elementary part of the universe escape. Enormous as is the amount of disconnection among things (for
these systematic influences and conjunctions follow rigidly
exclusive paths), everything that exists is influenced in *some*
way by something else, if you can only pick the way out
rightly. Loosely speaking, and in general, it may be said that
all things cohere and adhere to each other *somehow*, and that
the universe exists practically in reticulated or concatenated
forms which make of it a continuous or "integrated" affair.
Any kind of influence whatever helps to make the world one,
so far as you can follow it from next to next. You may then
say that "the world *is* One," meaning in these respects, namely,
and just so far as they obtain. But just as definitely is it *not*
One, so far as they do not obtain; and there is no species of
connection which will not fail, if, instead of choosing conductors for it you choose non-conductors. You are then
arrested at your very first step and have to write the world
down as a pure *many* from that particular point of view. If our
intellect had been as much interested in disjunctive as it is in

conjunctive relations, philosophy would have equally successfully celebrated the world's *disunion*.

The great point is to notice that the oneness and the manyness are absolutely co-ordinate here. Neither is primordial or more essential or excellent than the other. Just as with space, whose separating of things seems exactly on a par with its uniting of them, but sometimes one function and sometimes the other is what comes home to us most, so, in our general dealings with the world of influences, we now need conductors and now need non-conductors, and wisdom lies in knowing which is which at the appropriate moment.

4. All these systems of influence or non-influence may be listed under the general problem of the world's *causal unity*. If the minor causal influences among things should converge towards one common causal origin of them in the past, one great first cause for all that is, one might then speak of the absolute causal unity of the world. God's *fiat* on creation's day has figured in traditional philosophy as such an absolute cause and origin. Transcendental Idealism, translating "creation" into "thinking" (or "willing to think") calls the divine act "eternal" rather than "first," but the union of the many here is absolute, just the same—the many would not *be*, save for the One. Against this notion of the unity of origin of all things there has always stood the pluralistic notion of an eternal self-existing many in the shape of atoms or even of spiritual units of some sort. The alternative has doubtless a pragmatic meaning, but perhaps, as far as these lectures go, we had better leave the question of unity of origin unsettled.

5. The most important sort of union that obtains among things, pragmatically speaking, is their *generic unity*. Things exist in kinds, there are many specimens in each kind, and what the "kind" implies for one specimen, it implies also for every other specimen of that kind. We can easily conceive that every fact in the world might be singular, that is, unlike any other fact and sole of its kind. In such a world of singulars our logic would be useless, for logic works by predicating of the single instance what is true of all its kind. With no two things alike in the world, we should be unable to reason from our past experiences to our future ones. The existence of so much generic unity in things is thus perhaps the most momentous pragmatic specification of what it may mean to say "the world is One." *Absolute* generic unity would

obtain if there were one *summum genus* under which all things
without exception could be eventually subsumed. "Beings,"
"thinkables," "experiences," would be candidates for this
position. Whether the alternatives expressed by such words
have any pragmatic significance or not, is another question
which I prefer to leave unsettled just now.

6. Another specification of what the phrase "the world
is One" may mean is *unity of purpose*. An enormous number
of things in the world subserve a common purpose. All the
man-made systems, administrative, industrial, military, or
what not, exist each for its controlling purpose. Every living
being pursues its own peculiar purposes. They co-operate,
according to the degree of their development, in collective
or tribal purposes, larger ends thus enveloping lesser ones,
until an absolutely single, final and climacteric purpose sub-
served by all things without exception might conceivably be
reached. It is needless to say that the appearances conflict
with such a view. Any resultant, as I said in my third lecture,
may have been purposed in advance, but none of the results
we actually know in this world have in point of fact been
purposed in advance in all their details. Men and nations
start with a vague notion of being rich, or great, or good.
Each step they make brings unforeseen chances into sight, and
shuts out older vistas, and the specifications of the general
purpose have to be daily changed. What is reached in the
end may be better or worse than what was proposed, but it
is always more complex and different.

Our different purposes also are at war with each other.
Where one can't crush the other out, they compromise;
and the result is again different from what any one distinctly
proposed beforehand. Vaguely and generally, much of what
was purposed may be gained; but everything makes strongly
for the view that our world is incompletely unified teleologi-
cally and is still trying to get its unification better organized.

Whoever claims *absolute* teleological unity, saying that
there is one purpose that every detail of the universe sub-
serves, dogmatizes at his own risk. Theologians who dogmatize
thus find it more and more impossible, as our acquaintance
with the warring interests of the world's parts grows more
concrete, to imagine what the one climacteric purpose may
possibly be like. We see indeed that certain evils minister
to ulterior goods, that the bitter makes the cocktail better,

and that a bit of danger or hardship puts us agreeably to our trumps. We can vaguely generalize this into the doctrine that all the evil in the universe is but instrumental to its greater perfection. But the scale of the evil actually in sight defies all human tolerance; and transcendental idealism, in the pages of a Bradley or a Royce, brings us no farther than the book of Job did—God's ways are not our ways, so let us put our hands upon our mouth. A God who can relish such superfluities of horror is no God for human beings to appeal to. His animal spirits are too high. In other words the "Absolute" with his one purpose, is not the man-like God of common people.

7. *Aesthetic union* among things also obtains, and is very analogous to teleological union. Things tell a story. Their parts hang together so as to work out a climax. They play into each other's hands expressively. Retrospectively, we can see that altho no definite purpose presided over a chain of events, yet the events fell into a dramatic form, with a start, a middle, and a finish. In point of fact all stories end; and here again the point of view of a many is the more natural one to take. The world is full of partial stories that run parallel to one another, beginning and ending at odd times. They mutually interlace and interfere at points, but we can not unify them completely in our minds. In following your life-history, I must temporarily turn my attention from my own. Even a biographer of twins would have to press them alternately upon his reader's attention.

It follows that whoever says that the whole world tells one story utters another of those monistic dogmas that a man believes at his risk. It is easy to see the world's history pluralistically, as a rope of which each fibre tells a separate tale; but to conceive of each cross-section of the rope as an absolutely single fact, and to sum the whole longitudinal series into one being living an undivided life, is harder. We have indeed the analogy of embryology to help us. The microscopist makes a hundred flat cross-sections of a given embryo, and mentally unites them into one solid whole. But the great world's ingredients, so far as they are beings, seem like the rope's fibres, to be discontinuous, cross-wise, and to cohere only in the longitudinal direction. Followed in that direction they are many. Even the embryologist, when he follows the *development* of his object, has to treat the history of each single organ in turn. *Absolute* aesthetic union is thus another barely abstract ideal. The world appears as something more epic than dramatic.

So far, then, we see how the world is unified by its many systems, kinds, purposes, and dramas. That there is more union in all these ways than openly appears is certainly true. That there *may* be one sovereign purpose, system, kind, and story, is a legitimate hypothesis. All I say here is that it is rash to affirm this dogmatically without better evidence than we possess at present.

8. The *great* monistic *denkmittel* for a hundred years past has been the notion of *the one Knower*. The many exist only as objects for his thought—exist in his dream, as it were; and *as he knows* them, they have one purpose, form one system, tell one tale for him. This notion of an *all enveloping noetic unity* in things is the sublimest achievement of intellectualist philosophy. Those who believe in the Absolute, as the all-knower is termed, usually say that they do so for coercive reasons, which clear thinkers can not evade. The Absolute has far-reaching practical consequences, to some of which I drew attention in my second lecture. Many kinds of difference important to us would surely follow from its being true. I can not here enter into all the logical proofs of such a Being's existence, farther than to say that none of them seem to me sound. I must therefore treat the notion of an All-Knower simply as an hypothesis, exactly on a par logically with the pluralist notion that there is no point of view, no focus of information extant, from which the entire content of the universe is visible at once. "God's conscience," says Professor Royce,[2] "forms in its wholeness one luminously transparent conscious moment"—this is the type of noetic unity on which rationalism insists. Empiricism on the other hand is satisfied with the type of noetic unity that is humanly familiar. Everything gets known by *some* knower along with something else; but the knowers may in the end be irreducibly many, and the greatest knower of them all may yet not know the whole of everything, or even know what he does know at one single stroke—he may be liable to forget. Whichever type obtained, the world would still be a universe noetically. Its parts would be conjoined by knowledge, but in the one case the knowledge would be absolutely unified, in the other it would be strung along and overlapped.

The notion of one instantaneous or eternal Knower—either adjective here means the same thing—is, as I said, the great intellectualist achievement of our time. It has practically driven out that conception of "Substance" which earlier philosophers set such store by, and by which so much unifying work used to be done—universal substance which alone has being in and from itself, and of which all the particulars of experience are but forms to which it gives support. Substance has succumbed to the pragmatic criticisms of the English school. It appears now only as another name for the fact that phenomena as they come are actually grouped and given in coherent forms, the very forms in which we finite knowers experience or think them together. These forms of conjunction are as much parts of the tissue of experience as are the terms which they connect; and it is a great pragmatic achievement for recent idealism to have made the world hang together in these directly representable ways instead of drawing its unity from the "inherence" of its parts —whatever that may mean—in an unimaginable principle behind the scenes.

"The world is One," therefore, just so far as we experience it to be concatenated, One by as many definite conjunctions as appear. But then also *not* One by just as many definite *dis*-junctions as we find. The oneness and the manyness of it thus obtain in respects which can be separately named. It is neither a universe pure and simple nor a multiverse pure and simple. And its various manners of being One suggest, for their accurate ascertainment, so many distinct programs of scientific work. Thus the pragmatic question "What is the oneness known as? What practical difference will it make?" saves us from all feverish excitement over it as a principle of sublimity and carries us forward into the stream of experience with a cool head. The stream may indeed reveal far more connection and union than we now suspect, but we are not entitled on pragmatic principles to claim absolute oneness in any respect in advance.

It is so difficult to see definitely what absolute oneness can mean, that probably the majority of you are satisfied with the sober attitude which we have reached. Nevertheless there are possibly some radically monistic souls among you who are not content to leave the one and the many on a par. Union of various grades, union of diverse types, union that stops at non-conductors, union that merely goes from next to next, and means in many cases outer nextness only, and not a more internal bond, union of concatenation, in short; all that sort of thing seems to you a halfway stage of thought. The oneness of things, superior to their manyness, you think must also be more deeply true, must be the more real aspect of the world. The pragmatic view, you are sure, gives us a universe imperfectly rational. The real universe must form an unconditional unit of being, something consolidated, with its parts co-implicated through and through. Only then could we consider our estate completely rational.

There is no doubt whatever that this ultramonistic way of thinking means a great deal of many minds. "One Life, One Truth, One Love, One Principle, One Good, One God"—I quote from a Christian Science leaflet which the day's mail brings into my hands—beyond doubt such a confession of faith has pragmatically an emotional value, and beyond doubt the word "one" contributes to the value quite as much as the other words. But if we try to realize *intellectually* what we can possibly *mean* by such a glut of oneness we are thrown right back upon our pragmatistic determinations again. It means either the mere name One, the universe of discourse; or it means the sum total of all the ascertainable particular conjunctions and concatenations; or, finally, it means some one vehicle of conjunction treated as all-inclusive, like one origin, one purpose, or one knower. In point of fact it always means one *knower* to those who take it intellectually today. The one knower involves, they think, the other forms of conjunction. His world must have all its parts co-implicated in the one logical-aesthetical-teleological unit-picture which is his eternal dream.

The character of the absolute knower's picture is however so impossible for us to represent clearly, that we may fairly suppose that the authority which absolute monism undoubtedly possesses, and probably always will possess over some persons, draws its strength far less from intellectual than from mystical grounds. To interpret absolute monism worthily, be a mystic. Mystical states of mind in every degree are shown by history, usually tho not always, to make for the monistic view. This is no proper occasion to enter upon the general subject of mysticism, but I will quote one mystical pronouncement to show just what I mean. The paragon of all monistic systems is the Vedânta philosophy of Hindostan, and the paragon of Vedântist missionaries was the late Swami Vivekananda who visited our land some years ago. The method of Vedântism is the mystical method. You do not reason, but after going through a certain discipline *you see*, and having seen, you can report the truth. Vivekananda thus reports the truth in one of his lectures here:

"Where is there any more misery for him who sees this Oneness in the universe, this Oneness of life, Oneness of everything? . . . This separation between man and man, man and woman, man and child, nation from nation, earth from moon, moon from sun, this separation between atom and atom is the cause really of all the misery, and the Vedânta says this separation does not exist, it is not real. It is merely apparent, on the surface. In the heart of things there is unity still. If you go inside you find that unity between man and man, women and children, races and races, high and low, rich and poor, the gods and men: all are One, and animals too, if you go deep enough, and he who has attained to that has no more delusion. . . . Where is there any more delusion for him? What can delude him? He knows the reality of everything, the secret of everything. Where is there any more misery for him? What does he desire? He has traced the reality of everything unto the Lord, that center, the Unity of everything, and that is Eternal Bliss, Eternal Knowledge, Eternal Existence. Neither death nor disease nor sorrow nor misery nor discontent is There . . . In the Centre, the reality, there is no one to be mourned for, no one to be sorry for. He has penetrated everything, the Pure One, the Formless, the Bodiless, the Stainless, He the Knower, He the great Poet, the Self-Existent, He who is giving to every one what he deserves."

Observe how radical the character of the monism here is. Separation is not simply overcome by the One, it is denied to exist. There is no many. We are not parts of the One; It has no parts; and since in a sense we undeniably *are*, it must be that each of us *is* the One, indivisibly and totally. *An Absolute One, and I that One*, surely we have here a religion which, emotionally considered, has a high pragmatic value; it imparts a perfect sumptuosity of security. As our Swami says in another place:

"When man has seen himself as One with the infinite

Being of the universe, when all separateness has ceased, when all men, all women, all angels, all gods, all animals, all plants, the whole universe has been melted into that oneness, then all fear disappears. Whom to fear? Can I hurt myself? Can I kill myself? Can I injure myself? Do you fear yourself? Then will all sorrow disappear. What can cause me sorrow? I am the One Existence of the universe. Then all jealousies will disappear; of whom to be jealous? Of myself? Then all bad feelings disappear. Against whom shall I have this bad feeling? Against myself? There is none in the universe but me . . . kill out this differentiation, kill out this superstition that there are many. 'He who, in this world of many, sees that One; he who, in this mass of insentiency, sees that One Sentient Being; he who in this world of shadow, catches that Reality, unto him belongs eternal peace, unto none else, unto none else.' "

We all have some ear for this monistic music: it elevates and reassures. We all have at least the germ of mysticism in us. And when our idealists recite their arguments for the Absolute, saying that the slightest union admitted anywhere carries logically absolute Oneness with it, and that the slightest separation admitted anywhere logically carries disunion remediless and complete, I cannot help suspecting that the palpable weak places in the intellectual reasonings they use are protected from their own criticism by a mystical feeling that, logic or no logic, absolute Oneness must somehow at any cost be true. Oneness overcomes *moral* separateness at any rate. In the passion of love we have the mystic germ of what might mean a total union of all sentient life. This mystical germ wakes up in us on hearing the monistic utterances, acknowledges their authority, and assigns to intellectual considerations a secondary place.

I will dwell no longer on these religious and moral aspects of the question in this lecture. When I come to my final lecture there will be something more to say.

Leave then out of consideration for the moment the authority which mystical insights may be conjectured eventually to possess; treat the problem of the One and the Many in a purely intellectual way; and we see clearly enough where pragmatism stands. With her criterion of the practical differences that theories make, we see that she must equally abjure absolute monism and absolute pluralism. The world is

One just so far as its parts hang together by any definite connection. It is many just so far as any definite connection fails to obtain. And finally it is growing more and more unified by those systems of connection at least which human energy keeps framing as time goes on.

It is possible to imagine alternative universes to the one we know, in which the most various grades and types of union should be embodied. Thus the lowest grade of universe would be a world of mere *withness*, of which the parts were only strung together by the conjunction "and." Such a universe is even now the collection of our several inner lives. The spaces and times of your imagination, the objects and events of your day-dreams are not only more or less incoherent *inter se*, but are wholly out of definite relation with the similar contents of any one else's mind. Our various reveries now as we sit here compenetrate each other idly without influencing or interfering. They coexist, but in no order and in no receptacle, being the nearest approach to an absolute "many" that we can conceive. We can not even imagine any reason why they *should* be known all together, and we can imagine even less, if they were known together, how they could be known as one systematic whole.

But add our sensations and bodily actions, and the union mounts to a much higher grade. Our *audita et visa* and our acts fall into those receptacles of time and space in which each events finds its date and place. They form "things" and are of "kinds" too, and can be classed. Yet we can imagine a world of things and of kinds in which the causal interactions with which we are so familiar should not exist. Everything there might be inert towards everything else, and refuse to propagate its influence. Or gross mechanical influences might pass, but no chemical action. Such worlds would be far less unified than ours. Again there might be complete physico-chemical interaction, but no minds; or minds, but altogether private ones, with no social life; or social life limited to acquaintance, but no love; or love, but no customs or institutions that should systematize it. No one of these grades of universe would be absolutely irrational or disintegrated, inferior tho it might appear when looked at from the higher grades. For instance, if our minds should ever become "telepathically" connected, so that we knew immediately, or could under certain conditions know immediately, each what the other was thinking, the world we now live in would appear to the thinkers in that world to have been of an inferior grade.

With the whole of past eternity open for our conjectures to range in, it may be lawful to wonder whether the various kinds of union now realized in the universe that we inhabit may not possibly have been successively evolved after the fashion in which we now see human systems evolving in consequence of human needs. If such an hypothesis were legitimate, total oneness would appear at the end of things rather than at their origin. In other words the notion of the "Absolute" would have to be replaced by that of the "Ultimate." The two notions would have the same content—the maximally unified content of fact, namely—but their time-relations would be positively reversed.[3]

After discussing the unity of the universe in this pragmatic way, you ought to see why I said in my second lecture, borrowing the word from my friend G. Papini, that pragmatism tends to *unstiffen* all our theories. The world's oneness has generally been affirmed abstractly only, and as if any one who questioned it must be an idiot. The temper of monists has been so vehement, as almost at times to be convulsive; and this way of holding a doctrine does not easily go with reasonable discussion and the drawing of distinctions. The theory of the Absolute, in particular, has had to be an article of faith, affirmed dogmatically and exclusively. The One and All, first in the order of being and of knowing, logically necessary itself, and uniting all lesser things in the bonds of mutual necessity, how could it allow of any mitigation of its inner rigidity? The slightest suspicion of pluralism, the minutest wiggle of independence of any one of its parts from the control of the totality would ruin it. Absolute unity brooks no degrees, as well might you claim absolute purity for a glass of water because it contains but a single little choleragerm. The independence, however infinitesimal, of a part, however small, would be to the Absolute as fatal as a choleragerm.

Pluralism on the other hand has no need of this dogmatic rigoristic temper. Provided you grant *some* separation among things, some tremor of independence, some free play of parts on one another, some real novelty or chance, however minute, she is amply satisfied, and will allow you any amount, however great, of real union. How much of union there may be is a question that she thinks can only be decided empirically. The amount may be enormous, colossal; but absolute monism is shattered if, along with all the union, there has to be granted the slightest modicum, the most incipient nascency, or the most residual trace, of a separation that is not "overcome."

Pragmatism, pending the final empirical ascertainment of just what the balance of union and disunion among things may be, must obviously range herself upon the pluralistic side. Some day, she admits, even total union, with one knower, one origin, and a universe consolidated in every conceivable way, may turn out to be most acceptable of all hypotheses. Meanwhile the opposite hypothesis, of a world imperfectly unified still, and perhaps always to remain so, must be sincerely entertained. This latter hypothesis is pluralism's doctrine. Since absolute monism forbids its being even considered seriously, branding it as irrational from the start, it is clear that pragmatism must turn its back on absolute monism, and follow pluralism's more empirical path.

This leaves us with the common-sense world, in which we find things partly joined and partly disjoined. "Things," then, and their "conjunctions"—what do such words mean, pragmatically handled? In my next lecture, I will apply the pragmatic method to the stage of philosophizing known as Common Sense.

PRAGMATISM AND COMMON SENSE

In the last lecture we turned ourselves from the usual way of talking of the universe's oneness as a principle, sublime in all its blankness, towards a study of the special kinds of union which the universe enfolds. We found many of these to coexist with kinds of separation equally real. "How far am I verified?" is the question which each kind of union and each kind of separation asks us here, so as good pragmatists we have to turn our face towards experience, towards "facts."

Absolute oneness remains, but only as an hypothesis, and that hypothesis is reduced nowadays to that of an omniscient knower who sees all things without exception as forming one single systematic fact. But the knower in question may still be conceived either as an Absolute or as an Ultimate; and over against the hypothesis of him in either form the counter-hypothesis that the widest field of knowledge that ever was or will be still contains some ignorance, may be legitimately held. Some bits of information always may escape.

This is the hypothesis of *noetic pluralism,* which monists consider so absurd. Since we are bound to treat it as respectfully as noetic monism, until the facts shall have tipped the beam, we find that our pragmatism, tho originally nothing but a method, has forced us to be friendly to the pluralistic view. It *may* be that some parts of the world are connected so loosely with some other parts as to be strung along by nothing but the copula *and.* They might even come and go without those other parts suffering any internal change. This pluralistic view, of a world of *additive* constitution, is one that pragmatism is unable to rule out from serious consideration. But this view leads one to the farther hypothesis that the actual world, instead of being complete "eternally," as the

73

monists assure us, may be eternally incomplete, and at all times subject to addition or liable to loss.

It *is* at any rate incomplete in one respect, and flagrantly so. The very fact that we debate this question shows that *our knowledge* is incomplete at present and subject to addition. In respect of the knowledge it contains the world does genuinely change and grow. Some general remarks on the way in which our knowledge completes itself—when it does complete itself—will lead us very conveniently into our subject for this lecture, which is "Common Sense."

To begin with, our knowledge grows *in spots*. The spots may be large or small, but the knowledge never grows all over: some old knowledge always remains what it was. Your knowledge of pragmatism, let us suppose, is growing now. Later, its growth may involve considerable modification of opinions which you previously held to be true. But such modifications are apt to be gradual. To take the nearest possible example, consider these lectures of mine. What you first gain from them is probably a small amount of new information, a few new definitions, or distinctions, or points of view. But while these special ideas are being added, the rest of your knowledge stands still, and only gradually will you "line up" your previous opinions with the novelties I am trying to instil, and modify to some slight degree their mass.

You listen to me now, I suppose, with certain prepossessions as to my competency, and these affect your reception of what I say, but were I suddenly to break off lecturing, and to begin to sing "We won't go home till morning" in a rich baritone voice, not only would that new fact be added to your stock, but it would oblige you to define me differently, and that might alter your opinion of the pragmatic philosophy, and in general bring about a rearrangement of a number of your ideas. Your mind in such processes is strained, and sometimes painfully so, between its older beliefs and the novelties which experience brings along.

Our minds thus grow in spots; and like grease-spots, the spots spread. But we let them spread as little as possible we keep unaltered as much of our old knowledge, as many of our old prejudices and beliefs, as we can. We patch and tinker more than we renew. The novelty soaks in; it stains the ancient mass; but it is also tinged by what absorbs it. Our past apperceives and co-operates; and in the new equilibrium in which each step forward in the process of learning terminates, it happens relatively seldom that the new fact is added *raw*. More usually it is embedded cooked, as one might say, or stewed down in the sauce of the old.

New truths thus are resultants of new experiences and of old truths combined and mutually modifying one another. And since this is the case in the changes of opinion of today, there is no reason to assume that it has not been so at all times. It follows that very ancient modes of thought may have survived through all the later changes in men's opinions. The most primitive ways of thinking may not yet be wholly expunged. Like our five fingers, our ear-bones, our rudimentary caudal appendage, or our other "vestigial" peculiarities, they may remain as indelible tokens of events in our race-history. Our ancestors may at certain moments have struck into ways of thinking which they might conceivably not have found. But once they did so, and after the fact, the inheritance continues. When you begin a piece of music in a certain key, you must keep the key to the end. You may alter your house *ad libitum*, but the ground-plan of the first architect persists—you can make great changes, but you can not change a Gothic church into a Doric temple. You may rinse and rinse the bottle, but you can't get the taste of the medicine or whiskey that first filled it wholly out.

My thesis now is this, that *our fundamental ways of thinking about things are discoveries of exceedingly remote ancestors, which have been able to preserve themselves throughout the experience of all subsequent time.* They form one great stage of equilibrium in the human mind's development, the stage of *common sense.* Other stages have grafted themselves upon this stage, but have never succeeded in displacing it. Let us consider this common-sense stage first, as if it might be final.

In practical talk, a man's common sense means his good judgment, his freedom from eccentricity, his *gumption*, to use the vernacular word. In philosophy it means something entirely different, it means his use of certain intellectual forms or categories of thought. Were we lobsters, or bees, it might be that our organization would have led to our using quite different modes from these of apprehending our experiences. It *might* be too (we can not dogmatically deny this) that such categories, unimaginable by us today, would have proved on the whole as serviceable for handling our experiences mentally as those which we actually use.

If this sounds paradoxical to any one, let him think of analytical geometry. The identical figures which Euclid defined by intrinsic relations were defined by Descartes by the relations of their points to adventitious coordinates, the result being an absolutely different and vastly more potent way of handling curves. All our conceptions are what the Germans call *denkmittel*, means by which we handle facts by thinking them. Experience merely as such doesn't come ticketed and labelled, we have first to discover what it is. Kant speaks of it as being in its first intention a *gewühl der erscheinungen*, a *rhapsodie der wahrnehmungen*, a mere motley which we have to unify by our wits. What we usually do is first to frame some system of concepts mentally classified, serialized, or connected in some intellectual way, and then to use this as a tally by which we "keep tab" on the impressions that present themselves. When each is referred to some possible place in the conceptual system, it is thereby "understood." This notion of parallel "manifolds" with their elements standing reciprocally in "one-to-one relations," is proving so convenient nowadays in mathematics and logic as to supersede more and more the older classificatory conceptions. There are many conceptual systems of this sort; and the sense manifold is also such a system. Find a one-to-one relation for your sense-impressions *anywhere* among the concepts, and in so far forth you rationalize the impressions. But obviously you can rationalize them by using various conceptual systems.

The old common-sense way of rationalizing them is by a set of concepts of which the most important are these:

Thing
The same or different
Kinds
Minds
Bodies
One Time
One Space
Subjects and attributes
Causal influences
The fancied
The real

We are now so familiar with the order that these notions

have woven for us out of the everlasting weather of our
perceptions that we find it hard to realize how little of a
fixed routine the perceptions follow when taken by themselves.
The word weather is a good one to use here. In Boston,
for example, the weather has almost no routine, the only
law being that if you have had any weather for two days,
you will probably but not certainly have another weather on
the third. Weather-experience as it thus comes to Boston is
discontinuous, and chaotic. In point of temperature, of wind,
rain or sunshine, it *may* change three times a day. But the
Washington weather-bureau intellectualizes this disorder by
making each successive bit of Boston weather *episodic*. It
refers it to its place and moment in a continental cyclone, on
the history of which the local changes everywhere are strung
as beads are strung upon a cord.

Now it seems almost certain that young children and the
inferior animals take all their experiences very much as
uninstructed Bostonians take their weather. They know no
more of time, or space, as world-receptacles, or of permanent
subjects and changing predicates, or of causes, or kinds, or
thoughts, or things, than our common people know of continental cyclones. A baby's rattle drops out of his hand, but
the baby looks not for it. It has "gone out" for him, as a
candle-flame goes out; and it comes back, when you replace
it in his hand, as the flame comes back when relit. The idea
of its being a "thing," whose permanent existence by itself
he might interpolate between its successive apparitions has
evidently not occurred to him. It is the same with dogs. Out
of sight, out of mind, with them. It is pretty evident that
they have no *general* tendency to interpolate "things." Let
me quote here a passage from my colleague G. Santayana's
book.

"If a dog, while sniffing about contentedly, sees his master
arriving after a long absence . . . the poor brute asks for
no reason why his master went, why he has come again, why
he should be loved, or why presently while lying at his feet
you forget him and begin to grunt and dream of the chase—
all that is an utter mystery, utterly unconsidered. Such experience has variety, scenery, and a certain vital rhythm; its
story might be told in dithyrambic verse. It moves wholly by
inspiration; every event is providential, every act unpre-

78 • PRAGMATISM

meditated. Absolute freedom and absolute helplessness have met together: you depend wholly on divine favor, yet that unfathomable agency is not distinguishable from your own life. . . . [But] the figures even of that disordered drama have their exits and their entrances; and their cues can be gradually discovered by a being capable of fixing his attention and retaining the order of events. . . . In proportion as such understanding advances, each moment of experience becomes consequential and prophetic of the rest. The calm places in life are filled with power and its spasms with resource. No emotion can overwhelm the mind, for of none is the basis or issue wholly hidden; no event can disconcert it altogether, because it sees beyond. Means can be looked for to escape from the worst predicament; and whereas each moment had been formerly filled with nothing but its own adventures and surprised emotion, each now makes room for the lesson of what went before and surmises what may be the plot of the whole." [1]

Even today science and philosophy are still laboriously trying to part fancies from realities in our experience; and in primitive times they made only the most incipient distinctions in this line. Men believed whatever they thought with any liveliness, and they mixed their dreams with their realities inextricably. The categories of "thought" and "things" are indispensable here—instead of being realities we now call certain experiences only "thoughts." There is not a category, among those enumerated, of which we may not imagine the use to have thus originated historically and only gradually spread.

That one Time which we all believe in and in which each event has its definite date, that one Space in which each thing has its position, these abstract notions unify the world incomparably; but in their finished shape as concepts how different they are from the loose unordered time-and-space experiences of natural men! Everything that happens to us brings its own duration and extension, and both are vaguely surrounded by a marginal "more" that runs into the duration and extension of the next thing that comes. But we soon lose all our definite bearings; and not only do our children make no distinction between yesterday and the day before yesterday, the whole past being churned up together, but we adults still do so whenever the times are large. It is the same with spaces. On a map I can distinctly see the relation of London, Constantinople, and Peking to the place where I am; in reality I utterly fail to *feel* the facts which the map symbolizes. The directions and distances are vague, confused and mixed. Cosmic space and cosmic time, so far from being the intuitions that Kant said they were, are constructions as patently artificial as any that science can show. The great majority of the human race never use these notions, but live in plural times and spaces, interpenetrant and *durcheinander*.

Permanent "things" again; the "same" thing and its various "appearances" and "alterations," the different "kinds" of thing; with the "kind" used finally as a "predicate," of which the thing remains the "subject"—what a straightening of the tangle of our experience's immediate flux and sensible variety does this list of terms suggest! And it is only the smallest part of his experience's flux that any one actually does straighten out by applying to it these conceptual instruments. Out of them all our lowest ancestors probably used only, and then most vaguely and inaccurately, the notion of "the same again." But even then if you had asked them whether the same were a "thing" that had endured throughout the unseen interval, they would probably have been at a loss, and would have said that they had never asked that question, or considered matters in that light.

Kinds, and sameness of kind—what colossally useful *denkmittel* for finding our way among the many! The manyness might conceivably have been absolute. Experiences might have all been singulars, no one of them occurring twice. In such a world logic would have had no application; for kind and sameness of kind are logic's only instruments. Once we know that whatever is of a kind is also of that kind's kind, we can travel through the universe as if with seven-league boots. Brutes surely never use these abstractions, and civilized men use them in most various amounts.

Causal influence, again! This, if anything, seems to have been an antediluvian conception; for we find primitive men thinking that almost everything is significant and can exert influence of some sort. The search for the more definite influences seems to have started in the question: "Who, or what, is to blame?"—for any illness, namely, or disaster, or untoward thing. From this center the search for causal influences has spread. Hume and "Science" together have tried to eliminate the whole notion of influence, substituting the entirely different *denkmittel* of "law." But law is a comparatively recent invention, and influence reigns supreme in the older realm of common sense.

The "possible," as something less than the actual and more than the wholly unreal, is another of these magisterial notions of common sense. Criticise them as you may, they persist; and we fly back to them the moment critical pressure is relaxed. "Self," "body," in the substantial or metaphysical sense—no one escapes subjection to *those* forms of thought. In practice, the common-sense *denkmittel* are uniformly victorious. Every one, however instructed, still thinks of a "thing" in the common-sense way, as a permanent unit-subject that "supports" its attributes interchangeably. No one stably or sincerely uses the more critical notion, of a group of sense-qualities united by a law. With these categories in our hand, we make our plans and plot together, and connect all the remoter parts of experience with what lies before our eyes. Our later and more critical philosophies are mere fads and fancies compared with this natural mother tongue of thought.

Common sense appears thus as a perfectly definite stage in our understanding of things, a stage that satisfies in an extraordinarily successful way the purposes for which we think. "Things" do exist, even when we do not see them. Their "kinds" also exist. Their "qualities" are what they act by, and are what we act on; and these also exist. These lamps shed their quality of light on every object in this room. We intercept *it* on its way whenever we hold up an opaque screen. It is the very sound that my lips emit that travels into your ears. It is the sensible heat of the fire that migrates into the water in which we boil an egg; and we can change the heat into coolness by dropping in a lump of ice. At this stage of philosophy all non-European men without exception have remained. It suffices for all the necessary practical ends of life; and, among our race even, it is only the highly sophisticated specimens, the minds debauched by learning, as Berkeley calls them, who have ever even suspected common sense of not being absolutely true.

But when we look back, and speculate as to how the common-sense categories may have achieved their wonderful supremacy, no reason appears why it may not have been by

a process just like that by which the conceptions due to
Democritus, Berkeley, or Darwin, achieved their similar
triumphs in more recent times. In other words, they may have
been successfully *discovered* by prehistoric geniuses whose
names the night of antiquity has covered up; they may have
been verified by the immediate facts of experience which they
first fitted; and then from fact to fact and from man to man
they may have *spread*, until all language rested on them and
we are now incapable of thinking naturally in any other terms.
Such a view would only follow the rule that has proved elsewhere so fertile, of assuming the vast and remote to conform
to the laws of formation that we can observe at work in the
small and near.

For all utilitarian practical purposes these conceptions
amply suffice; but that they began at special points of discovery and only gradually spread from one thing to another,
seems proved by the exceedingly dubious limits of their
application today. We assume for certain purposes one "objective" Time that *aequabiliter fluit*, but we don't livingly
believe in or realize any such equally-flowing time. "Space"
is a less vague notion; but "things," what are they? Is a constellation properly a thing? or an army? or is an *ens rationis*
such as space or justice a thing? Is a knife whose handle and
blade are changed the "same?" Is the "changeling," whom
Locke so seriously discusses, of the human "kind?" Is "telepathy" a "fancy" or a "fact?" The moment you pass beyond
the practical use of these categories (a use usually suggested
sufficiently by the circumstances of the special case) to a
merely curious or speculative way of thinking, you find it
impossible to say within just what limits of fact any one of
them shall apply.

The peripatetic philosophy, obeying rationalist propensities,
has tried to eternalize the common-sense categories by treating them very technically and articulately. A "thing" for instance is a being, or *ens*. An *ens* is a subject in which qualities
"inhere." A subject is a substance. Substances are of kinds,
and kinds are definite in number, and discrete. These distinctions are fundamental and eternal. As terms of *discourse* they
are indeed magnificently useful, but what they mean, apart
from their use in steering our discourse to profitable issues,
does not appear. If you ask a scholastic philosopher what a
substance may be in itself, apart from its being the support

of attributes, he simply says that your intellect knows perfectly what the word means.

But what the intellect knows clearly is only the word itself and its steering function. So it comes about that intellects *sibi permissi*, intellects only curious and idle, have forsaken the common-sense level for what in general terms may be called the "critical" level of thought. Not merely *such* intellects either—your Humes and Berkeleys and Hegels; but practical observers of facts, your Galileos, Daltons, Faradays, have found it impossible to treat the *naïfs* sense-termini of common sense as ultimately real. As common sense interpolates her constant "things" between our intermittent sensations, so science *extra*polates her world of "primary" qualities, her atoms, her ether, her magnetic fields, and the like, beyond the common-sense world. The "things" are now invisible impalpable things; and the old visible common-sense things are supposed to result from the mixture of these invisibles. Or else the whole *naïf* conception of thing gets superseded, and a thing's name is interpreted as denoting only the law or *regel der verbindung* by which certain of our sensations habitually succeed or coexist.

Science and critical philosophy thus burst the bounds of common sense. With science *naïf* realism ceases: "Secondary" qualities become unreal; primary ones alone remain. With critical philosophy, havoc is made of everything. The common-sense categories one and all cease to represent anything in the way of *being;* they are but sublime tricks of human thought, our ways of escaping bewilderment in the midst of sensation's irremediable flow.

But the scientific tendency in critical thought, tho inspired at first by purely intellectual motives, has opened an entirely unexpected range of practical utilities to our astonished view. Galileo gave us accurate clocks and accurate artillery-practice; the chemists flood us with new medicines and dye-stuffs; Ampère and Faraday have endowed us with the New York subway and with Marconi telegrams. The hypothetical things that such men have invented, defined as they have defined them, are showing an extraordinary fertility in consequences verifiable by sense. Our logic can deduce from them a consequence due under certain conditions, we can then bring about the conditions, and presto, the consequence is there before our eyes. The scope of the practical control of nature newly put into our hand by scientific ways of thinking vastly exceeds the scope of the old control grounded on common sense. Its rate of increase accelerates so that no one can trace the limit; one may even fear that the *being* of man may be crushed by his own powers, that his fixed nature as an organism may not prove adequate to stand the strain of the ever increasingly tremendous functions, almost divine creative functions, which his intellect will more and more enable him to wield. He may drown in his wealth like a child in a bathtub, who has turned on the water and who can not turn it off.

The philosophic stage of criticism, much more thorough in its negations than the scientific stage, so far gives us no new range of practical power. Locke, Hume, Berkeley, Kant, Hegel, have all been utterly sterile, so far as shedding any light on the details of nature goes, and I can think of no invention or discovery that can be directly traced to anything in their peculiar thought, for neither with Berkeley's tar-water nor with Kant's nebular hypothesis had their respective philosophic tenets anything to do. The satisfactions they yield to their disciples are intellectual, not practical; and even then we have to confess that there is a large minus-side to the account.

There are thus at least three well-characterized levels, stages or types of thought about the world we live in, and the notions of one stage have one kind of merit, those of another stage another kind. It is impossible, however, to say that any stage as yet in sight is absolutely more *true* than any other. Common sense is the more *consolidated* stage, because it got its innings first, and made all language into its ally. Whether it or science be the more *august* stage may be left to private judgment. But neither consolidation nor augustness are decisive marks of truth. If common sense were true, why should science have had to brand the secondary qualities, to which our world owes all its living interest, as false, and to invent an invisible world of points and curves, and mathematical equations instead? Why should it have needed to transform causes and activities into laws of "functional variation"? Vainly did scholasticism, common sense's college-trained younger sister, seek to stereotype the forms the human family had always talked with, to make them definite and fix them for eternity. Substantial forms (in other words our secondary qualities) hardly outlasted the year of our Lord

1600. People were already tired of them then; and Galileo, and Descartes, with his "new philosophy," gave them only a little later their *coup de grâce*.

But now if the new kinds of scientific "thing," the corpuscular and etheric world, were essentially more "true," why should they have excited so much criticism within the body of science itself? Scientific logicians are saying on every hand that these entities and their determinations, however definitely conceived, should not be held for literally real. It is *as if* they existed; but in reality they are like co-ordinates or logarithms, only artificial short-cuts for taking us from one part to another of experience's flux. We can cipher fruitfully with them; they serve us wonderfully; but we must not be their dupes.

There is no *ringing* conclusion possible when we compare these types of thinking, with a view to telling which is the more absolutely true. Their naturalness, their intellectual economy, their fruitfulness for practice, all start up as distinct tests of their veracity, and as a result we get confused. Common sense is *better* for one sphere of life, science for another, philosophic criticism for a third; but whether either be *truer* absolutely, Heaven only knows. Just now, if I understand the matter rightly, we are witnessing a curious reversion to the common sense way of looking at physical nature, in the philosophy of science favored by such men as Mach, Ostwald and Duhem. According to these teachers no hypothesis is truer than any other in the sense of being a more literal copy of reality. They are all but ways of talking on our part, to be compared solely from the point of view of their *use*. The only literally true thing is *reality;* and the only reality we know is, for these logicians, sensible reality, the flux of our sensations and emotions as they pass. "Energy" is the collective name (according to Ostwald) for the sensations just as they present themselves (the movement, heat, magnetic pull, or light, or whatever it may be) when they are measured in certain ways. So measuring them, we are enabled to describe the correlated changes which they show us, in formulas matchless for their simplicity and fruitfulness for human use. They are sovereign triumphs of economy in thought.

No one can fail to admire the "energetic" philosophy. But the hypersensible entities, the corpuscles and vibrations, hold their own with most physicists and chemists, in spite of its appeal. It seems too economical to be all-sufficient. Profusion, not economy, may after all be reality's key-note.

I am dealing here with highly technical matters, hardly suitable for popular lecturing, and in which my own competence is small. All the better for my conclusion, however, which at this point is this. The whole notion of truth, which naturally and without reflexion we assume to mean the simple duplication by the mind of a ready-made and given reality, proves hard to understand clearly. There is no simple test available for adjudicating off-hand between the divers types of thought that claim to possess it. Common sense, common science or corpuscular philosophy, ultra-critical science, or energetics, and critical or idealistic philosophy, all seem insufficiently true in some regard and leave some dissatisfaction. It is evident that the conflict of these so widely differing systems obliges us to overhaul the very idea of truth, for at present we have no definite notion of what the word may mean. I shall face that task in my next lecture, and will add but a few words, in finishing the present one.

There are only two points that I wish you to retain from the present lecture. The first one relates to common sense. We have seen reason to suspect it, to suspect that in spite of their being so venerable, of their being so universally used and built into the very structure of language, its categories may after all be only a collection of extraordinarily successful hypotheses (historically discovered or invented by single men, but gradually communicated, and used by everybody) by which our forefathers have from time immemorial unified and straightened the discontinuity of their immediate experiences, and put themselves into an equilibrium with the surface of nature so satisfactory for ordinary practical purposes that it certainly would have lasted forever, but for the excessive intellectual vivacity of Democritus, Archimedes, Galileo, Berkeley, and of other eccentric geniuses whom the example of such men inflamed. Retain, I pray you, this suspicion about common sense.

The other point is this. Ought not the existence of the various types of thinking which we have reviewed, each so splendid for certain purposes, yet all conflicting still, and neither one of them able to support a claim of absolute veracity, to awaken a presumption favorable to the pragmatistic view that all our theories are *instrumental*, are mental modes of *adaption* to reality, rather than revelations or gnostic answers to some divinely instituted world-enigma? I expressed this view as clearly as I could in the second of these lectures. Certainly the restlessness of the actual theoretic situation, the value for some purposes of each thought-level, and the inability of either to expel the others decisively, suggest this pragmatistic view, which I hope that the next lectures may soon make entirely convincing. May there not after all be a possible ambiguity in truth?

PRAGMATISM'S CONCEPTION
OF TRUTH

When Clerk-Maxwell was a child it is written that he had a mania for having everything explained to him, and that when people put him off with vague verbal accounts of any phenomenon he would interrupt them impatiently by saying, "Yes; but I want you to tell me the *particular go* of it!" Had his question been about truth, only a pragmatist could have told him the particular go of it. I believe that our contemporary pragmatists, especially Messrs. Schiller and Dewey, have given the only tenable account of this subject. It is a very ticklish subject, sending subtle rootlets into all kinds of crannies, and hard to treat in the sketchy way that alone befits a public lecture. But the Schiller-Dewey view of truth has been so ferociously attacked by rationalistic philosophers, and so abominably misunderstood, that here, if anywhere, is the point where a clear and simple statement should be made.

I fully expect to see the pragmatist view of truth run through the classic stages of a theory's career. First, you know, a new theory is attacked as absurd; then it is admitted to be true, but obvious and insignificant; finally it is seen to be so important that its adversaries claim that they themselves discovered it. Our doctrine of truth is at present in the first of these three stages, with symptoms of the second stage having begun in certain quarters. I wish that this lecture might help it beyond the first stage in the eyes of many of you.

Truth, as any dictionary will tell you, is a property of certain of our ideas. It means their "agreement," as falsity means their disagreement, with "reality." Pragmatists and intellectualists both accept this definition as a matter of course. They begin to quarrel only after the question is raised as to what may precisely be meant by the term "agreement," and

87

what by the term "reality," when reality is taken as something for our ideas to agree with.

In answering these questions the pragmatists are more analytic and painstaking, the intellectualists more offhand and irreflective. The popular notion is that a true idea must copy its reality. Like other popular views, this one follows the analogy of the most usual experience. Our true ideas of sensible things do indeed copy them. Shut your eyes and think of yonder clock on the wall, and you get just such a true picture or copy of its dial. But your idea of its "works" (unless you are a clockmaker) is much less of a copy, yet it passes muster, for it in no way clashes with the reality. Even though it should shrink to the mere word "works," that word still serves you truly; and when you speak of the "time-keeping function" of the clock, or of its spring's "elasticity," it is hard to see exactly what your ideas can copy.

You perceive that there is a problem here. Where our ideas cannot copy definitely their object, what does agreement with that object mean? Some idealists seem to say that they are true whenever they are what God means that we ought to think about that object. Others hold the copy-view all through, and speak as if our ideas possessed truth just in proportion as they approach to being copies of the Absolute's eternal way of thinking.

These views, you see, invite pragmatistic discussion. But the great assumption of the intellectualists is that truth means essentially an inert static relation. When you've got your true idea of anything, there's an end of the matter. You're in possession; you *know;* you have fulfilled your thinking destiny. You are where you ought to be mentally; you have obeyed your categorical imperative; and nothing more need follow on that climax of your rational destiny. Epistemologically you are in stable equilibrium.

Pragmatism, on the other hand, asks its usual question. "Grant an idea or belief to be true," it says, "what concrete difference will its being true make in any one's actual life? How will the truth be realized? What experiences will be different from those which would obtain if the belief were false? What, in short, is the truth's cash-value in experiential terms?"

The moment pragmatism asks this question, it sees the answer: *True ideas are those that we can assimilate, validate, corroborate and verify. False ideas are those that we can not.* That is the practical difference it makes to us to have true ideas; that, therefore, is the meaning of truth, for it is all that truth is known-as.

This thesis is what I have to defend. The truth of an idea is not a stagnant property inherent in it. Truth *happens* to an idea. It *becomes* true, is *made* true by events. Its verity *is* in fact an event, a process: the process namely of its verifying itself, its veri-*fication*. Its validity is the process of its vali-*dation*.

But what do the words verification and validation themselves pragmatically mean? They again signify certain practical consequences of the verified and validated idea. It is hard to find any one phrase that characterizes these consequences better than the ordinary agreement-formula—just such consequences being what we have in mind whenever we say that our ideas "agree" with reality. They lead us, namely, through the acts and other ideas which they instigate, into or up to, or towards, other parts of experience with which we feel all the while—such feeling being among our potentialities—that the original ideas remain in agreement. The connections and transitions come to us from point to point as being progressive, harmonious, satisfactory. This function of agreeable leading is what we mean by an idea's verification. Such an account is vague and it sounds at first quite trivial, but it has results which it will take the rest of my hour to explain.

Let me begin by reminding you of the fact that the possession of true thoughts means everywhere the possession of invaluable instruments of action; and that our duty to gain truth, so far from being a blank command from out of the blue, or a "stunt" self-imposed by our intellect, can account for itself by excellent practical reasons.

The importance to human life of having true beliefs about matters of fact is a thing too notorious. We live in a world of realities that can be infinitely useful or infinitely harmful. Ideas that tell us which of them to expect count as the true ideas in all this primary sphere of verification, and the pursuit of such ideas is a primary human duty. The possession of truth, so far from being here an end in itself, is only a preliminary means towards other vital satisfactions. If I am lost in the woods and starved, and find what looks like a cow-path, it is of the utmost importance that I should think of a human habitation at the end of it, for if I do so and follow it, I save myself. The true thought is useful here because the house which is its object is useful. The practical value of true ideas is thus primarily derived from the practical importance of their objects to us. Their objects are, indeed, not important at all times. I may on another occasion have no use for the house; and then my idea of it, however verifiable, will be practically irrelevant, and had better remain latent. Yet since almost any object may some day become temporarily important, the advantage of having a general stock of *extra* truths, of ideas that shall be true of merely possible situations, is obvious. We store such extra truths away in our memories, and with the overflow we fill our books of reference. Whenever such an extra truth becomes practically relevant to one of our emergencies, it passes from cold-storage to do work in the world and our belief in it grows active. You can say of it then either that "it is useful because it is true" or that "it is true because it is useful." Both these phrases mean exactly the same thing, namely that here is an idea that gets fulfilled and can be verified. True is the name for whatever idea starts the verification-process, useful is the name for its completed function in experience. True ideas would never have been singled out as such, would never have acquired a class-name, least of all a name suggesting value, unless they had been useful from the outset in this way.

From this simple cue pragmatism gets her general notion of truth as something essentially bound up with the way in which one moment in our experience may lead us towards other moments which it will be worth while to have been led to. Primarily, and on the common-sense level, the truth of a state of mind means this function of *a leading that is worth while*. When a moment in our experience, of any kind whatever, inspires us with a thought that is true, that means that sooner or later we dip by that thought's guidance into the particulars of experience again and make advantageous connection with them. This is a vague enough statement, but I beg you to retain it, for it is essential.

Our experience meanwhile is all shot through with regularities. One bit of it can warn us to get ready for another bit, can "intend" or be "significant of" that remoter object. The object's advent is the significance's verification. Truth, in these cases, meaning nothing but eventual verification, is manifestly incompatible with waywardness on our part. Woe to him whose beliefs play fast and loose with the order which realities follow in his experience; they will lead him nowhere or else make false connections.

By "realities" or "objects" here, we mean either things of common sense, sensibly present, or else common sense relations, such as dates, places, distances, kinds, activities. Following our mental image of a house along the cow-path, we actually come to see the house; we get the image's full verification. *Such simply and fully verified leadings are certainly the originals and prototypes of the truth-process.* Experience offers indeed other forms of truth-process, but they are all conceivable as being primary verifications arrested, multiplied or substituted one for another.

Take, for instance, yonder object on the wall. You and I consider it to be a "clock," altho no one of us has seen the hidden works that make it one. We let our notion pass for true without attempting to verify. If truths mean verification-process essentially, ought we then to call such unverified truths as this abortive? No, for they form the overwhelmingly large number of the truths we live by. Indirect as well as direct verifications pass muster. Where circumstantial evidence is sufficient, we can go without eye-witnessing. Just as we here assume Japan to exist without ever having been there, because it *works* to do so, everything we know conspiring with the belief, and nothing interfering, so we assume that thing to be a clock. We *use* it as a clock, regulating the length of our lecture by it. The verification of the assumption here means its leading to no frustration or contradiction. Verifi-*ability* of wheels and weights and pendulum is as good as verification. For one truth-process completed there are a million in our lives that function in this state of nascency. They turn us *towards* direct verification; lead us into the *surroundings* of the objects they envisage; and then, if everything runs on harmoniously, we are so sure that verification is possible that we omit it, and are usually justified by all that happens.

Truth lives, in fact, for the most part on a credit system. Our thoughts and beliefs "pass," so long as nothing challenges them, just as bank-notes pass so long as nobody refuses them. But this all points to direct face-to-face verifications somewhere, without which the fabric of truth collapses like a financial system with no cash-basis whatever. You accept my verification of one thing, I yours of another. We trade on each other's truth. But beliefs verified concretely by *somebody* are the posts of the whole superstructure.

Another great reason—beside economy of time—for waiving complete verification in the usual business of life is that all things exist in kinds and not singly. Our world is found once for all to have that peculiarity. So that when we have once directly verified our ideas about one specimen of a kind, we consider ourselves free to apply them to other specimens without verification. A mind that habitually discerns the kind of thing before it, and acts by the law of the kind immediately, without pausing to verify, will be a "true" mind in ninety-nine out of a hundred emergencies, proved so by its conduct fitting everything it meets, and getting no refutation.

Indirectly or only potentially verifying processes may thus be true as well as full verification-processes. They work as true processes would work, give us the same advantages, and claim our recognition for the same reasons. All this on the common-sense level of matters of fact, which we are alone considering.

But matters of fact are not our only stock in trade. *Relations among purely mental ideas* form another sphere where true and false beliefs obtain, and here the beliefs are absolute, or unconditional. When they are true they bear the name either of definitions or of principles. It is either a principle or a definition that 1 and 1 make 2, that 2 and 1 make 3, and so on; that white differs less from gray than it does from black; that when the cause begins to act the effect also commences. Such propositions hold of all possible "ones," of all conceivable "whites" and "grays" and "causes." The objects here are mental objects. Their relations are perceptually obvious at a glance, and no sense-verification is necessary. Moreover, once true, always true, of those same mental objects. Truth here has an "eternal" character. If you can find a concrete thing anywhere that is "one" or "white" or "gray" or an "effect," then your principles will everlastingly apply to it. It is but a case of ascertaining the kind, and then applying the law of its kind to the particular object. You are sure to get truth if you can but name the kind rightly, for your mental relations hold good of everything of that kind without exception. If you then, nevertheless, failed to get truth concretely, you would say that you had classed your real objects wrongly.

In this realm of mental relations, truth again is an affair of leading. We relate one abstract idea with another, framing in the end great systems of logical and mathematical truth, under the respective terms of which the sensible facts of experience eventually arrange themselves, so that our eternal truths hold good of realities also. This marriage of fact and theory is endlessly fertile. What we say is here already true in advance of special verification, *if we have subsumed our objects rightly.* Our ready-made ideal framework for all sorts of possible objects follows from the very structure of our thinking. We can no more play fast and loose with these abstract relations than we can do so with our sense-experiences. They coerce us; we must treat them consistently, whether or not we like the results. The rules of addition apply to our debts as rigorously as to our assets. The hundredth decimal of π, the ratio of the circumference to its diameter, is predetermined ideally now, tho no one may have computed it. If we should ever need the figure in our dealings with an actual circle we should need to have it given rightly, calculated by the usual rules; for it is the same kind of truth that those rules elsewhere calculate.

Between the coercions of the sensible order and those of the ideal order, our mind is thus wedged tightly. Our ideas must agree with realities, be such realities concrete or abstract, be they facts or be they principles, under penalty of endless inconsistency and frustration.

So far, intellectualists can raise no protest. They can only say that we have barely touched the skin of the matter.

Realities mean, then, either concrete facts, or abstract kinds of thing and relations perceived intuitively between them. They furthermore and thirdly mean, as things that new ideas of ours must no less take account of, the whole body of other truths already in our possession. But what now does "agreement" with such threefold realities mean?—to use again the definition that is current.

Here it is that pragmatism and intellectualism begin to part company. Primarily, no doubt, to agree means to copy, but we saw that the mere word "clock" would do instead of a mental picture of its works, and that of many realities our ideas can only be symbols and not copies. "Past time," "power," "spontaneity"—how can our mind copy such realities?

To "agree" in the widest sense with a reality *can only mean to be guided either straight up to it or into its surroundings, or to be put into such working touch with it as to handle either it or something connected with it better than if we disagreed.* Better either intellectually or practically! And often agreement will only mean the negative fact that nothing contradictory from the quarter of that reality comes to interfere with the way in which our ideas guide us elsewhere. To copy a reality is, indeed, one very important way of agreeing with it, but it is far from being essential. The essential thing is the process of being guided. Any idea that helps us to *deal*, whether practically or intellectually, with either the reality or its belongings, that doesn't entangle our progress in frustrations, that *fits*, in fact, and adapts our life to the reality's whole setting, will agree sufficiently to meet the requirement. It will hold true of that reality.

Thus, *names* are just as "true" or "false" as definite mental pictures are. They set up similar verification-processes, and lead to fully equivalent practical results.

All human thinking gets discursified; we exchange ideas; we lend and borrow verifications, get them from one another by means of social intercourse. All truth thus gets verbally built out, stored up, and made available for every one. Hence, we must *talk* consistently just as we must *think* consistently: for both in talk and thought we deal with kinds. Names are arbitrary, but once understood they must be kept to. We mustn't now call Abel "Cain" or Cain "Abel." If we do, we ungear ourselves from the whole book of Genesis, and from all its connections with the universe of speech and fact down to the present time. We throw ourselves out of whatever truth that entire system of speech and fact may embody.

The overwhelming majority of our true ideas admit of no direct or face-to-face verification—those of past history, for example, as of Cain and Abel. The stream of time can be remounted only verbally, or verified indirectly by the present prolongations or effects of what the past harbored. Yet if they agree with these verbalities and effects, we can know that our ideas of the past are true. *As true as past time itself was*, so

true was Julius Caesar, so true were antediluvian
all in their proper dates and settings. That past time i
is guaranteed by its coherence with everything that's
True as the present *is*, the past *was* also.

Agreement thus turns out to be essentially an affair of
leading—leading that is useful because it is into quarters that
contain objects that are important. True ideas lead us into useful verbal and conceptual quarters as well as directly up to
useful sensible termini. They lead to consistency, stability and
flowing human intercourse. They lead away from eccentricity
and isolation, from foiled and barren thinking. The untram-
melled flowing of the leading-process, its general freedom from
clash and contradiction, passes for its indirect verification; but
all roads lead to Rome, and in the end and eventually, all true
processes must lead to the face of directly verifying sensible
experiences *somewhere*, which somebody's ideas have copied.

Such is the large loose way in which the pragmatist interprets the word agreement. He treats it altogether practically.
He lets it cover any process of conduction from a present idea
to a future terminus, provided only it run prosperously. It is
only thus that "scientific" ideas, flying as they do beyond
common sense, can be said to agree with their realities. It is,
as I have already said, *as if* reality were made of ether, atoms
or electrons, but we mustn't think so literally. The term
"energy" doesn't even pretend to stand for anything "objective." It is only a way of measuring the surface of phenomena
so as to string their changes on a simple formula.

Yet in the choice of these man-made formulas we can not
be capricious with impunity any more than we can be capri-
ous on the common-sense practical level. We must find a
theory that will *work;* and that means something extremely
difficult; for our theory must mediate between all previous
truths and certain new experiences. It must derange common
sense and previous belief as little as possible, and it must lead
to some sensible terminus or other that can be verified exactly.
To "work" means both these things; and the squeeze is so
tight that there is little loose play for any hypothesis. Our
theories are wedged and controlled as nothing else is. Yet
sometimes alternative theoretic formulas are equally compatible with all the truths we know, and then we choose
between them for subjective reasons. We choose the kind of
theory to which we are already partial; we follow "elegance"

"economy." Clerk-Maxwell somewhere says it would be "poor scientific taste" to choose the more complicated of two equally well-evidenced conceptions; and you will all agree with him. Truth in science is what gives us the maximum possible sum of satisfactions, taste included, but consistency both with previous truth and with novel fact is always the most imperious claimant.

I have led you through a very sandy desert. But now, if I may be allowed so vulgar an expression, we begin to taste the milk in the coconut. Our rationalist critics here discharge their batteries upon us, and to reply to them will take us out from all this dryness into full sight of a momentous philosophical alternative.

Our account of truth is an account of truths in the plural, of processes of leading, realized *in rebus*, and having only this quality in common, that they *pay*. They pay by guiding us into or towards some part of a system that dips at numerous points into sense-percepts, which we may copy mentally or not, but with which at any rate we are now in the kind of commerce vaguely designated as verification. Truth for us is simply a collective name for verification-processes, just as health, wealth, strength, etc., are names for other processes connected with life, and also pursued because it pays to pursue them. Truth is *made*, just as health, wealth and strength are made, in the course of experience.

Here rationalism is instantaneously up in arms against us. I can imagine a rationalist to talk as follows:

"Truth is not made," he will say; "it absolutely obtains, being a unique relation that does not wait upon any process, but shoots straight over the head of experience, and hits its reality every time. Our belief that yon thing on the wall is a clock is true already, altho no one in the whole history of the world should verify it. The bare quality of standing in that transcendent relation is what makes any thought true that possesses it, whether or not there be verification. You pragmatists put the cart before the horse in making truth's being reside in verification-processes. These are merely signs of its being, merely our lame ways of ascertaining after the fact, which of our ideas already has possessed the wondrous quality. The quality itself is timeless, like all essences and natures. Thoughts partake of it directly, as they partake of falsity or of irrelevancy. It can't be analyzed away into pragmatic consequences."

The whole plausibility of this rationalist tirade is due to the fact to which we have already paid so much attention. In our world, namely, abounding as it does in things of similar kinds and similarly associated, one verification serves for others of its kind, and one great use of knowing things is to be led not so much to them as to their associates, especially to human talk about them. The quality of truth, obtaining *ante rem*, pragmatically means, then, the fact that in such a world innumerable ideas work better by their indirect or possible than by their direct and actual verification. Truth *ante rem* means only verifiability, then; or else it is a case of the stock rationalist trick of treating the *name* of a concrete phenomenal reality as an independent prior entity, and placing it behind the reality as its explanation. Professor Mach quotes somewhere an epigram of Lessing's:

> Sagt Hänschen Schlau zu Vetter Fritz,
> "Wie kommt es, Vetter Fritzen,
> Dass grad' die Reichsten in der Welt,
> Das meiste Geld besitzen?"

Hänschen Schlau here treats the principle "wealth" as something distinct from the facts denoted by the man's being rich. It antedates them; the facts become only a sort of secondary coincidence with the rich man's essential nature.

In the case of "wealth" we all see the fallacy. We know that wealth is but a name for concrete processes that certain men's lives play a part in, and not a natural excellence found in Messrs. Rockefeller and Carnegie, but not in the rest of us.

Like wealth, health also lives *in rebus*. It is a name for processes, as digestion, circulation, sleep, etc., that go on happily, tho in this instance we are more inclined to think of it as a principle and to say the man digests and sleeps so well *because* he is so healthy.

With "strength" we are, I think, more rationalistic still, and decidedly inclined to treat it as an excellence pre-existing in the man and explanatory of the herculean performances of his muscles.

With "truth" most people go over the border entirely, and treat the rationalistic account as self-evident. But really all these words in *th* are exactly similar. Truth exists *ante rem* just as much and as little as the other things do.

The scholastics, following Aristotle, made much of the distinction between habit and act. Health *in actu* means, among other things, good sleeping and digesting. But a healthy man need not always be sleeping, or always digesting, any more than a wealthy man need be always handling money, or a strong man always lifting weights. All such qualities sink to the status of "habits" between their times of exercise; and similarly truth becomes a habit of certain of our ideas and beliefs in their intervals of rest from their verifying activities. But those activities are the root of the whole matter, and the condition of there being any habit to exist in the intervals.

"The true," to put it very briefly, is only the expedient in the way of our thinking, just as "the right" is only the expedient in the way of our behaving. Expedient in almost any fashion; and expedient in the long run and on the whole of course; for what meets expediently all the experience in sight won't necessarily meet all farther experiences equally satisfactorily. Experience, as we know, has ways of *boiling over,* and making us correct our present formulas.

The "absolutely" true, meaning what no farther experience will ever alter, is that ideal vanishing-point towards which we imagine that all our temporary truths will some day converge. It runs on all fours with the perfectly wise man, and with the absolutely complete experience; and, if these ideals are ever realized, they will all be realized together. Meanwhile we have to live today by what truth we can get today, and be ready tomorrow to call it falsehood. Ptolemaic astronomy, Euclidean space, Aristotelian logic, scholastic metaphysics, were expedient for centuries, but human experience has boiled over those limits, and we now call these things only relatively true, or true within those borders of experience. "Absolutely" they are false; for we know that those limits were casual, and might have been transcended by past theorists just as they are by present thinkers.

When new experiences lead to retrospective judgments, using the past tense, what these judgments utter *was* true, even tho no past thinker had been led there. We live forwards, a Danish thinker has said, but we understand backwards. The present sheds a backward light on the world's previous processes. They may have been truth-processes for the actors in them. They are not so for one who knows the later revelations of the story.

This regulative notion of a potential better truth to be established later, possibly to be established some day absolutely, and having powers of retroactive legislation, turns its face, like all pragmatist notions, towards concreteness of fact, and towards the future. Like the half-truths, the absolute truth will have to be *made,* made as a relation incidental to the growth of a mass of verification-experience, to which the half-true ideas are all along contributing their quota.

I have already insisted on the fact that truth is made largely out of previous truths. Men's beliefs at any time are so much experience *funded.* But the beliefs are themselves parts of the sum total of the world's experience, and become matter, therefore, for the next day's funding operations. So far as reality means experienceable reality, both it and the truths men gain about it are everlastingly in process of mutation—mutation towards a definite goal, it may be—but still mutation.

Mathematicians can solve problems with two variables. On the Newtonian theory, for instance, acceleration varies with distance, but distance also varies with acceleration. In the realm of truth-processes facts come independently and determine our beliefs provisionally. But these beliefs make us act, and as fast as they do so, they bring into sight or into existence new facts which re-determine the beliefs accordingly. So the whole coil and ball of truth, as it rolls up, is the product of a double influence. Truths emerge from facts; but they dip forward into facts again and add to them; which facts again create or reveal new truth (the word is indifferent) and so on indefinitely. The "facts" themselves meanwhile are not *true.* They simply *are.* Truth is the function of the beliefs that start and terminate among them.

The case is like a snowball's growth, due as it is to the distribution of the snow on the one hand, and to the successive pushes of the boys on the other, with these factors co-determining each other incessantly.

The most fateful point of difference between being a rationalist and being a pragmatist is now fully in sight. Experience is in mutation, and our psychological ascertainments of truth are in mutation—so much rationalism will allow; but never that either reality itself or truth itself is mutable. Reality stands complete and ready-made from all eternity, rationalism insists, and the agreement of our ideas with it is that unique unanalyzable virtue in them of which she has already told us. As that intrinsic excellence, their truth has nothing to do with our experiences. It adds nothing to the content of experience. It makes no difference to reality itself; it is supervenient, inert, static, a reflection merely. It doesn't *exist*, it *holds* or *obtains*, it belongs to another dimension from that of either facts or fact-relations, belongs, in short, to the epistemological dimension—and with that big word rationalism closes the discussion.

Thus, just as pragmatism faces forward to the future, so does rationalism here again face backward to a past eternity. True to her inveterate habit, rationalism reverts to "principles," and thinks that when an abstraction once is named, we own an oracular solution.

The tremendous pregnancy in the way of consequences for life of this radical difference of outlook will only become apparent in my later lectures. I wish meanwhile to close this lecture by showing that rationalism's sublimity does not save it from inanity.

When, namely, you ask rationalists, instead of accusing pragmatism of desecrating the notion of truth, to define it themselves by saying exactly what *they* understand by it, the only positive attempts I can think of are these two:

1. "Truth is the system of propositions which have an un-conditional claim to be recognized as valid." [1]

2. Truth is a name for all those judgments which we find ourselves under obligation to make by a kind of imperative duty. [2]

The first thing that strikes one in such definitions is their unutterable triviality. They are absolutely true, of course, but absolutely insignificant until you handle them pragmatically. What do you mean by "claim" here, and what do you mean by "duty"? As summary names for the concrete reasons why thinking in true ways is overwhelmingly expedient and good for mortal men, it is all right to talk of claims on reality's part to be agreed with, and of obligations on our part to agree. We feel both the claims and the obligations, and we feel them for just those reasons.

But the rationalists who talk of claim and obligation *ex-pressly say that they have nothing to do with our practical interests or personal reasons.* Our reasons for agreeing are psychological facts, they say, relative to each thinker, and to the accidents of his life. They are his evidence merely, they are no part of the life of truth itself. That life transacts itself in a purely logical or epistemological, as distinguished from a psychological, dimension, and its claims antedate and exceed all personal motivations whatsoever. Tho neither man nor God should ever ascertain truth, the word would still have to be defined as that which *ought* to be ascertained and recognized.

There never was a more exquisite example of an idea abstracted from the concretes of experience and then used to oppose and negate what it was abstracted from.

Philosophy and common life abound in similar instances. The "sentimentalist fallacy" is to shed tears over abstract justice and generosity, beauty, etc., and never to know these qualities when you meet them in the street, because the circumstances make them vulgar. Thus I read in the privately printed biography of an eminently rationalistic mind: "It was strange that with such admiration for beauty in the abstract, my brother had no enthusiasm for fine architecture, for beautiful painting, or for flowers." And in almost the last philosophic work I have read, I find such passages as the following: "Justice is ideal, solely ideal. Reason conceives that it ought to exist, but experience shows that it can not. . . . Truth, which ought to be, can not be. . . . Reason is deformed by experience. As soon as reason enters experience it becomes contrary to reason."

The rationalist's fallacy here is exactly like the sentimentalist's. Both extract a quality from the muddy particulars of experience, and find it so pure when extracted that they contrast it with each and all its muddy instances as an opposite and higher nature. All the while it is *their* nature. It is the nature of truths to be validated, verified. It pays for our ideas to be validated. Our obligation to seek truth is part of our general obligation to do what pays. The payments true ideas bring are the sole why of our duty to follow them. Identical whys exist in the case of wealth and health.

Truth makes no other kind of claim and imposes no other kind of thought than health and wealth do. All these claims are conditional; the concrete benefits we gain are what we mean by calling the pursuit a duty. In the case of truth, untrue beliefs work as perniciously in the long run as true beliefs work beneficially. Talking abstractly, the quality "true" may thus be said to grow absolutely precious and the quality "untrue" absolutely damnable: the one may be called good, the other bad, unconditionally. We ought to think the true, we ought to shun the false, imperatively.

But if we treat all this abstraction literally and oppose it to its mother soil in experience, see what a preposterous position we work ourselves into.

We can not then take a step forward in our actual thinking. When shall I acknowledge this truth and when that? Shall the acknowledgment be loud?—or silent? If sometimes loud, sometimes silent, which *now*? When may a truth go into cold-storage in the encyclopedia? and when shall it come out for battle? Must I constantly be repeating the truth "twice two are four" because of its eternal claim on recognition? or is it sometimes irrelevant? Must my thoughts dwell night and day on my personal sins and blemishes, because I truly have them? —or may I sink and ignore them in order to be a decent social unit, and not a mass of morbid melancholy and apology?

It is quite evident that our obligation to acknowledge truth, so far from being unconditional, is tremendously conditioned. Truth with a big T, and in the singular, claims abstractly to be recognized, of course; but concrete truths in the plural need be recognized only when their recognition is expedient. A truth must always be preferred to a falsehood when both relate to the situation; but when neither does, truth is as little of a duty as falsehood. If you ask me what o'clock it is and I tell you that I live at 95 Irving Street, my answer may indeed be true, but you don't see why it is my duty to give it. A false address would be as much to the purpose.

With this admission that there are conditions that limit the application of the abstract imperative, *the pragmatistic treatment of truth sweeps back upon us in its fulness*. Our duty to agree with reality is seen to be grounded in a perfect jungle of concrete expediencies.

When Berkeley had explained what people meant by matter, people thought that he denied matter's existence. When Messrs. Schiller and Dewey now explain what people mean by truth, they are accused of denying *its* existence. These pragmatists destroy all objective standards, critics say, and put foolishness and wisdom on one level. A favorite formula for describing Mr. Schiller's doctrines and mine is that we are persons who think that by saying whatever you find it pleasant to say and calling it truth you fulfil every pragmatistic requirement.

I leave it to you to judge whether this be not an impudent slander. Pent in, as the pragmatist more than any one else sees himself to be, between the whole body of funded truths squeezed from the past and the coercions of the world of sense about him, who so well as he feels the immense pressure of objective control under which our minds perform their operations? If any one imagines that this law is lax, let him keep its commandment one day, says Emerson. We have heard much of late of the uses of the imagination in science. It is high time to urge the use of a little imagination in philosophy. The unwillingness of some of our critics to read any but the silliest of possible meanings into our statements is as discreditable to their imaginations as anything I know in recent philosophic history. Schiller says the true is that which "works." Thereupon he is treated as one who limits verification to the lowest material utilities. Dewey says truth is what gives "satisfaction." He is treated as one who believes in calling everything true which, if it were true, would be pleasant.

Our critics certainly need more imagination of realities. I have honestly tried to stretch my own imagination and to read the best possible meaning into the rationalist conception, but I have to confess that it still completely baffles me. The notion of a reality calling on us to "agree" with it, and that for no reason, but simply because its claim is "unconditional" or "transcendent," is one that I can make neither head nor tail of. I try to imagine myself as the sole reality in the world, and then to imagine what more I would "claim" if I were allowed to. If you suggest the possibility of my claiming that a mind should come into being from out of the void inane and stand and *copy* me, I can indeed imagine what the copying might mean, but I can conjure up no motive. What good it would do me to be copied, or what good it would do that mind to copy me, if further consequences are expressly and in principle ruled out as motives for the claim (as they are by our rationalist authorities) I can not fathom. When the Irishman's admirers ran him along to the place of banquet in a sedan chair with no bottom, he said, "Faith, if it wasn't for the honor of the thing, I might as well have come on foot." So here: but for the honor of the thing, I might as well have remained uncopied. Copying is one genuine mode of knowing (which for some strange reason our contemporary transcendentalists seem to be tumbling over each other to repudiate); but when we get beyond copying, and fall back on unnamed forms of agreeing that are expressly denied to be either copyings or leadings or fittings, or any other processes pragmatically definable, the *what* of the "agreement" claimed becomes as unintelligible as the why of it. Neither content nor motive can be imagined for it. It is an absolutely meaningless abstraction.[3]

Surely in this field of truth it is the pragmatists and not the rationalists who are the more genuine defenders of the universe's rationality.

PRAGMATISM AND HUMANISM

What hardens the heart of every one I approach with the view of truth sketched in my last lecture is that typical idol of the tribe, the notion of *the* Truth, conceived as the one answer, determinate and complete, to the one fixed enigma which the world is believed to propound. For popular tradition, it is all the better if the answer be oracular, so as itself to awaken wonder as an enigma of the second order, veiling rather than revealing what its profundities are supposed to contain. All the great single-word answers to the world's riddle, such as God, the One, Reason, Law, Spirit, Matter, Nature, Polarity, the Dialectic Process, the Idea, the Self, the Oversoul, draw the admiration that men have lavished on them from this oracular rôle. By amateurs in philosophy and professionals alike, the universe is represented as a queer sort of petrified sphinx whose appeal to men consists in a monotonous challenge to his divining powers. *The* Truth: what a perfect idol of the rationalistic mind! I read in an old letter—from a gifted friend who died too young—these words: "In everything, in science, art, morals and religion, there *must* be one system that is right and *every* other wrong." How characteristic of the enthusiasm of a certain stage of youth! At twenty-one we rise to such a challenge and expect to find the system. It never occurs to most of us even later that the question "what is *the* truth?" is no real question (being irrelative to all conditions) and that the whole notion of *the* truth is an abstraction from the fact of truths in the plural, a mere useful summarizing phrase like *the* Latin Language or *the* Law.

Common-law judges sometimes talk about the law, and schoolmasters talk about the Latin tongue, in a way to make their hearers think they mean entities pre-existent to the de-

cisions or to the words and syntax, determining them unequivocally and requiring them to obey. But the slightest
exercise of reflection makes us see that, instead of being principles of this kind, both law and Latin are results. Distinctions
between the lawful and the unlawful in conduct, or between
the correct and incorrect in speech, have grown up incidentally
among the interactions of men's experiences in detail; and in
no other way do distinctions between the true and the false in
belief ever grow up. Truth grafts itself on previous truth,
modifying it in the process, just as idiom grafts itself on
previous idiom, and law on previous law. Given previous law
and a novel case, and the judge will twist them into fresh
law. Previous idiom; new slang or metaphor or oddity that hits
the public taste; and presto, a new idiom is made. Previous
truth; fresh facts: and our mind finds a new truth.

All the while, however, we pretend that the eternal is un-
rolling, that the one previous justice, grammar or truth are
simply fulgurating and not being made. But imagine a youth
in the courtroom trying cases with his abstract notion of "the"
law, or a censor of speech let loose among the theatres with
his idea of "the" mother tongue, or a professor setting up to
lecture on the actual universe with his rationalistic notion of
"the Truth" with a big T, and what progress do they make?
Truth, law, and language fairly boil away from them at the
least touch of novel fact. These things *make themselves* as
we go. Our rights, wrongs, prohibitions, penalties, words,
forms, idioms, beliefs, are so many new creations that add
themselves as fast as history proceeds. Far from being antecedent principles that animate the process, law, language,
truth are but abstract names for its results.

Laws and languages at any rate are thus seen to be man-
made things. Mr. Schiller applies the analogy to beliefs, and
proposes the name of "Humanism" for the doctrine that to an
unascertainable extent our truths are man-made products too.
Human motives sharpen all our questions, human satisfactions
lurk in all our answers, all our formulas have a human twist.
This element is so inextricable in the products that Mr.
Schiller sometimes seems almost to leave it an open question
whether there be anything else. "The world," he says, "is
essentially λυη, it is what we make it. It is fruitless to define
it by what it originally was or by what it is apart from us; it
is what is made of it. Hence . . . the world is plastic." [1] He

adds that we can learn the limits of the plasticity only by trying, and that we ought to start as if it were wholly plastic, acting methodically on that assumption, and stopping only when we are decisively rebuked.

This is Mr. Schiller's butt-end-foremost statement of the humanist position, and it has exposed him to severe attack. I mean to defend the humanist position in this lecture, so I will insinuate a few remarks at this point.

Mr. Schiller admits as emphatically as any one the presence of resisting factors in every actual experience of truth-making, of which the new-made special truth must take account, and with which it has perforce to "agree." All our truths are beliefs about "Reality;" and in any particular belief the reality acts as something independent, as a thing *found*, not manufactured. Let me here recall a bit of my last lecture.

"Reality" is in general what truths have to take account of;[2] and the *first* part of reality from this point of view is the flux of our sensations. Sensations are forced upon us, coming we know not whence. Over their nature, order and quantity we have as good as no control. *They* are neither true nor false; they simply *are*. It is only what we say about them, only the names we give them, our theories of their source and nature and remote relations, that may be true or not.

The *second* part of reality, as something that our beliefs must also obediently take account of is the *relations* that obtain between our sensations or between their copies in our minds. This part falls into two subparts: 1) the relations that are mutable and accidental, as those of date and place; and 2) those that are fixed and essential because they are grounded on the inner natures of their terms. Both sorts of relation are matters of immediate perception. Both are "facts." But it is the latter kind of fact that forms the more important subpart of reality for our theories of knowledge. Inner relations namely are "eternal," are perceived whenever their sensible terms are compared; and of them our thought—mathematical and logical thought so-called—must eternally take account.

The *third* part of reality, additional to these perceptions (tho largely based upon them), is the *previous truths* of which every new inquiry takes account. This third part is a much less obdurately resisting factor: it often ends by giving way. In speaking of these three portions of reality as at all times controlling our belief's formation, I am only reminding you of what we heard in our last hour.

Now however fixed these elements of reality may be, we still have a certain freedom in our dealings with them. Take our sensations. *That* they are is undoubtedly beyond our control; but *which* we attend to, note, and make emphatic in our conclusions depends on our own interests; and, according as we lay the emphasis here or there, quite different formulations of truth result. We read the same facts differently. "Waterloo," with the same fixed details, spells a "victory" for an Englishman; for a Frenchman it spells a "defeat." So, for an optimist philosopher the universe spells victory, for a pessimist, defeat.

What we say about reality thus depends on the perspective into which we throw it. The *that* of it is its own; but the *what* depends on the *which;* and the which depends on *us.* Both the sensational and the relational parts of reality are dumb; they say absolutely nothing about themselves. We it is who have to speak for them. This dumbness of sensations has led such intellectualists as T. H. Green and Edward Caird to shove them almost beyond the pale of philosophic recognition, but pragmatists refuse to go so far. A sensation is rather like a client who has given his case to a lawyer and then has passively to listen in the courtroom to whatever account of his affairs, pleasant or unpleasant, the lawyer finds it most expedient to give.

Hence, even in the field of sensation, our minds exert a certain arbitrary choice. By our inclusions and omissions we trace the field's extent; by our emphasis we mark its foreground and its background; by our order we read it in this direction or in that. We receive in short the block of marble, but we carve the statue ourselves.

This applies to the "eternal" parts of reality as well: we shuffle our perceptions of intrinsic relation and arrange them just as freely. We read them in one serial order or another, class them in this way or in that, treat one or the other as more fundamental, until our beliefs about them form those bodies of truth known as logics, geometrics, or arithmetics, in each and all of which the form and order in which the whole is cast is flagrantly man-made.

Thus, to say nothing of the new *facts* which men add to the matter of reality by the acts of their own lives, they have already impressed their mental forms on that whole third of reality which I have called "previous truths." Every hour brings its new percepts, its own facts of sensation and relation, to be truly taken account of; but the whole of our *past* dealings with such facts is already founded in the previous truths. It is therefore only the smallest and recentest fraction of the first two parts of reality that comes to us without the human touch, and that fraction has immediately to become humanized in the sense of being squared, assimilated, or in some way adapted, to the humanized mass already there. As a matter of fact we can hardly take in an impression at all, in the absence of a preconception of what impressions there may possibly be.

When we talk of reality "independent" of human thinking, then, it seems a thing very hard to find. It reduces to the notion of what is just entering into experience and yet to be named, or else to some imagined aboriginal presence in experience, before any belief about the presence had arisen, before any human conception had been applied. It is what is absolutely dumb and evanescent, the merely ideal limit of our minds. We may glimpse it, but we never grasp it; what we grasp is always some substitute for it which previous human thinking has peptonized and cooked for our consumption. If so vulgar an expression were allowed us, we might say that wherever we find it, it has been already *faked*. This is what Mr. Schiller has in mind when he calls independent reality a mere unresisting λνη, which *is* only to be made over by us.

That is Mr. Schiller's belief about the sensible core of reality. We "encounter" it (in Mr. Bradley's words) but don't possess it. Superficially this sounds like Kant's view; but between categories fulminated before nature began, and categories gradually forming themselves in nature's presence, the whole chasm between rationalism and empiricism yawns. To the genuine "Kantianer" Schiller will always be to Kant as a satyr to Hyperion.

Other pragmatists may reach more positive beliefs about the sensible core of reality. They may think to get at it in its independent nature, by peeling off the successive man-made wrappings. They may make theories that tell us where it comes from and all about it; and *if these theories work satisfactorily they will be true*. The transcendental idealists say there is no core, the finally completed wrapping being reality and truth in one. Scholasticism still teaches that the core is "matter." Professor Bergson, Heymans, Strong, and others believe in the core and bravely try to define it. Messrs. Dewey and Schiller treat it as a "limit." Which is the truer of all these diverse accounts, or of others comparable with them, unless it be the one that finally proves the most satisfactory? On the one hand there will stand reality, on the other an account of it which it proves impossible to better or to alter. If the impossibility prove permanent, the truth of the account will be absolute. Other content of truth than this I can find nowhere. If the antipragmatists have any other meaning, let them for heaven's sake reveal it, let them grant us access to it!

Not *being* reality, but only our belief *about* reality, it will contain human elements, but these will *know* the non-human element, in the only sense in which there can be knowledge of anything. Does the river make its banks, or do the banks make the river? Does a man walk with his right leg or with his left leg more essentially? Just as impossible may it be to separate the real from the human factors in the growth of our cognitive experience.

Let this stand as a first brief indication of the humanistic position. Does it seem paradoxical? If so, I will try to make it plausible by a few illustrations, which will lead to a fuller acquaintance with the subject.

In many familiar objects every one will recognize the human element. We conceive a given reality in this way or in that, to suit our purpose, and the reality passively submits to the conception. You can take the number 27 as the cube of 3, or as the product of 3 and 9, or as 26 *plus* 1, or 100 *minus* 73, or in countless other ways, of which one will be just as true as another. You can take a chess-board as black squares on a white ground, or as white squares on a black ground, and neither conception is a false one.

You can treat the adjoined figure as a star, as two big triangles crossing each other, as a hexagon with legs set up on its angles, as six equal triangles hanging together by their tips, etc. All these treatments are true treatments—the sensible *that* upon the paper resists no one of them. You can say of a line that it runs east, or you can say that it runs west, and the line *per se* accepts both descriptions without rebelling at the inconsistency.

We carve out groups of stars in the heavens, and call them constellations, and the stars patiently suffer us to do so, though if they knew what we were doing, some of them might feel much surprised at the partners we had given them. We name the same constellation diversely, as Charles's Wain, the Great Bear, or the Dipper. None of the names will be false, and one will be as true as another, for all are applicable.

In all these cases we humanly make an *addition* to some sensible reality, and that reality tolerates the addition. All the additions "agree" with the reality; they fit it, while they build it out. No one of them is false. Which may be treated as the *more* true, depends altogether on the human use of it. If the 27 is a number of dollars which I find in a drawer where I had left 28, it is 28 minus 1. If it is the number of inches in a board which I wish to insert as a shelf into a cupboard 26 inches wide, it is 26 plus 1. If I wish to ennoble the heavens by the constellations I see there, "Charles's Wain" would be more true than "Dipper." My friend Frederick Myers was humorously indignant that that prodigious star-group should remind us Americans of nothing but a culinary utensil.

What shall we call a *thing* anyhow? It seems quite arbitrary, for we carve out everything, just as we carve out constellations, to suit our human purposes. For me, this whole "audience" is one thing, which grows now restless, now attentive. I have no use at present for its individual units, so I don't consider them. So of an "army," of a "nation." But in your own eyes, ladies and gentlemen, to call you "audience" is an accidental way of taking you. The permanently real things for you are your individual persons. To an anatomist, again, those persons are but organisms, and the real things are the organs. Not the organs, so much as their constituent cells, say the histologists; not the cells, but their molecules, say in turn the chemists.

We break the flux of sensible reality into things, then, at our will. We create the subjects of our true as well as of our false propositions.

We create the predicates also. Many of the predicates of things express only the relations of the things to us and to our feelings. Such predicates of course are human additions. Caesar crossed the Rubicon, and was a menace to Rome's freedom. He is also an American schoolroom pest, made into one by the reaction of our schoolboys to his writings. The added predicate is as true of him as the earlier ones.

You see how naturally one comes to the humanistic principle: you can't weed out the human contribution. Our nouns
and adjectives are all humanized heirlooms, and in the theories
we build them into, the inner order and arrangement is wholly
dictated by human considerations, intellectual consistency
being one of them. Mathematics and logic themselves are fer-
menting with human rearrangements; physics, astronomy and
biology follow massive cues of preference. We plunge forward into the field of fresh experience with the beliefs our
ancestors and we have made already; these determine what
we notice; what we notice determines what we do; what we
do again determines what we experience; so from one thing
to another, altho the stubborn fact remains that there *is* a
sensible flux, what is *true of it* seems from first to last to be
largely a matter of our own creation.

We build the flux out inevitably. The great question is:
does it, with our additions, *rise or fall in value?* Are the additions *worthy* or *unworthy?* Suppose a universe composed of
seven stars, and nothing else but three human witnesses and
their critic. One witness names the stars "Great Bear," one
calls them "Charles's Wain;" one calls them the "Dipper."
Which human addition has made the best universe of the
given stellar material? If Frederick Myers were the critic, he
would have no hesitation in "turning down" the American
witness.

Lotze has in several places made a deep suggestion. We
naïvely assume, he says, a relation between reality and our
minds which may be just the opposite of the true one. Reality,
we naturally think, stands ready-made and complete, and our
intellects supervene with the one simple duty of describing it
as it is already. But may not our descriptions, Lotze asks, be
themselves important additions to reality? And may not previous reality itself be there, far less for the purpose of re-
appearing unaltered in our knowledge, than for the very purpose of stimulating our minds to such additions as shall en-
hance the universe's total value. *"Die erhöhung des vorgefundenen daseins"* is a phrase used by Professor Eucken somewhere, which reminds one of this suggestion by the great
Lotze.

It is identically our pragmatistic conception. In our cognitive
as well as in our active life we are creative. We *add,* both to
the subject and to the predicate part of reality. The world

stands really malleable, waiting to receive its final touches at our hands. Like the kingdom of heaven, it suffers human violence willingly. Man *engenders* truths upon it.

No one can deny that such a rôle would add both to our dignity and to our responsibility as thinkers. To some of us it proves a most inspiring notion. Signore Papini, the leader of Italian pragmatism, grows fairly dithyrambic over the view that it opens of man's divinely-creative functions.

The import of the difference between pragmatism and rationalism is now in sight throughout its whole extent. The essential contrast is that *for rationalism reality is ready-made and complete from all eternity, while for pragmatism it is still in the making, and awaits part of its complexion from the future.* On the one side the universe is absolutely secure, on the other it is still pursuing its adventures.

We have got into rather deep water with this humanistic view, and it is no wonder that misunderstanding gathers round it. It is accused of being a doctrine of caprice. Mr. Bradley, for example, says that a humanist, if he understood his own doctrine, would have to "hold any end, however perverted, to be rational, if I insist on it personally, and any idea, however mad, to be the truth if only some one is resolved that he will have it so." The humanist view of "reality," as something resisting, yet malleable, which controls our thinking as an energy that must be taken "account" of incessantly (tho not necessarily merely *copied*) is evidently a difficult one to introduce to novices. The situation reminds me of one that I have personally gone through. I once wrote an essay on our right to believe, which I unluckily called the *Will* to Believe. All the critics, neglecting the essay, pounced upon the title. Psychologically it was impossible, morally it was iniquitous. The "will to deceive," the "will to make-believe," were wittily proposed as substitutes for it.

The alternative between pragmatism and rationalism, in the shape in which we now have it before us, is no longer a question in the theory of knowledge, it concerns the structure of the universe itself.

On the pragmatist side we have only one edition of the universe, unfinished, growing in all sorts of places, especially in the places where thinking beings are at work.

On the rationalist side we have a universe in many editions, one real one, the infinite folio, or *édition de luxe,* eternally complete; and then the various finite editions, full of false readings, distorted and mutilated each in its own way.

So the rival metaphysical hypotheses of pluralism and monism here come back upon us. I will develop their differences during the remainder of our hour.

And first let me say that it is impossible not to see a temperamental difference at work in the choice of sides. The rationalist mind, radically taken, is of a doctrinaire and authoritative complexion: the phrase "*must* be" is ever on its lips. The bellyband of its universe must be tight. A radical pragmatist on the other hand is a happy-go-lucky anarchistic sort of creature. If he had to live in a tub like Diogenes he wouldn't mind at all if the hoops were loose and the staves let in the sun.

Now the idea of this loose universe affects your typical rationalists in much the same way as "freedom of the press" might affect a veteran official in the Russian bureau of censorship; or as "simplified spelling" might affect an elderly schoolmistress. It affects him as the swarm of protestant sects affects a papist onlooker. It appears as backboneless and devoid of principle as "opportunism" in politics appears to an old-fashioned French legitimist, or to a fanatical believer in the divine right of the people.

For pluralistic pragmatism, truth grows up inside of all the finite experiences. They lean on each other, but the whole of them, if such a whole there be, leans on nothing. All "homes" are in finite experience; finite experience as such is homeless. Nothing outside of the flux secures the issue of it. It can hope salvation only from its own intrinsic promises and potencies.

To rationalists this describes a tramp and vagrant world, adrift in space, with neither elephant nor tortoise to plant the sole of its foot upon. It is a set of stars hurled into heaven without even a center of gravity to pull against. In other spheres of life it is true that we have got used to living in a state of relative insecurity. The authority of "the State," and that of an absolute "moral law," have resolved themselves into expediencies, and holy church has resolved itself into "meeting-houses." Not so as yet within the philosophic classrooms. A universe with such as *us* contributing to create its truth, a world delivered to *our* opportunisms and our private judgments! Home-rule for Ireland would be a millennium in comparison. We're no more fit for such a part than the Filipinos are "fit for self-government." Such a world would not be *respectable* philosophically. It is a trunk without a tag, a dog without a collar in the eyes of most professors of philosophy.

What then would tighten this loose universe, according to the professors?

Something to support the finite many, to tie it to, to unify and anchor it. Something *un-*exposed to accident, something eternal and unalterable. The mutable in experience must be founded on immutability. Behind our *de facto* world, our world in act, there must be a *de jure* duplicate fixed and previous, with all that can happen here already there *in posse*, every drop of blood, every smallest item, appointed and provided, stamped and branded, without chance of variation. The negatives that haunt our ideals here below must be themselves negated in the absolutely Real. This alone makes the universe solid. This is the resting deep. We live upon the stormy surface; but with this our anchor holds, for it grapples rock bottom. This is Wordsworth's "eternal peace abiding at the heart of endless agitation." This is Vivekananda's mystic One of which I read to you. This is Reality with the big R, reality that makes the timeless claim, reality to which defeat can't happen. This is what the men of principles, and in general all the men whom I called tender-minded in my first lecture, think themselves obliged to postulate.

And this, exactly this, is what the tough-minded of that lecture find themselves moved to call a piece of perverse abstraction-worship. The tough-minded are the men whose alpha and omega are *facts*. Behind the bare phenomenal facts, as my tough-minded old friend Chauncey Wright, the great Harvard empiricist of my youth, used to say, there is *nothing*. When a rationalist insists that behind the facts there is the *ground* of the facts, the *possibility* of the facts, the tougher empiricists accuse him of taking the mere name and nature of a fact and clapping it behind the fact as a duplicate entity to make it possible. That such sham grounds are often invoked is notorious. At a surgical operation I once heard a bystander ask a doctor why the patient breathed so deeply. "Because ether is a respiratory stimulant," the doctor answered. "Ah!" said the questioner, as if that were a good explanation. But this is like saying that cyanide of potassium kills because it is a "poison," or that it is so cold tonight because it is "winter," or that we have five fingers because we are "pentadactyls."

These are but names for the facts, taken from the facts, and then treated as previous and explanatory. The tender-minded notion of an absolute reality is, according to the radically tough-minded, framed on just this pattern. It is but our summarizing name for the whole spread-out and strung-along mass of phenomena, treated as if it were a different entity, both one and previous.

You see how differently people take things. The world we live in exists diffused and distributed, in the form of an indefinitely numerous lot of *eaches*, coherent in all sorts of ways and degrees; and the tough-minded are perfectly willing to keep them at that valuation. They can *stand* that kind of world, their temper being well adapted to its insecurity. Not so the tender-minded party. They must back the world we find ourselves born into by "another and a better" world in which the eaches form an All and the All a One that logically presupposes, co-implicates, and secures each *each* without exception.

Must we as pragmatists be radically tough-minded? or can we treat the absolute edition of the world as a legitimate hypothesis? It is certainly legitimate, for it is thinkable, whether we take it in its abstract or in its concrete shape.

By taking it abstractly I mean placing it behind our finite life as we place the word "winter" behind tonight's cold weather. "Winter" is only the name for a certain number of days which we find generally characterized by cold weather, but it guarantees nothing in that line, for our thermometer tomorrow may soar into the 70's. Nevertheless the word is a useful one to plunge forward with into the stream of our experience. It cuts off certain probabilities and sets up others. You can put away your straw hats; you can unpack your arctics. It is a summary of things to look for. It names a part of nature's habits, and gets you ready for their continuation. It is a definite instrument abstracted from experience, a conceptual reality that you must take account of, and which reflects you totally back into sensible realities. The pragmatist is the last person to deny the reality of such abstractions. They are so much past experience funded.

But taking the absolute edition of the world concretely means a different hypothesis. Rationalists take it concretely and *oppose* it to the world's finite editions. They give it a particular nature. It is perfect, finished. Everything known there is known along with everything else; here, where ignorance reigns, far otherwise. If there is want there, there also is the satisfaction provided. Here all is process; that world is timeless. Possibilities obtain in our world; in the absolute world, where all that is *not* is from eternity impossible, and all that *is* is necessary, the category of possibility has no application. In this world crimes and horrors are regrettable. In that totalized world regret obtains not, for "the existence of ill in the temporal order is the very condition of the perfection of the eternal order."

Once more, either hypothesis is legitimate in pragmatist eyes, for either has its uses. Abstractly, or taken like the word winter, as a memorandum of past experience that orients us towards the future, the notion of the absolute world is indispensable. Concretely taken, it is also indispensable, at least to certain minds, for it determines them religiously, being often a thing to change their lives by, and by changing their lives, to change whatever in the outer order depends on them.

We can not therefore methodically join the tough minds in their rejection of the whole notion of a world beyond our finite experience. One misunderstanding of pragmatism is to identify it with positivistic tough-mindedness, to suppose that it scorns every rationalistic notion as so much jabber and gesticulation, that it loves intellectual anarchy as such and prefers a sort of wolf-world absolutely unpent and wild and without a master or a collar to any philosophic classroom product whatsoever. I have said so much in these lectures against the over-tender forms of rationalism, that I am prepared for some misunderstanding here, but I confess that the amount of it that I have found in this very audience surprises me, for I have simultaneously defended rationalistic hypotheses, so far as these re-direct you fruitfully into experience.

For instance I receive this morning this question on a post-card: "Is a pragmatist necessarily a complete materialist and agnostic?" One of my oldest friends, who ought to know me better, writes me a letter that accuses the pragmatism I am recommending of shutting out all wider metaphysical views and condemning us to the most *terre-à-terre* naturalism. Let me read you some extracts from it.

"It seems to me," my friend writes, "that the pragmatic objection to pragmatism lies in the fact that it might accentuate the narrowness of narrow minds.

"Your call to the rejection of the namby-pamby and the wishy-washy is of course inspiring. But altho it is salutary and stimulating to be told that one should be responsible for the immediate issues and bearings of his words and thoughts, I decline to be deprived of the pleasure and profit of dwelling also on remoter bearings and issues, and it is the *tendency* of pragmatism to refuse this privilege.

"In short, it seems to me that the limitations, or rather the dangers, of the pragmatic tendency, are analogous to those which beset the unwary followers of the 'natural sciences.' Chemistry and physics are eminently pragmatic; and many of their devotees, smugly content with the data that their weights and measures furnish, feel an infinite pity and disdain for all students of philosophy and metaphysics whomsoever. And of course everything can be expressed—after a fashion, and 'theoretically'—in terms of chemistry and physics, that is, *everything except the vital principle of the whole*, and that, they say, there is no pragmatic use in trying to express; it has no bearings—for *them*. I for my part refuse to be persuaded that we can not look beyond the obvious pluralism of the naturalist and the pragmatist to a logical unity in which they take no interest."

How is such a conception of the pragmatism I am advocating possible, after my first and second lectures? I have all along been offering it expressly as a mediator between tough-mindedness and tender-mindedness. If the notion of a world *ante rem*, whether taken abstractly like the word winter, or concretely as the hypothesis of an Absolute, can be shown to have any consequences whatever for our life, it has a meaning. If the meaning works, it will have *some* truth that ought to be held to through all possible reformulations, for pragmatism.

The absolutistic hypothesis, that perfection is eternal, aboriginal, and most real, has a perfectly definite meaning, and it works religiously. To examine how, will be the subject of my next and final lecture.

PRAGMATISM AND RELIGION

At the close of the last lecture I reminded you of the first one, in which I had opposed tough-mindedness to tender-mindedness and recommended pragmatism as their mediator. Tough-mindedness positively rejects tender-mindedness's hypothesis of an eternal perfect edition of the universe co-existing with our finite experience.

On pragmatic principles we can not reject any hypothesis if consequences useful to life flow from it. Universal conceptions, as things to take account of, may be as real for pragmatism as particular sensations are. They have, indeed, no meaning and no reality if they have no use. But if they have any use they have that amount of meaning. And the meaning will be true if the use squares well with life's other uses.

Well, the use of the Absolute is proved by the whole course of men's religious history. The eternal arms are then beneath. Remember Vivekananda's use of the Atman—not indeed a scientific use, for we can make no particular deductions from it. It is emotional and spiritual altogether.

It is always best to discuss things by the help of concrete examples. Let me read therefore some of those verses entitled "To You" by Walt Whitman—"You" of course meaning the reader or hearer of the poem whosoever he or she may be.

Whoever you are, now I place my hand upon you that you
    be my poem;
I whisper with my lips close to your ear,
I have loved many men and women and men, but I love none
    better than you.

O I have been dilatory and dumb;
I should have made my way to you long ago;
I should have blabbed nothing but you, I should have chanted
    nothing but you.

I will leave all and come and make the hymns of you;
None have understood you, but I understand you;
None have done justice to you—you have not done justice to
    yourself;
None but have found you imperfect—I only find no imper-
    fection in you.
O I could sing such glories and grandeurs about you;
You have not known what you are—you have slumbered upon
    yourself all your life;
What you have done returns already in mockeries.

But the mockeries are not you;
Underneath them and within them, I see you lurk;
I pursue you where none else has pursued you.
Silence, the desk, the flippant expression, the night, the ac-
    customed routine, if these conceal you from others, or
    from yourself, they do not conceal you from me;
The shaved face, the unsteady eye, the impure complexion,
    if these balk others, they do not balk me;
The pert apparel, the deformed attitude, drunkenness, greed,
    premature death, all these I part aside.

There is no endowment in man or woman that is not tallied
    in you;
There is no virtue, no beauty, in man or woman, but as good
    is in you;
No pluck nor endurance in others, but as good is in you;
No pleasure waiting for others, but an equal pleasure waits
    for you.

Whoever you are! claim your own at any hazard!
These shows of the east and west are tame, compared with
    you;
These immense meadows—these interminable rivers—you are
    immense and interminable as they;

You are he or she who is master or mistress over them,
Master or mistress in your own right over Nature, elements,
    pain, passion, dissolution.

The hopples fall from your ankles—you find an unfailing suf-
    ficiency;
Old or young, male of female, rude, low, rejected by the
    rest whatever you are promulges itself;
Through birth, life, death, burial, the means are provided,
    nothing is scanted;
Through angers, losses, ambition, ignorance, ennui, what you
    are picks its way.

Verily a fine and moving poem, in any case, but there
are two ways of taking it, both useful.

One is the monistic way, the mystical way of pure cosmic
emotion. The glories and grandeurs, they are yours absolutely,
even in the midst of your defacements. Whatever may happen
to you, whatever you may appear to be, inwardly you are safe.
Look back, *lie* back, on your true principle of being! This is
the famous way of quietism, of indifferentism. Its enemies
compare it to a spiritual opium. Yet pragmatism must respect
this way, for it has massive historic vindication.

But pragmatism sees another way to be respected also,
the pluralistic way of interpreting the poem. The you so
glorified, to which the hymn is sung, may mean your better
possibilities phenomenally taken, or the specific redemptive
effects even of your failures, upon yourself or others. It
may mean your loyalty to the possibilities of others whom
you admire and love so that you are willing to accept your
own poor life, for it is that glory's partner. You can at least
appreciate, applaud, furnish the audience, of so brave a total
world. Forget the low in yourself, then, think only of the
high. Identify your life therewith; then, through angers, losses,
ignorance, ennui, whatever you thus make yourself, whatever
you thus most deeply are, picks its way.

In either way of taking the poem, it encourages fidelity to
ourselves. Both ways satisfy; both sanctify the human flux.
Both paint the portrait of the *you* on a gold background. But
the background of the first way is the static One, while in
the second way it means possibles in the plural, genuine
possibles, and it has all the restlessness of that conception.

Noble enough is either way of reading the poem; but plainly the pluralistic way agrees with the pragmatic temper best, for it immediately suggests an infinitely larger number of the details of future experience to our mind. It sets definite activities in us at work. Altho this second way seems prosaic and earth-born in comparison with the first way, yet no one can accuse it of tough-mindedness in any brutal sense of the term. Yet if, as pragmatists, you should positively set up the second way *against* the first way, you would very likely be misunderstood. You would be accused of denying nobler conceptions, and of being an ally of tough-mindedness in the worst sense.

You remember the letter from a member of this audience from which I read some extracts at our previous meeting. Let me read you an additional extract now. It shows a vagueness in realizing the alternatives before us which I think is very widespread.

"I believe," writes my friend and correspondent, "in pluralism; I believe that in our search for truth we leap from one floating cake of ice to another, on an infinite sea, and that by each of our acts we make new truths possible and old ones impossible; I believe that each man is responsible for making the universe better, and that if he does not do this it will be in so far left undone.

"Yet at the same time I am willing to endure that my children should be incurably sick and suffering (as they are not) and I myself stupid and yet with brains enough to see my stupidity, only on one condition, namely, that through the construction, in imagination and by reasoning, of a *rational unity of all things,* I can conceive my acts and my thoughts and my troubles as *supplemented by all the other phenomena of the world, and as forming—when thus supplemented—a scheme which I approve and adopt as my own;* and for my part I refuse to be persuaded that we can not look beyond the obvious pluralism of the naturalist and pragmatist to a logical unity in which they take no interest or stock."

Such a fine expression of personal faith warms the heart of the hearer. But how much does it clear his philosophic head? Does the writer consistently favor the monistic, or the pluralistic, interpretation of the world's poem? His troubles become atoned for *when thus supplemented,* he says, supplemented, that is, by all the remedies that *the other phenomena* may supply. Obviously here the writer faces forward into the particulars of experience, which he interprets in a pluralistic-melioristic way.

But he believes himself to face backward. He speaks of what he calls the rational *unity* of things, when all the while he really means their possible empirical *unification*. He supposes at the same time that the pragmatist, because he criticizes rationalism's abstract One, is cut off from the consolation of believing in the saving possibilities of the concrete many. He fails in short to distinguish between taking the world's perfection as a necessary principle, and taking it only as a possible *terminus ad quem*.

I regard the writer of the letter as a genuine pragmatist, but as a pragmatist *sans le savoir*. He appears to me as one of that numerous class of philosophic amateurs whom I spoke of in my first lecture, as wishing to have all the good things going, without being too careful as to how they agree or disagree. "Rational unity of all things" is so inspiring a formula, that he brandishes it off-hand, and abstractly accuses pluralism of conflicting with it (for the bare names do conflict), altho concretely he means by it just the pragmatistically unified and ameliorated world. Most of us remain in this essential vagueness, and it is well that we should; but in the interest of clearheadedness it is well that some of us should go farther, so I will try now to focus a little more discriminatingly on this particular religious point.

Is then this you of yous, this absolutely real world, this unity that yields the moral inspiration and has the, religious value, to be taken monistically or pluralistically? Is it *ante rem* or *in rebus*? Is it a principle or an end, an absolute or an ultimate, a first or a last? Does it make you look forward or lie back? It is certainly worth while not to clump the two things together, for if discriminated, they have decidedly diverse meanings for life.

Please observe that the whole dilemma revolves pragmatically about the notion of the world's possibilities. Intellectually, rationalism invokes its absolute principle of unity, as a ground of possibility for the many facts. Emotionally, it sees it as a container and limiter of possibilities, a guarantee that the upshot shall be good. Taken in this way, the absolute makes all good things certain, and all bad things impossible (in the eternal, namely), and may be said to transmute the entire category of possibility into categories more secure. One sees at this point that the great religious differences lies between the men who insist that the world *must and shall be,* and those who are contented with believing that the world *may be,* saved. The whole clash of rationalistic and empiricist religion is thus over the validity of possibility. It is necessary therefore to begin by focusing upon that word. What may the word "possible" definitely mean? To unreflecting men it means a sort of third estate of being, less real than existence, more real than non-existence, a twilight realm, a hybrid status, a limbo into which and out of which realities ever and anon are made to pass.

Such a conception is of course too vague and nondescript to satisfy us. Here, as elsewhere, the only way to extract a term's meaning is to use the pragmatic method on it. When you say that a thing is possible, what difference does it make? It makes at least this difference that if any one calls it impossible you can contradict him, if any one calls it actual you can contradict *him,* and if any one calls it necessary you can contradict him too.

But these privileges of contradiction don't amount to much. When you say a thing is possible, does not that make some farther difference in terms of actual fact?

It makes at least this negative difference that if the statement be true, it follows that *there is nothing extant capable of preventing* the possible thing. The absence of real grounds of interference may thus be said to make things *not impossible,* possible therefore in the *bare* or *abstract* sense.

But most possibles are not bare, they are concretely grounded, or well-grounded, as we say. What does this mean pragmatically? It means not only that there are no preventive conditions present, but that some of the conditions of production of the possible thing actually are here. Thus a concretely possible chicken means: (1) that the idea of chicken contains no essential self-contradiction; (2) that no boys, skunks, or other enemies are about; and (3) that at least an actual egg exists. Possible chicken means actual egg—plus actual sitting hen, or incubator, or what not. As the actual conditions approach completeness the chicken becomes a better-and-better-grounded possibility. When the conditions are entirely complete, it ceases to be a possibility, and turns into an actual fact.

Let us apply this notion to the salvation of the world. What does it pragmatically mean to say that this is possible? It means that some of the conditions of the world's deliverance do actually exist. The more of them there are existent, the fewer preventing conditions you can find, the better-grounded is the salvation's possibility, the more *probable* does the fact of the deliverance become.

So much for our preliminary look at possibility.

Now it would contradict the very spirit of life to say that our minds must be indifferent and neutral in questions like that of the world's salvation. Any one who pretends to be neutral writes himself down here as a fool and a sham. We all do wish to minimize the insecurity of the universe; we are and ought to be unhappy when we regard it as exposed to every enemy and open to every life-destroying draft. Nevertheless there are unhappy men who think the salvation of the world impossible. Theirs is the doctrine known as pessimism.

Optimism in turn would be the doctrine that thinks the world's salvation inevitable.

Midway between the two there stands what may be called the doctrine of meliorism, tho it has hitherto figured less as a doctrine than as an attitude in human affairs. Optimism has always been the regnant *doctrine* in European philosophy. Pessimism was only recently introduced by Schopenhauer and counts few systematic defenders as yet. Meliorism treats salvation as neither necessary nor impossible. It treats it as a possibility, which becomes more and more of a probability the more numerous the actual conditions of salvation become.

It is clear that pragmatism must incline towards meliorism. Some conditions of the world's salvation are actually extant, and she can not possibly close her eyes to this fact: and should the residual conditions come, salvation would become an accomplished reality. Naturally the terms I use here are exceedingly summary. You may interpret the word "salvation" in any way you like, and make it as diffuse and distributive, or as climacteric and integral a phenomenon as you please.

Take, for example, any one of us in this room with the ideals which he cherishes and is willing to live and work for. Every such ideal realized will be one moment in the world's salvation. But these particular ideals are not bare abstract possibilities. They are grounded, they are *live* possibilities, for we are their live champions and pledges, and if the complementary conditions come and add themselves, our ideals will become actual things. What now are the complementary conditions? They are first such a mixture of things as will in the fullness of time give us a chance, a gap that we can spring into, and, finally, *our act*.

Does our act then *create* the world's salvation so far as it makes room for itself, so far as it leaps into the gap? Does it create, not the whole world's salvation of course, but just so much of this as itself covers of the world's extent?

Here I take the bull by the horns, and in spite of the whole crew of rationalists and monists, of whatever brand they be, I ask *why not*? Our acts, our turning-places, where we seem to ourselves to make ourselves and grow, are the parts of the world to which we are closest, the parts of which our knowledge is the most intimate and complete. Why should we not take them at their face value? Why may they not be the actual turning-places and growing-places which they seem to be, of the world—why not the workshop of being, where we catch fact in the making, so that nowhere may the world grow in any other kind of way than this?

Irrational! we are told. How can new being come in local spots and patches which add themselves or stay away at random, independently of the rest? There must be a reason for our acts, and where in the last resort can any reason be looked for save in the material pressure or the logical compulsion of the total nature of the world? There can be but one real agent of growth, or seeming growth, anywhere, and that agent is the integral world itself. It may grow all-over, if growth there be, but that single parts should grow *per se* is irrational.

But if one talks of rationality—and of reasons for things, and insists that they can't just come in spots, what *kind* of a reason can there ultimately be why anything should come at all? Talk of logic and necessity and categories and the absolute and the contents of the whole philosophical machine-shop as you will, the only *real* reason I can think of why anything should ever come is that *some one wishes it to be here*. It is *demanded*—demanded, it may be, to give relief to no matter how small a fraction of the world's mass. This is *living reason*, and compared with it material causes and logical necessities are spectral things.

In short the only fully rational world would be the world of wishing-caps, the world of telepathy, where every desire is fulfilled instanter, without having to consider or placate surrounding or intermediate powers. This is the Absolute's own world. He calls upon the phenomenal world to be, and it *is*, exactly as he calls for it, no other condition being required. In our world, the wishes of the individual are only one condition. Other individuals are there with other wishes and they must be propitiated first. So Being grows under all sorts of resistances in this world of the many, and, from compromise to compromise, only gets organized gradually into what may be called secondarily rational shape. We approach the wishing-cap type of organization only in a few departments of life. We want water and we turn a faucet. We want a kodak-picture and we press a button. We want information and we telephone. We want to travel and we buy a ticket. In these and similar cases, we hardly need to do more than the wishing—the world is rationally organized to do the rest.

But this talk of rationality is a parenthesis and a digression. What we were discussing was the idea of a world growing not integrally but piecemeal by the contributions of its several parts. Take the hypothesis seriously and as a live one. Suppose that the world's author put the case to you before creation, saying: "I am going to make a world not certain to be saved, a world the perfection of which shall be conditional merely, the condition being that each several agent does its own 'level best.' I offer you the chance of taking part in such a world. Its safety, you see, is unwarranted. It is a real adventure, with real danger, yet it may win through. It is a social scheme of co-operative work genuinely to be done. Will you join the procession? Will you trust yourself and trust the other agents enough to face the risk?"

Should you in all seriousness, if participation in such a world were proposed to you, feel bound to reject it as not safe enough? Would you say that, rather than be part and parcel of so fundamentally pluralistic and irrational a universe, you preferred to relapse into the slumber of nonentity from which you had been momentarily aroused by the tempter's voice?

Of course if you are normally constituted, you would do nothing of the sort. There is a healthy-minded buoyancy in most of us which such a universe would exactly fit. We would therefore accept the offer—"Top! und schlag auf schlag!" It would be just like the world we practically live in; and loyalty to our old nurse Nature would forbid us to say no. The world proposed would seem "rational" to us in the most living way.

Most of us, I say, would therefore welcome the proposition and add our *fiat* to the *fiat* of the creator. Yet perhaps some would not; for there are morbid minds in every human collection, and to them the prospect of a universe with only a fighting chance of safety would probably make no appeal. There are moments of discouragement in us all, when we are sick of self and tired of vainly striving. Our own life breaks down, and we fall into the attitude of the prodigal son. We mistrust the chances of things. We want a universe where we can just give up, fall on our father's neck, and be absorbed into the absolute life as a drop of water melts into the river or the sea.

The peace and rest, the security desiderated at such moments is security against the bewildering accidents of so much finite experience. Nirvana means safety from this everlasting round of adventures of which the world of sense consists. The Hindoo and the Buddhist, for this is essentially their attitude, are simply afraid, afraid of more experience, afraid of life.

And to men of this complexion, religious monism comes with its consoling words: "All is needed and essential—even you with your sick soul and heart. All are one with God, and with God all is well. The everlasting arms are beneath, whether in the world of finite appearance you seem to fail or to succeed." There can be no doubt that when men are reduced to their last sick extremity absolutism is the only saving scheme. Pluralistic moralism simply makes their teeth chatter, it refrigerates the very heart within their breast.

So we see concretely two types of religion in sharp contrast. Using our old terms of comparison, we may say that the absolutistic scheme appeals to the tender-minded while the pluralistic scheme appeals to the tough. Many persons would refuse to call the pluralistic scheme religious at all. They would call it moralistic, and would apply the word religious to the monistic scheme alone. Religion in the sense of self-surrender, and moralism in the sense of self-sufficingness, have been pitted against each other as incompatibles frequently enough in the history of human thought.

We stand here before the final question of philosophy. I said in my fourth lecture that I believed the monistic-pluralistic alternative to be the deepest and most pregnant question that our minds can frame. Can it be that the disjunction is a final one? that only one side can be true? Are a pluralism and monism genuine incompatibles? So that, if the world were really pluralistically constituted, if it really existed distributively and were made up of a lot of eaches, it could only be saved piecemeal and *de facto* as the result of their behavior, and its epic history in no wise short-circuited by some essential oneness in which the severalness were already "taken up" beforehand and eternally "overcome"? If this were so, we should have to choose one philosophy or the other. We could not say "yes, yes" to both alternatives. There would have to be a "no" in our relations with the possible. We should confess an ultimate disappointment: we could not remain healthy-minded and sick-minded in one indivisible act.

Of course as human beings we can be healthy minds on one day and sick souls on the next; and as amateur dabblers in philosophy we may perhaps be allowed to call ourselves monistic pluralists, or free-will determinists, or whatever else may occur to us of a reconciling kind. But as philosophers aiming at clearness and consistency, and feeling the pragmatistic need of squaring truth with truth, the question is forced upon us of frankly adopting either the tender or the robustious type of thought. In particular *this* query has always come home to me: May not the claims of tender-mindedness go too far? May not the notion of a world already saved *in toto* anyhow, be too saccharine to stand? May not religious optimism be too idyllic? Must *all* be saved? Is *no* price to be paid in the work of salvation? Is the last word sweet? Is all "yes, yes" in the universe? Doesn't the fact of "no" stand at the very core of life? Doesn't the very "seriousness" that we attribute to life mean that ineluctable no's and losses form a part of it, that there are genuine sacrifices somewhere, and that something permanently drastic and bitter always remains at the bottom of its cup?

I can not speak officially as a pragmatist here; all I can say is that my own pragmatism offers no objection to my taking sides with this more moralistic view, and giving up the claim of total reconciliation. The possibility of this is involved in the pragmatistic willingness to treat pluralism as a serious hypothesis. In the end it is our faith and not our logic that decides such questions, and I deny the right of any pretended logic to veto my own faith. I find myself willing to take the universe to be really dangerous and adventurous, without therefore backing out and crying "no play." I am willing to think that the prodigal-son attitude, open to us as it is in many vicissitudes, is not the right and final attitude towards the whole of life. I am willing that there should be real losses and real losers, and no total preservation of all that is. I can believe in the ideal as an ultimate, not as an origin, and as an extract, not the whole. When the cup is poured off, the dregs are left behind for ever, but the possibility of what is poured off is sweet enough to accept.

As a matter of fact countless human imaginations live in this moralistic and epic kind of a universe, and find its disseminated and strung-along successes sufficient for their rational needs. There is a finely translated epigram in the Greek anthology which admirably expresses this state of mind, this acceptance of loss as unatoned for, even though the lost element might be one's self:

> A shipwrecked sailor, buried on this coast,
>   Bids you set sail.
> Full many a gallant bark, when we were lost,
>   Weathered the gale.

Those puritans who answered "yes" to the question: Are you willing to be damned for God's glory? were in this objective and magnanimous condition of mind. The way of escape from evil on this system is *not* by getting it "aufgehoben," or preserved in the whole as an element essential but "overcome." *It is by dropping it out altogether, throwing it overboard and getting beyond it, helping to make a universe that shall forget its very place and name.*

It is then perfectly possible to accept sincerely a drastic kind of a universe from which the element of "seriousness" is not to be expelled. Whoso does so is, it seems to me, a genuine pragmatist. He is willing to live on a scheme of uncertified possibilities which he trusts; willing to pay with his own person, if need be, for the realization of the ideals which he frames.

What now actually *are* the other forces which he trusts to co-operate with him, in a universe of such a type? They are at least his fellow men, in the stage of being which our actual universe has reached. But are there not superhuman forces also, such as religious men of the pluralistic type we have been considering have always believed in? Their words may have sounded monistic when they said "there is no God but God;" but the original polytheism of mankind has only imperfectly and vaguely sublimated itself into monotheism, and monotheism itself, so far as it was religious and not a scheme of classroom instruction for the metaphysicians, has always viewed God as but one helper, *primus inter pares*, in the midst of all the shapers of the great world's fate.

I fear that my previous lectures, confined as they have been to human and humanistic aspects, may have left the impression on many of you that pragmatism means methodically to leave the superhuman out. I have shown small respect indeed for the Absolute, and I have until this moment spoken of no other superhuman hypothesis but that. But I trust that you see sufficiently that the Absolute has nothing but its superhumanness in common with the theistic God. On pragmatistic principles, if the hypothesis of God works satisfactorily in the widest sense of the word, it is true. Now whatever its residual difficulties may be, experience shows that it certainly does work, and that the problem is to build it out and determine it so that it will combine satisfactorily with all the other working truths. I can not start upon a whole theology at the end of this last lecture; but when I tell you that I have written a book on men's religious experience, which on the whole has been regarded as making for the reality of God, you will perhaps exempt my own pragmatism from the charge of being an atheistic system. I firmly disbelieve, myself, that our human experience is the highest form of experience extant in the universe. I believe rather that we stand in much the same relation to the whole of the universe as our canine and feline pets do to the whole of human life. They inhabit our drawing-rooms and libraries. They take part in scenes of whose significance they have no inkling. They are merely tangent to curves of history the beginnings and ends and forms of which pass wholly beyond their ken. So we are tangent to the wider life of things. But, just as many of the dog's and cat's ideals coincide with our ideals, and the dogs and cats have daily living proof of the fact, so we may well believe, on the proofs that religious experience affords, that higher powers exist and are at work to save the world on ideal lines similar to our own.

You see that pragmatism can be called religious, if you allow that religion can be pluralistic or merely melioristic in type. But whether you will finally put up with that type of religion or not is a question that only you yourself can decide. Pragmatism has to postpone dogmatic answer, for we do not yet know certainly which type of religion is going to work best in the long run. The various overbeliefs of men, their several faith-ventures, are in fact what are needed to bring the evidence in. You will probably make your own ventures severally. If radically tough, the hurly-burly of the sensible facts of nature will be enough for you, and you will need no religion at all. If radically tender, you will take up with the more monistic form of religion: the pluralistic form, with its reliance on possibilities that are not necessities, will not seem to afford you security enough.

But if you are neither tough nor tender in an extreme and radical sense, but mixed as most of us are, it may seem to you that the type of pluralistic and moralistic religion that I have offered is as good a religious synthesis as you are likely to find. Between the two extremes of crude naturalism on the one hand and transcendental absolutism on the other, you may find that what I take the liberty of calling the pragmatistic or melioristic type of theism is exactly what you require.

AUTHOR'S PREFACE TO
THE MEANING OF TRUTH

The pivotal part of my book named *Pragmatism* is its account
of the relation called "truth" which may obtain between an
idea (opinion, belief, statement, or what not) and its object.
"Truth," I there say, "is a property of certain of our ideas.
It means their agreement, as falsity means their disagreement,
with reality. Pragmatists and intellectualists both accept this
definition as a matter of course.

"Where our ideas [do] not copy definitely their object, what
does agreement with that object mean? . . . Pragmatism asks
its usual question: 'Grant an idea or belief to be true,' it says,
'what concrete difference will its being true make in any one's
actual life? What experiences [may] be different from those
which would obtain if the belief were false? How will the
truth be realized? What, in short, is the truth's cash-value
in experiential terms?' The moment pragmatism asks this
question, it sees the answer: *True ideas are those that we
can assimilate, validate, corroborate, and verify. False ideas
are those that we cannot.* That is the practical difference it
makes to us to have true ideas; that therefore is the meaning
of truth, for it is all that truth is known as.

"The truth of an idea is not a stagnant property inherent
in it. Truth *happens* to an idea. It *becomes* true, is *made* true
by events. Its verity *is* in fact an event, a process, the process
namely of its verifying itself, its *verification*. Its validity is the
process of its *validation*.[1]

"To agree in the widest sense with a reality can only mean
to be guided either straight up to it or into its surroundings,
or to be put into such working touch with it as to handle either
it or something connected with it better than if we disagreed.
Better either intellectually or practically. . . . Any idea that

helps us to deal, whether practically or intellectually, with either the reality or its belongings, that doesn't entangle our progress in frustrations, that *fits,* in fact, and adapts our life to the reality's whole setting, will agree sufficiently to meet the requirement. It will be true of that reality.

"*The true,* to put it very briefly, *is only the expedient in the way of our thinking, just as the right is only the expedient in the way of our behaving.* Expedient in almost any fashion, and expedient in the long run and on the whole, of course; for what meets expediently all the experience in sight won't necessarily meet all farther experiences equally satisfactorily. Experience, as we know, has ways of *boiling over,* and making us correct our present formulas."

This account of truth, following upon the similar ones given by Messrs. Dewey and Schiller, has occasioned the liveliest discussion. Few critics have defended it, most of them have scouted it. It seems evident that the subject is a hard one to understand, under its apparent simplicity; and evident also, I think, that the definitive settlement of it will mark a turning-point in the history of epistemology, and consequently in that of general philosophy. In order to make my own thought more accessible to those who hereafter may have to study the question, I have collected in the volume that follows all the work of my pen that bears directly on the truth-question. My first statement was in 1884, in the article that begins the present volume. The other papers follow in the order of their publication. Two or three appear now for the first time.

One of the accusations which I oftenest have had to meet is that of making the truth of our religious beliefs consist in their "feeling good" to us, and in nothing else. I regret to have given some excuse for this charge, by the unguarded language in which, in the book *Pragmatism,* I spoke of the truth of the belief of certain philosophers in the absolute. Explaining why I do not believe in the absolute myself yet finding that it may secure "moral holidays" to those who need them, and is true in so far forth (if to gain moral holidays be a good),[2] I offered this as a conciliatory olive-branch to my enemies. But they, as is only too common with such offerings, trampled the gift under foot and turned and rent the giver. I had counted too much on their good will—oh for the rarity of christian charity under the sun! Oh for the rarity of ordinary secular intelligence also! I had supposed it to be matter of common observation that, of two competing views of the universe which in all other respects are equal, but of which the first denies some vital human need while the second satisfies it, the second will be favored by sane men for the simple reason that it makes the world seem more rational. To choose the first view under such circumstances would be an ascetic act, an act of philosophic self-denial of which no normal human being would be guilty. Using the pragmatic test of the meaning of concepts, I had shown the concept of the absolute to *mean* nothing but the holiday giver, the banisher of cosmic fear. One's objective deliverance, when one says "the absolute exists," amounted, on my showing, just to this, that "some justification of a feeling of security in presence of the universe," exists, and that systematically to refuse to cultivate a feeling of security would be to do violence to a tendency in one's emotional life which might well be respected as prophetic.

Apparently my absolutist critics fail to see the workings of their own minds in any such picture, so all that I can do is to apologize, and take my offering back. The absolute is true in *no* way then, and least of all, by the verdict of the critics, in the way which I assigned!

My treatment of "God," "freedom," and "design" was similar. Reducing, by the pragmatic test, the meaning of each of these concepts to its positive experienceable operation, I showed them all to mean the same thing, viz., the presence of "promise" in the world. "God or no God?" means "promise or no promise?" It seems to me that the alternative is objective enough, being a question as to whether the cosmos has one character or another, even though our own provisional answer be made on subjective grounds. Nevertheless christian and non-christian critics alike accuse me of summoning people to say "God exists," *even when he doesn't exist,* because forsooth in my philosophy the "truth" of the saying doesn't really mean that he exists in any shape whatever, but only that to say so feels good.

Most of the pragmatist and anti-pragmatist warfare is over what the word "truth" shall be held to signify, and not over any of the facts embodied in truth-situations; for both pragmatists and anti-pragmatists believe in existent objects, just as they believe in our ideas of them. The difference is that when the pragmatists speak of truth, they mean exclusively something about the ideas, namely their workableness; whereas when anti-pragmatists speak of truth they seem most often to mean something about the objects. Since the pragmatist, if he agrees that an idea is "really" true, also agrees to whatever it says about its object; and since most anti-pragmatists have already come round to agreeing that, if the object exists, the idea that it does so is workable; there would seem so little left to fight about that I might well be asked why instead of reprinting my share in so much verbal wrangling, I do not show my sense of "values" by burning it all up.

I understand the question and I will give my answer. I am interested in another doctrine in philosophy to which I give the name of radical empiricism, and it seems to me that the establishment of the pragmatist theory of truth is a step of first-rate importance in making radical empiricism prevail. Radical empiricism consists first of a postulate, next of a statement of fact, and finally of a generalized conclusion.

The postulate is that the only things that shall be debatable among philosophers shall be things definable in terms drawn from experience. [Things of an unexperienceable nature may exist *ad libitum*, but they form no part of the material for philosophic debate.]

The statement of fact is that the relations between things, conjunctive as well as disjunctive, are just as much matters of direct particular experience, neither more so nor less so, than the things themselves.

The generalized conclusion is that therefore the parts of experience hold together from next to next by relations that are themselves parts of experience. The directly apprehended universe needs, in short, no extraneous trans-empirical connective support, but possesses in its own right a concatenated or continuous structure.

The great obstacle to radical empiricism in the contemporary mind is the rooted rationalist belief that experience as immediately given is all disjunction and no conjunction, and that to make one world out of this separateness, a higher unifying agency must be there. In the prevalent idealism this agency is represented as the absolute all-witness which "relates" things together by throwing "categories" over them like a net. The most peculiar and unique, perhaps, of all these categories is supposed to be the truth-relation, which connects parts of reality in pairs, making of one of them a knower, and of the other a thing known, yet which is itself content-less experientially, neither describable, explicable, nor reduce-able to lower terms, and denotable only by uttering the name "truth."

The pragmatist view, on the contrary, of the truth-relation is that it has a definite content, and that everything in it is experienceable. Its whole nature can be told in positive terms. The "workableness" which ideas must have, in order to be true, means particular workings, physical or intellectual, actual or possible, which they may set up from next to next inside of concrete experience. Were this pragmatic contention ad-mitted, one great point in the victory of radical empiricism would also be scored, for the relation between an object and the idea that truly knows it, is held by rationalists to be nothing of this describable sort, but to stand outside of all possible temporal experience; and on the relation, so inter-preted, rationalism is wonted to make its last most obdurate rally.

Now the anti-pragmatist contentions which I try to meet in this volume can be so easily used by rationalists as weapons of resistance, not only to pragmatism but to radical empiricism also (for if the truth-relation were transcendent, others might be so too), that I feel strongly the strategical importance of having them definitely met and got out of the way. What our critics most persistently keep saying is that though workings go with truth, yet they do not constitute it. It is numerically additional to them, prior to them, explanatory *of* them, and in no wise to be explained *by* them, we are incessantly told. The first point for our enemies to establish, therefore, is that *some-thing* numerically additional and prior to the workings is involved in the truth of an idea. Since the *object* is additional, and usually prior, most rationalists plead *it*, and boldly accuse us of denying it. This leaves on the bystanders the impres-sion—since we cannot reasonably deny the existence of the object—that our account of truth breaks down, and that our critics have driven us from the field. Altho in various places in this volume I try to refute the slanderous charge that we deny real existence, I will say here again, for the sake of emphasis, that the existence of the object, whenever the idea asserts it "truly," is the only reason, in innumerable cases, why the idea does work successfully, if it work at all; and that it seems an abuse of language, to say the least, to transfer the word "truth" from the idea to the object's existence, when the false-hood of ideas that won't work is explained by that existence as well as the truth of those that will.

I find this abuse prevailing among my most accomplished adversaries. But once establish the proper verbal custom, let the word "truth" represent a property of the idea, cease to make it something mysteriously connected with the object known, and the path opens fair and wide, as I believe, to the discussion of radical empiricism on its merits. The truth of an idea will then mean only its workings, or that in it which by ordinary psychological laws sets up those workings; it will mean neither the idea's object, nor anything "saltatory" inside the idea, that terms drawn from experience cannot describe.

One word more, ere I end this preface. A distinction is sometimes made between Dewey, Schiller and myself, as if I, in supposing the object's existence, made a concession to popular prejudice which they, as more radical pragmatists, refuse to make. As I myself understand these authors, we all three absolutely agree in admitting the transcendency of the object (provided it be an experienceable object) to the sub-ject, in the truth-relation. Dewey in particular has insisted al-most *ad nauseam* that the whole meaning of our cognitive states and processes lies in the way they intervene in the control and revaluation of independent existences or facts. His account of knowledge is not only absurd, but meaningless, unless independent existences be there of which our ideas take account, and for the transformation of which they work. But because he and Schiller refuse to discuss objects and rela-tions "transcendent" in the sense of being *altogether trans-experiential*, their critics pounce on sentences in their writings to that effect to show that they deny the existence *within the realm of experience* of objects external to the ideas that de-clare their presence there.[2] It seems incredible that educated and apparently sincere critics should so fail to catch their ad-versary's point of view.

What misleads so many of them is possibly also the fact that the universes of discourse of Schiller, Dewey, and myself are panoramas of different extent, and that what the one postulates explicitly the other provisionally leaves only in a state of implication, while the reader thereupon considers it to be denied. Schiller's universe is the smallest being essen-tially a psychological one. He starts with but one sort of thing, truth-claims, but is led ultimately to the independent objective facts which they assert, inasmuch as the most successfully validated of all claims is that such facts are there. My universe is more essentially epistemological. I start with two things, the objective facts and the claims, and indicate which claims, the facts being there, will work successfully as the latter's substitutes and which will not. I call the former claims true. Dewey's panorama, if I understand this colleague, is the widest of the three, but I refrain from giving my own account of its complexity. Suffice it that he holds as firmly as I do to objects independent of our judgments. If I am wrong in saying this, he must correct me. I decline in this matter to be corrected at second hand.

I have not pretended in the following pages to consider all the critics of my account of truth, such as Messrs. Taylor, Lovejoy, Gardiner, Bakewell, Creighton, Hibben, Parodi, Salter, Carus, Lalande, Mentré, McTaggart, G. E. Moore, Ladd and others, especially not Professor Schinz, who has published under the title of *Anti-pragmatisme* an amusing sociological romance. Some of these critics seem to me to labor under an inability, almost pathetic, to understand the thesis which they seek to refute. I imagine that most of their difficulties have been answered by anticipation elsewhere in this volume, and I am sure that my readers will thank me for not adding more repetition to the fearful amount that is already there.

95 IRVING ST., CAMBRIDGE (MASS.),
August, 1909.

THE FUNCTION OF COGNITION [1]

The following inquiry is (to use a distinction familiar to readers of Mr. Shadworth Hodgson) not an inquiry into the "how it comes," but into the "what it is" of cognition. What we call acts of cognition are evidently realized through what we call brains and their events, whether there be "souls" dynamically connected with the brains or not. But with neither brains nor souls has this essay any business to transact. In it we shall simply assume that cognition *is* produced, somehow, and limit ourselves to asking what elements it contains, what factors it implies.

Cognition is a function of consciousness. The first factor it implies is therefore a state of consciousness wherein the cognition shall take place. Having elsewhere used the word "feeling" to designate generically all states of consciousness considered subjectively, or without respect to their possible function, I shall then say that, whatever elements an act of cognition may imply besides, it at least implies the existence of a *feeling*. [If the reader share the current antipathy to the word "feeling," he may substitute for it, wherever I use it, the word "idea," taken in the old broad Lockian sense, or he may use the clumsy phrase "state of consciousness," or finally he may say "thought" instead.]

Now it is to be observed that the common consent of mankind has agreed that some feelings are cognitive and some are simple facts having a subjective, or, what one might almost call a physical, existence, but no such self-transcendent function as would be implied in their being pieces of knowledge. Our task is again limited here. We are not to ask, "How is self-transcendence possible?" We are only to ask, "How comes it that common sense has assigned a number of cases in which it is assumed not only to be possible but actual? And what are the marks used by common sense to distinguish those cases from the rest?" In short, our inquiry is a chapter in descriptive psychology, hardly anything more.

Condillac embarked on a quest similar to this by his famous hypothesis of a statue to which various feelings were successively imparted. Its first feeling was supposed to be one of fragrance. But to avoid all possible complication with the question of genesis, let us not attribute even to a statue the possession of our imaginary feeling. Let us rather suppose it attached to no matter, nor localized at any point in space, but left swinging *in vacuo*, as it were, by the direct creative *fiat* of a god. And let us also, to escape entanglement with difficulties about the physical or psychical nature of its "object," not call it a feeling of fragrance or of any other determinate sort, but limit ourselves to assuming that it is a feeling of q. What is true of it under this abstract name will be no less true of it in any more particular shape (such as fragrance, pain, hardness) which the reader may suppose.

Now, if this feeling of q be the only creation of the god, it will of course form the entire universe. And if, to escape the cavils of that large class of persons who believe that *semper idem sentire ac non sentire* are the same,[2] we allow the feeling to be of as short a duration as they like, that universe will only need to last an infinitesimal part of a second. The feeling in question will thus be reduced to its fighting weight, and all that befalls it in the way of a cognitive function must be held to befall in the brief instant of its quickly snuffed-out life—a life, it will also be noticed, that has no other moment of consciousness either preceding or following it.

Well now, can our little feeling, thus left alone in the universe—for the god and we psychological critics may be supposed left out of the account—can the feeling, I say, be said to have any sort of a cognitive function? For it to *know*, there must be something to be known. What is there, on the present supposition? One may reply, "the feeling's content q." But does it not seem more proper to call this the feeling's *quality* than its content? Does not the word "content" suggest that the feeling has already dirempted itself as an act from its content as an object? And would it be quite safe to assume so promptly that the quality q of a feeling is one and the same thing with a feeling of the quality q? The quality q, so far, is an entirely subjective fact which the feeling carries so to speak endogenously, or in its pocket. If any one pleases to dignify so simple a fact as this by the name of knowledge, of course nothing can prevent him. But let us keep closer to the path of common usage, and reserve the name knowledge for the cognition of "realities," meaning by realities things that exist independently of the feeling through which their cognition occurs. If the content of the feeling occur nowhere in the universe outside of the feeling itself, and perish with the feeling, common usage refuses to call it a reality, and brands it as a subjective feature of the feeling's constitution, or at the most as the feeling's *dream*.

For the feeling to be cognitive in the specific sense, then, it must be self-transcendent; and we must prevail upon the god to *create a reality outside of it* to correspond to its intrinsic quality q. Thus only can it be redeemed from the condition of being a solipsism. If now the new-created reality *resemble* the feeling's quality q, I say that the feeling may be held by us *to be cognizant of that reality*.

This first instalment of my thesis is sure to be attacked. But one word before defending it. "Reality" has become our warrant for calling a feeling cognitive; but what becomes our warrant for calling anything reality? The only reply is—the faith of the present critic or inquirer. At every moment of his life he finds himself subject to a belief in *some* realities, even though his realities of this year should prove to be his illusions of the next. Whenever he finds that the feeling he is studying contemplates what he himself regards as a reality, he must of course admit the feeling itself to be truly cognitive. We are ourselves the critics here; and we shall find our burden much lightened by being allowed to take reality in this relative and provisional way. Every science must make some assumptions. *Erkenntnisstheoretiker* are but fallible mortals. When they study the function of cognition, they do it by means of the same function in themselves. And knowing that the fountain cannot be higher than its source, we should promptly confess that our results in this field are affected by our own liability to err. *The most we can claim is, that what we say about cognition may be counted as true as what we say about anything else.* If our hearers agree with us about what are to be held "realities," they will perhaps also agree to the reality of our doctrine of the way in which they are known. We cannot ask for more.

Our terminology shall follow the spirit of these remarks. We will deny the function of knowledge to any feeling whose quality or content we do not ourselves believe to exist outside of that feeling as well as in it. We may call such a feeling a dream if we like; we shall have to see later whether we can call it a fiction or an error.

To revert now to our thesis. Some persons will immediately cry out, "How *can* a reality resemble a feeling?" Here we find how wise we were to name the quality of the feeling by an algebraic letter q. We flank the whole difficulty of resemblance between an inner state and an outward reality, by leaving it free to any one to postulate as the reality whatever sort of thing he thinks *can* resemble a feeling—if not an outward thing, then another feeling like the first one—the mere feeling q in the critic's mind for example. Evading thus this objection, we turn to another which is sure to be urged.

It will come from those philosophers to whom "thought," in the sense of a knowledge of relations, is the all in all of mental life; and who hold a merely feeling consciousness to be no better—one would sometimes say from their utterances, a good deal worse—than no consciousness at all. Such phrases as these, for example, are common today in the mouths of those who claim to walk in the footprints of Kant and Hegel rather than in the ancestral English paths: "A perception detached from all others, 'left out of the heap we call a mind,' being out of all relation, has no qualities—is simply nothing. We can no more consider it than we can see vacancy." "It is simply in itself fleeting, momentary, unnameable (because while we name it it has become another), and for the very same reason unknowable, the very negation of knowability." "Exclude from what we have considered real all qualities constituted by relation, we find that none are left."

Altho such citations as these from the writings of Professor Green might be multiplied almost indefinitely, they would hardly repay the pains of collection, so egregiously false is the doctrine they teach. Our little supposed feeling, whatever it may be, from the cognitive point of view, whether a bit of knowledge or a dream, is certainly no psychical zero. It is a most positively and definitely qualified inner fact, with a complexion all its own. Of course there are many mental facts which it is *not*. It knows *q*, if *q* be a reality, with a very minimum of knowledge. It neither dates nor locates it. It neither classes nor names it. And it neither knows itself as a feeling, nor contrasts itself with other feelings, nor estimates its own duration or intensity. It is, in short, if there is no more of it than this, a most dumb and helpless and useless kind of thing.

But if we must describe it by so many negations, and if it can say nothing *about* itself or *about* anything else, by what right do we deny that it is a psychical zero? And may not the "relationists" be right after all?

In the innocent looking word "about" lies the solution of this riddle; and a simple enough solution it is when frankly looked at. A quotation from a too seldom quoted book, the *Exploratio Philosophica* of John Grote (London, 1865), p. 60, will form the best introduction to it.

"Our knowledge," writes Grote, "may be contemplated in either of two ways, or, to use other words, we may speak in a double manner of the 'object' of knowledge. That is, we may either use language thus: we *know* a thing, a man, etc.; or we may use it thus: we know such and such things *about* the thing, the man, etc. Language in general, following its true logical instinct, distinguishes between these two applications of the notion of knowledge, the one being γνῶναι, *noscere, kennen, connaître,* the other being εἰδέναι, *scire, wissen, savoir.* In the origin, the former may be considered more what I have called phenomenal—it is the notion of knowledge as *acquaintance* or familiarity with what is known; which notion is perhaps more akin to the phenomenal bodily communication, and is less purely intellectual than the other; it is the kind of knowledge which we have of a thing by the presentation to the senses or the representation of it in picture or type, a *Vorstellung.* The other, which is what we express in judgments or propositions, what is embodied in *Begriffe* or concepts without any necessary imaginative representation, is in its origin the more intellectual notion of knowledge. There is no reason, however, why we should not express our knowledge, whatever its kind, in either manner, provided only we do not confusedly express it, in the same proposition or piece of reasoning, in both."

Now obviously if our supposed feeling of *q* is (if knowledge at all) only knowledge of the mere acquaintance-type, it is

milking a he-goat, as the ancients would have said, to try to
extract from it any deliverance *about* anything under the sun,
even about itself. And it is as unjust, after our failure, to turn
upon it and call it a psychical nothing, as it would be, after
our fruitless attack upon the billy-goat, to proclaim the non-
lactiferous character of the whole goat-tribe. But the entire
industry of the Hegelian school in trying to shove simple sensation out of the pale of philosophic recognition is founded
on this false issue. It is always the "speechlessness" of sensation, its inability to make any "statement," [3] that is held to
make the very notion of it meaningless, and to justify the
student of knowledge in scouting it out of existence. "Significance," in the sense of standing as the sign of other mental
states, is taken to be the sole function of what mental states
we have; and from the perception that our little primitive
sensation has as yet no significance in this literal sense, it is an
easy step to call it first meaningless, next senseless, then
vacuous, and finally to brand it as absurd and inadmissible.
But in this universal liquidation, this everlasting slip, slip, slip,
of direct acquaintance into knowledge-*about,* until at last
nothing is left about which the knowledge can be supposed
to obtain, does not all "significance" depart from the situation?
And when our knowledge about things has reached its never
so complicated perfection, must there not needs abide alongside of it and inextricably mixed in with it some acquaintance
with *what* things all this knowledge is about?

Now, our supposed little feeling gives a *what;* and if other
feelings should succeed which remembered the first, its *what*
may stand as subject or predicate of some piece of knowledge-
about, of some judgment, perceiving relations between it and
other *whats* which the other feelings may know. The hitherto
dumb *q* will then receive a name and be no longer speechless.
But every name, as students of logic know, has its "denotation," and the denotation always means some reality or content, relationless *ab extra* or with its internal relations un-
analyzed, like the *q* which our primitive sensation is supposed
to know. No relation-expressing proposition is possible except
on the basis of a preliminary acquaintance with such "facts,"
with such contents, as this. Let the *q* be fragrance, let it be
toothache, or let it be a more complex kind of feeling, like
that of the full moon swimming in her blue abyss, it must
first come in that simple shape, and be held fast in that first

intention, before any knowledge *about* it can be attained. The knowledge *about* it is *it* with a context added. Undo *it*, and what is added cannot be *context*.[4]

Let us say no more then about this objection, but enlarge our thesis, thus: If there be in the universe a *q* other than the *q* in the feeling, the latter may have acquaintance with an entity ejective to itself; an acquaintance moreover, which, as mere acquaintance, it would be hard to imagine susceptible either of improvement or increase, being in its way complete; and which would oblige us (so long as we refuse not to call acquaintance knowledge) to say not only that the feeling is cognitive, but that all qualities of feeling, *so long as there is anything outside of them which they resemble,* are feelings *of* qualities of existence, and perceptions of outward fact.

The point of this vindication of the cognitive function of the first feeling lies, it will be noticed, in the discovery that *q* does exist elsewhere than in it. In case this discovery were not made, we could not be sure the feeling was cognitive; and in case there were nothing outside to be discovered, we should have to call the feeling a dream. But the feeling itself cannot make a discovery. Its own *q* is the only *q* it grasps; and its own nature is not a particle altered by having the self-transcendent function of cognition either added to it or taken away. The function is accidental; synthetic, not analytic; and falls outside and not inside its being.[5]

A feeling feels as a gun shoots. If there be nothing to be felt or hit, they discharge themselves *ins blaue hinein.* If, however, something starts up opposite them, they no longer simply shoot or feel, they hit and know.

But with this arises a worse objection than any yet made. We the critics look on and see a real *q* and a feeling of *q;* and because the two resemble each other, we say the one knows the other. But what right have we to say this until we know that the feeling of *q* means to stand for or represent just that *same* other *q?* Suppose, instead of one *q*, a number of real *q's* in the field. If the gun shoots and hits, we can easily see which one of them it hits. But how can we distinguish which one the feeling knows? It knows the one it stands for. But which one *does* it stand for? It declares no intention in this respect. It merely resembles; it resembles all indifferently; and resembling, *per se*, is not necessarily representing or standing-for at all. Eggs resemble each other, but do not on that account represent, stand for, or know each other. And if you say this is because neither of them is a *feeling*, then imagine the world to consist of nothing but toothaches, which *are* feelings, feelings resembling each other exactly, would they know each other the better for all that?

The case of *q* being a bare quality like that of toothache-pain is quite different from that of its being a concrete individual thing. There is practically no test for deciding whether the feeling of a bare quality means to represent it or not. It can *do* nothing to the quality beyond resembling it, simply because an abstract quality is a thing to which nothing can be done. Being without context or environment or *principium individuationis*, a quiddity with no haecceity, a platonic idea, even duplicate editions of such a quality (were they possible), would be indiscernible, and no sign could be given, no result altered, whether the feeling meant to stand for this edition or for that, or whether it simply resembled the quality without meaning to stand for it at all.

If now we grant a genuine pluralism of editions to the quality *q*, by assigning to each a *context* which shall distinguish it from its mates, we may proceed to explain which edition of it the feeling knows, by extending our principle of resemblance to the context too, and saying the feeling knows the particular *q* whose context it most exactly duplicates. But here again the theoretic doubt recurs: duplication and coincidence, are they knowledge? The gun shows which *q* it points to and hits, by *breaking* it. Until the feeling can show us which *q* it points to and knows, by some equally flagrant token, why are we not free to deny that it either points to or knows any one of the *real q*'s at all, and to affirm that the word "resemblance" exhaustively describes its relation to the reality?

Well, as a matter of fact, every actual feeling *does* show us, quite as flagrantly as the gun, which *q* it points to; and practically in concrete cases the matter is decided by an element we have hitherto left out. Let us pass from abstractions to possible instances, and ask our obliging *deus ex machina* to frame for us a richer world. Let him send me, for example, a dream of the death of a certain man, and let him simultaneously cause the man to die. How would our practical instinct spontaneously decide whether this were a case of cognition of the reality, or only a sort of marvellous coincidence of a re-sembling reality with my dream? Just such puzzling cases as this are what the "society for psychical research" is busily collecting and trying to interpret in the most reasonable way.

If my dream were the only one of the kind I ever had in my life, if the context of the death in the dream differed in many particulars from the real death's context, and if my dream led me to no action about the death, unquestionably we should all call it a strange coincidence, and naught besides. But if the death in the dream had a long context, agreeing point for point with every feature that attended the real death; if I were constantly having such dreams, all equally perfect, and if on awaking I had a habit of *acting* immediately as if they were true and so getting "the start" of my more tardily instructed neighbors, we should in all probability have to admit that I had some mysterious kind of clairvoyant power, that my dreams in an inscrutable way meant just those realities they figured, and that the word "coincidence" failed to touch the root of the matter. And whatever doubts any one preserved would completely vanish, if it should appear that from the midst of my dream I had the power of *interfering* with the course of the reality, and making the events in it turn this way or that, according as I dreamed they should. Then at least it would be certain that my waking critics and my dreaming self were dealing with the *same*.

And thus do men invariably decide such a question. *The falling of the dream's practical consequences* into the real world, and the *extent* of the resemblance between the two worlds are the criteria they instinctively use.[6] All feeling is for the sake of action, all feeling results in action—to-day no argument is needed to prove these truths. But by a most singular disposition of nature which we may conceive to have been different, *my feelings act upon the realities within my critic's world.* Unless, then, my critic can prove that my feel-ing does not "point to" those realities which it acts upon, how can he continue to doubt that he and I are alike cognizant of one and the same real world? If the action is performed in one world, that must be the world the feeling intends; if in another world, *that* is the world the feeling has in mind. If your feeling bear no fruits in my world, I call it utterly detached from my world; I call it a solipsism, and call its world a dream-world. If your toothache does not prompt you to *act* as if I had a toothache, nor even as if I had a separate existence; if you neither say to me, "I know now how you must suffer!" nor tell me of a remedy, I deny that your feeling, however it may resemble mine, is really cognizant of mine. It gives no *sign* of being cognizant, and such a sign is absolutely necessary to my admission that it is.

Before I can think you to mean my world, you must affect my world; before I can think you to mean much of it, you must affect much of it; and before I can be sure you mean it *as I do*, you must affect it *just as I should* if I were in your place. Then I, your critic, will gladly believe that we are thinking, not only of the same reality, but that we are thinking it *alike*, and thinking of much of its extent.

Without the practical effects of our neighbor's feelings on our own world, we should never suspect the existence of our neighbor's feelings at all, and of course should never find ourselves playing the critic as we do in this article. The constitution of nature is very peculiar. In the world of each of us are certain objects called human bodies, which move about and act on all the other objects there, and the occasions of their action are in the main what the occasions of our action would be, were they our bodies. They use words and gestures, which, if we used them, would have thoughts behind them—no mere thoughts *überhaupt*, however, but strictly determinate thoughts. I think you have the notion of fire in general, because I see you act towards this fire in my room just as I act towards it—poke it and present your person towards it, and so forth. But that binds me to believe that if you feel "fire" at all, *this* is the fire you feel. As a matter of fact, whenever we constitute ourselves into psychological critics, it is not by dint of discovering which reality a feeling "resembles" that we find out which reality it means. We become first aware of which one it means, and then we suppose that to be the one it resembles. We see each other looking at the same objects, pointing to them and turning them over in various ways, and thereupon we hope and trust that all of our several feelings resemble the reality and each other. But this is a thing of which we are never theoretically sure. Still, it would practically be a case of *grübelsucht*, if a ruffian were assaulting and drubbing my body, to spend much time in subtle speculation either as to whether his vision of my body resembled mine, or as to whether the body he really *meant* to insult were not

some body in his mind's eye, altogether other from my own.
The practical point of view brushes such metaphysical cob-
webs away. If what he have in mind be not *my* body, why call
we it a body at all? His mind is inferred by me as a term, to
whose existence we trace the things that happen. The in-
ference is quite void if the term, once inferred, be separated
from its connection with the body that made me infer it, and
connected with another that is not mine at all. No matter for
the metaphysical puzzle of how our two minds, the ruffian's
and mine, *can* mean the same body. Men who see each other's
bodies sharing the same space, treading the same earth,
splashing the same water, making the same air resonant, and
pursuing the same game and eating out of the same dish, will
never practically believe in a pluralism of solipsistic worlds.

Where, however, the actions of one mind seem to take no
effect in the world of the other, the case is different. This is
what happens in poetry and fiction. Every one knows *Ivanhoe*,
for example; but so long as we stick to the story pure and
simple without regard to the facts of its production, few would
hesitate to admit that there are as many different Ivanhoes
as there are different minds cognizant of the story.[7] The fact
that all these Ivanhoes *resemble* each other does not prove the
contrary. But if an alteration invented by one man in his
version were to reverberate immediately through all the other
versions, and produce changes therein, we should then easily
agree that all these thinkers were thinking the *same* Ivanhoe,
and that, fiction or no fiction, it formed a little world common
to them all.

Having reached this point, we may take up our thesis and
improve it again. Still calling the reality by the name of q
and letting the critic's feeling vouch for it, we can say that
any other feeling will be held cognizant of q, provided it both
resemble q, and refer to q, as shown by its either modifying
q directly, or modifying some other reality, p or r, which the
critic knows to be continuous with q. Or more shortly, thus:
*The feeling of q knows whatever reality it resembles, and
either directly or indirectly operates on.* If it resemble without operating, it is a dream; if it operate without resembling,
it is an error.[8]

It is to be feared that the reader may consider this formula
rather insignificant and obvious, and hardly worth the labor of
so many pages, especially when he considers that the only

cases to which it applies are *percepts,* and that the whole field
of symbolic or conceptual thinking seems to elude its grasp.
Where the reality is either a material thing or act, or a state
of the critic's consciousness, I may both mirror it in my mind
and operate upon it—in the latter case indirectly, of course—
as soon as I perceive it. But there are many cognitions, universally allowed to be such, which neither mirror nor operate
on their realities.

In the whole field of symbolic thought we are universally
held both to intend, to speak of, and to reach conclusions
about—to know in short—particular realities, without having
in our subjective consciousness any mindstuff that resembles
them even in a remote degree. We are instructed about them
by language which awakens no consciousness beyond its
sound; and we know *which* realities they are by the faintest
and most fragmentary glimpse of some remote context they
may have and by no direct imagination of themselves. As
minds may differ here, let me speak in the first person. I am
sure that my own current thinking has *words* for its almost
exclusive subjective material, words which are made intelligible by being referred to some reality that lies beyond the
horizon of direct consciousness, and of which I am only aware
as of a terminal *more* existing in a certain direction, to which
the words might lead but do not lead yet. The *subject,* or
topic, of the words is usually something towards which I
mentally seem to pitch them in a backward way, almost as I
might jerk my thumb over my shoulder to point at something,
without looking round, if I were only entirely sure that it was
there. The *up-shot,* or *conclusion,* of the words is something
towards which I seem to incline my head forwards, as if giving assent to its existence, tho all my mind's eye catches sight
of may be some tatter of an image connected with it, which
tatter, however, if only endued with the feeling of familiarity
and reality, makes me feel that the whole to which it belongs
is rational and real, and fit to be let pass.

Here then is cognitive consciousness on a large scale, and
yet what it knows, it hardly resembles in the least degree.
The formula last laid down for our thesis must therefore be
made more complete. We may now express it thus: *A percept
knows whatever reality it directly or indirectly operates on
and resembles; a conceptional feeling, or thought knows*° *a
reality, whenever it actually or potentially terminates in a per-*

cept that operates on, or resembles that reality, or is otherwise connected with it or with its context. The latter percept may be either sensation or sensorial idea; and when I say the thought must *terminate* in such a percept, I mean that it must ultimately be capable of leading up thereto, by the way of practical experience, if the terminal feeling be a sensation; by the way of logical or habitual suggestion, if it be only an image in the mind.

Let an illustration make this plainer. I open the first book I take up, and read the first sentence that meets my eye: "Newton saw the handiwork of God in the heavens as plainly as Paley in the animal kingdom." I immediately look back and try to analyze the subjective state in which I rapidly apprehended this sentence as I read it. In the first place there was an obvious feeling that the sentence was intelligible and rational and related to the world of realities. There was also a sense of agreement or harmony between "Newton," "Paley," and "God." There was no apparent image connected with the words "heavens," or "handiwork," or "God;" they were words merely. With "animal kingdom" I think there was the faintest consciousness (it may possibly have been an image of the steps) of the Museum of Zoölogy in the town of Cambridge where I write. With "Paley" there was an equally faint consciousness of a small dark leather book; and with "Newton" a pretty distinct vision of the right-hand lower corner of a curling periwig. This is all the mind-stuff I can discover in my first consciousness of the meaning of this sentence, and I am afraid that even not all of this would have been present had I come upon the sentence in a genuine reading of the book, and not picked it out for an experiment. And yet my consciousness was truly cognitive. The sentence is "about realities" which my psychological critic—for we must not forget him—acknowledges to be such, even as he acknowledges my distinct feeling that they *are* realities, and my acquiescence in the general rightness of what I read of them, to be true knowledge on my part.

Now what justifies my critic in being as lenient as this? This singularly inadequate consciousness of mine, made up of symbols that neither resemble nor affect the realities they stand for—how can he be sure it is cognizant of the very realities he has himself in mind?

He is sure because in countless like cases he has seen such

inadequate and symbolic thoughts, by developing themselves, terminate in percepts that practically modified and presumably resembled his own. By "developing" themselves is meant obeying their tendencies, following up the suggestions nascently present in them, working in the direction in which they seem to point, clearing up the penumbra, making distinct the halo, unravelling the fringe, which is part of their composition, and in the midst of which their more substantive kernel of subjective content seems consciously to lie. Thus I may develop my thought in the Paley direction by procuring the brown leather volume and bringing the passages about the animal kingdom before the critic's eyes. I may satisfy him that the words mean for me just what they mean for him, by showing him *in concreto* the very animals and their arrangements, of which the pages treat. I may get Newton's works and portraits; or if I follow the line of suggestion of the wig, I may smother my critic in seventeenth-century matters pertaining to Newton's environment, to show that the word "Newton" has the same *locus* and relations in both our minds. Finally I may, by act and word, persuade him that what I mean by God and the heavens and the analogy of the handiworks, is just what he means also.

My demonstration in the last resort is to his *senses*. My thought makes me act on his senses much as he might himself act on them, were he pursuing the consequences of a perception of his own. Practically then *my* thought terminates in *his* realities. He willingly supposes it, therefore, to be *of* them, and inwardly to *resemble* what his own thought would be, were it of the same symbolic sort as mine. And the pivot and fulcrum and support of his mental persuasion, is the sensible operation which my thought leads me, or may lead, to effect— the bringing of Paley's book, of Newton's portrait, etc., before his very eyes.

In the last analysis, then, we believe that we all know and think about and talk about the same world, because *we believe our* PERCEPTS *are possessed by us in common.* And we believe this because the percepts of each one of us seem to be changed in consequence of changes in the percepts of some one else. What I am for you is in the first instance a percept of your own. Unexpectedly, however, I open and show you a book, uttering certain sounds the while. These acts are also your percepts, but they so resemble acts of yours with feelings prompting them, that you cannot doubt I have the feelings too, or that the book is one book felt in both our worlds. That it is felt in the same way, that my feelings of it resemble yours, is something of which we never can be sure, but which we assume as the simplest hypothesis that meets the case. As a matter of fact, we never *are* sure of it, and, as *erkenntnisstheoretiker*, we can only say that of feelings that should *not* resemble each other, both could not know the the same thing at the same time in the same way.¹⁰ If each holds to its own percept as the reality, it is bound to say of the other percept, that, though it may *intend* that reality, and prove this by working change upon it, yet, if it do not resemble it, it is all false and wrong.¹¹

If this be so of percepts, how much more so of higher modes of thought! Even in the sphere of sensation individuals are probably different enough. Comparative study of the simplest conceptual elements seems to show a wider divergence still. And when it comes to general theories and emotional attitudes towards life, it is indeed time to say with Thackeray, "My friend, two different universes walk about under your hat and under mine."

What can save us at all and prevent us from flying asunder into a chaos of mutually repellent solipsisms? Through what can our several minds commune? Through nothing but the mutual resemblance of those of our perceptual feelings which have this power of modifying one another, *which are mere dumb knowledges-of-acquaintance*, and which must also resemble their realities or not know them aright at all. In such pieces of knowledge-of-acquaintance all our knowledge-about must end, and carry a sense of this possible termination as part of its content. These percepts, these *termini*, these sensible things, these mere matters of acquaintance, are the only realities we ever directly know, and the whole history of our thought is the history of our substitution of one of them for another, and the reduction of the substitute to the status of a conceptual sign. Contemned though they be by some thinkers, these sensations are the mother-earth, the anchorage, the stable rock, the first and last limits, the *terminus a quo* and the *terminus ad quem* of the mind. To find such sensational *termini* should be our aim with all our higher thought. They end discussion; they destroy the false conceit of knowledge; and without them we are all at sea with each other's meaning. If two men act alike on a percept, they believe themselves to feel alike about it; if not, they may suspect they know it in differing ways. We can never be sure we understand each other till we are able to bring the matter to this test.[12] This is why metaphysical discussions are so much like fighting with the air; they have no practical issue of a sensational kind. "Scientific" theories, on the other hand, always terminate in definite percepts. You can deduce a possible sensation from your theory and, taking me into your laboratory, prove that your theory is true of my world by giving me the sensation then and there. Beautiful is the flight of conceptual reason through the upper air of truth. No wonder philosophers are dazzled by it still, and no wonder they look with some disdain at the low earth of feeling from which the goddess launched herself aloft. But woe to her if she return not home to its acquaintance; *Nirgends haften dann die unsichern Sohlen*— every crazy wind will take her, and, like a fire-balloon at night, she will go out among the stars.

NOTE—The reader will easily see how much of the account of the truth-function developed later in *Pragmatism* was already explicit in this earlier article, and how much came to be defined later. In this earlier article we find distinctly asserted:

1. The reality, external to the true idea;
2. The critic, reader, or epistemologist, with his own belief, as warrant for this reality's existence;
3. The experienceable environment, as the vehicle or medium connecting knower with known, and yielding the cognitive *relation;*
4. The notion of *pointing*, through this medium, to the reality, as one condition of our being said to know it;
5. That of *resembling* it, and eventually *affecting* it, as determining the pointing to *it* and not to something else.
6. The elimination of the "epistemological gulf," so that the whole truth-relation falls inside of the continuities of concrete experience, and is constituted of particular processes, varying with every object and subject, and susceptible of being described in detail.

The defects in this earlier account are:

1. The possibly undue prominence given to resembling, which altho a fundamental function in knowing truly, is so often dispensed with;
2. The undue emphasis laid upon operating on the object itself, which in many cases is indeed decisive of that being what we refer to, but which is often lacking, or replaced by operations on other things related to the object.

3. The imperfect development of the generalized notion of the *workability* of the feeling or idea as equivalent to that *satisfactory adaptation* to the particular reality, which constitutes the truth of the idea. It is this more generalized notion, as covering all such specifications as pointing, fitting, operating or resembling, that distinguishes the developed view of Dewey, Schiller, and myself.

4. The treatment of percepts as the only realm of reality. I now treat concepts as a co-ordinate realm.

The next paper represents a somewhat broader grasp of the topic on the writer's part.

THE TIGERS IN INDIA [1]

There are two ways of knowing things, knowing them immediately or intuitively, and knowing them conceptually or representatively. Altho such things as the white paper before our eyes can be known intuitively, most of the things we know, the tigers now in India, for example, or the scholastic system of philosophy, are known only representatively or symbolically.

Suppose, to fix our ideas, that we take first a case of conceptual knowledge; and let it be our knowledge of the tigers in India, as we sit here. Exactly what do we *mean* by saying that we here know the tigers? What is the precise fact that the cognition so confidently claimed is *known-as*, to use Shadworth Hodgson's inelegant but valuable form of words?

Most men would answer that what we mean by knowing the tigers is having them, however absent in body, become in some way present to our thought; or that our knowledge of them is known as presence of our thought to them. A great mystery is usually made of this peculiar presence in absence; and the scholastic philosophy, which is only common sense grown pedantic, would explain it as a peculiar kind of existence, called *intentional inexistence*, of the tigers in our mind. At the very least, people would say that what we mean by knowing the tigers is mentally *pointing* towards them as we sit here.

But now what do we mean by *pointing*, in such a case as this? What is the pointing known-as, here?

To this question I shall have to give a very prosaic answer —one that traverses the prepossessions not only of common sense and scholasticism, but also those of nearly all the epistemological writers whom I have ever read. The answer, made brief, is this: The pointing of our thought to the tigers is known simply and solely as a procession of mental associates and motor consequences that follow on the thought, and that would lead harmoniously, if followed out, into some ideal or real context, or even into the immediate presence, of the tigers. It is known as our rejection of a jaguar, if that beast were shown. It is known as our ability to utter all sorts of propositions which don't contradict other propositions that are true of the real tigers. It is even known, if we take the tigers very seriously, as actions of ours which may terminate in directly intuited tigers, as they would if we took a voyage to India for the purpose of tiger-hunting and brought back a lot of skins of the striped rascals which we had laid low. In all this there is no self-transcendency in our mental images *taken by themselves*. They are one phenomenal fact; the tigers are another; and their pointing to the tigers is a perfectly commonplace intra-experiential relation, *if you once grant a connecting world to be there*. In short, the ideas and the tigers are in themselves as loose and separate, to use Hume's language, as any two things can be; and pointing means here an operation as external and adventitious as any that nature yields.²

I hope you may agree with me now that in representative knowledge there is no special inner mystery, but only an outer chain of physical or mental intermediaries connecting thought and thing. *To know an object is here to lead to it through a context which the world supplies.* All this was most instructively set forth by our colleague D. S. Miller at our meeting in New York last Christmas, and for re-confirming my sometime wavering opinion, I owe him this acknowledgment.³

Let us next pass on to the case of immediate or intuitive acquaintance with an object, and let the object be the white paper before our eyes. The thought-stuff and the thing-stuff are here indistinguishably the same in nature, as we saw a moment since, and there is no context of intermediaries or associates to stand between and separate the thought and thing. There is no "presence in absence" here, and no "pointing," but rather an allround embracing of the paper by the thought; and it is clear that the knowing cannot now be explained exactly as it was when the tigers were its object. Dotted all through our experience are states of immediate acquaintance just like this. Somewhere our belief always does rest on ultimate data like the whiteness, smoothness, or squareness of this paper. Whether such qualities be truly ultimate aspects of being, or only provisional suppositions of ours, held-to till we get better informed, is quite immaterial for our present inquiry. So long as it is believed in, we see our object face to face. What now do we mean by "knowing" such a sort of object as this? For this is also the way in which we should know the tiger if our conceptual idea of him were to terminate by having led us to his lair?

This address must not become too long, so I must give my answer in the fewest words. And let me first say this: So far as the white paper or other ultimate datum of our experience is considered to enter also into some one else's experience, and we, in knowing it, are held to know it there as well as here; so far, again, as it is considered to be a mere mask for hidden molecules that other now impossible experiences of our own might some day lay bare to view; so far it is a case of tigers in India again—the things known being absent experiences, the knowing can only consist in passing smoothly towards them through the intermediary context that the world supplies. But if our own private vision of the paper be considered in abstraction from every other event, as if it constituted by itself the universe (and it might perfectly well do so, for aught we can understand to the contrary), then the paper seen and the seeing of it are only two names for one indivisible fact which, properly named, is *the datum, the phenomenon, or the experience*. The paper is in the mind and the mind is around the paper, because paper and mind are only two names that are given later to the one experience, when, taken in a larger world of which it forms a part, its connections are traced in different directions.[4] *To know immediately, then, or intuitively, is for mental content and object to be identical.* This is a very different definition from that which we gave of representative knowledge; but neither definition involves those mysterious notions of self-transcendency and presence in absence which are such essential parts of the ideas of knowledge, both of philosophers and of common men.[5]

HUMANISM AND TRUTH [1]

Receiving from the Editor of *Mind* an advance proof of Mr. Bradley's article on "Truth and Practice," I understand this as a hint to me to join in the controversy over "Pragmatism" which seems to have seriously begun. As my name has been coupled with the movement, I deem it wise to take the hint, the more so as in some quarters greater credit has been given me than I deserve, and probably undeserved discredit in other quarters falls also to my lot.

First, as to the word "pragmatism." I myself have only used the term to indicate a method of carrying on abstract discussion. The serious meaning of a concept, says Mr. Peirce, lies in the concrete difference to some one which its being true will make. Strive to bring all debated conceptions to that "pragmatic" test, and you will escape vain wrangling: if it can make no practical difference which of two statements be true, then they are really one statement in two verbal forms; if it can make no practical difference whether a given statement be true or false, then the statement has no real meaning. In neither case is there anything fit to quarrel about: we may save our breath, and pass to more important things.

All that the pragmatic method implies, then, is that truths should *have* practical [2] consequences. In England the word has been used more broadly still, to cover the notion that the truth of any statement *consists* in the consequences, and particularly in their being good consequences. Here we get beyond affairs of method altogether; and since my pragmatism and this wider pragmatism are so different, and both are important enough to have different names, I think that Mr. Schiller's proposal to call the wider pragmatism by the name of "humanism" is excellent and ought to be adopted. The narrower pragmatism may still be spoken of as the "pragmatic method."

I have read in the past six months many hostile reviews of Schiller's and Dewey's publications; but with the exception of Mr. Bradley's elaborate indictment, they are out of reach where I write, and I have largely forgotten them. I think that a free discussion of the subject on my part would in any case be more useful than a polemic attempt at rebutting these criticisms in detail. Mr. Bradley in particular can be taken care of by Mr. Schiller. He repeatedly confesses himself unable to comprehend Schiller's views, he evidently has not sought to do so sympathetically, and I deeply regret to say that his laborious article throws, for my mind, absolutely no useful light upon the subject. It seems to me on the whole an *ignoratio elenchi,* and I feel free to disregard it altogether.

The subject is unquestionably difficult. Messrs. Dewey's and Schiller's thought is eminently an induction, a generalization working itself free from all sorts of entangling particulars. If true, it involves much restatement of traditional notions. This is a kind of intellectual product that never attains a classic form of expression when first promulgated. The critic ought therefore not to be too sharp and logic-chopping in his dealings with it, but should weigh it as a whole, and especially weigh it against its possible alternatives. One should also try to apply it first to one instance, and then to another to see how it will work. It seems to me that it is emphatically not a case for instant execution, by conviction of intrinsic absurdity or of self-contradiction, or by caricature of what it would look like if reduced to skeleton shape. Humanism is in fact much more like one of those secular changes that come upon public opinion overnight, as it were, borne upon tides "too deep for sound or foam," that survive all the crudities and extravagances of their advocates, that you can pin to no one absolutely essential statement, nor kill by any one decisive stab.

Such have been the changes from aristocracy to democracy, from classic to romantic taste, from theistic to pantheistic feeling, from static to evolutionary ways of understanding life—changes of which we all have been spectators. Scholasticism still opposes to such changes the method of confutation by single decisive reasons, showing that the new view involves self-contradiction, or traverses some fundamental principle. This is like stopping a river by planting a stick in the middle of its bed. Round your obstacle flows the water and "gets there all the same." In reading some of our opponents, I am not a little reminded of those catholic writers who refute darwinism by telling us that higher species cannot come from lower because _minus nequit gignere plus,_ or that the notion of transformation is absurd, for it implies that species tend to their own destruction, and that would violate the principle that every reality tends to persevere in its own shape. The point of view is too myopic, too tight and close to take in the inductive argument. Wide generalizations in science always meet with these summary refutations in their early days; but they outlive them, and the refutations then sound oddly antiquated and scholastic. I cannot help suspecting that the humanistic theory is going through this kind of would-be refutation at present.

The one condition of understanding humanism is to become inductive-minded oneself, to drop rigorous definitions, and follow lines of least resistance "on the whole." "In other words," an opponent might say, "resolve your intellect into a kind of slush." "Even so," I make reply, "if you will consent to use no politer word." For humanism, conceiving the more "true" as the more "satisfactory" (Dewey's term), has sincerely to renounce rectilinear arguments and ancient ideals of rigor and finality. It is in just this temper of renunciation, so different from that of pyrrhonistic scepticism, that the spirit of humanism essentially consists. Satisfactoriness has to be measured by a multitude of standards, of which some, for aught we know, may fail in any given case; and what is more satisfactory than any alternative in sight, may to the end be a sum of _pluses_ and _minuses,_ concerning which we can only trust that by ulterior corrections and improvements a maximum of the one and a minimum of the other may some day be approached. It means a real change of heart, a break with absolutistic hopes, when one takes up this inductive view of the conditions of belief.

As I understand the pragmatist way of seeing things, it owes its being to the break-down which the last fifty years have brought about in the older notions of scientific truth. "God geometrizes," it used to be said; and it was believed that Euclid's elements literally reproduced his geometrizing. There is an eternal and unchangeable "reason;" and its voice was supposed to reverberate in _Barbara_ and _Celarent._ So also of the "laws of nature," physical and chemical, so of natural history classifications—all were supposed to be exact and exclusive duplicates of pre-human archetypes buried in the structure of things, to which the spark of divinity hidden in our intellect enables us to penetrate. The anatomy of the world is logical, and its logic is that of a university professor, it was thought. Up to about 1850 almost every one believed that sciences expressed truths that were exact copies of a definite code of non-human realities. But the enormously rapid multiplication of theories in these latter days has well-nigh upset the notion of any one of them being a more literally objective kind of thing than another. There are so many geometries, so many logics, so many physical and chemical hypotheses, so many classifications, each one of them good for so much and yet not good for everything, that the notion that even the truest formula may be a human device and not a literal transcript has dawned upon us. We hear scientific laws now treated as so much "conceptual shorthand," true so far as they are useful but no farther. Our mind has become tolerant of symbol instead of reproduction, of approximation instead of exactness, of plasticity instead of rigor. "Energetics," measuring the bare face of sensible phenomena so as to describe in a single formula all their changes of "level," is the last word of his scientific humanism, which indeed leaves queries enough outstanding as to the reason for so curious a congruence between the world and the mind, but which at any rate makes our whole notion of scientific truth more flexible and genial than it used to be.

It is to be doubted whether any theorizer today, either in mathematics, logic, physics or biology, conceives himself to be literally re-editing processes of nature or thoughts of God. The main forms of our thinking, the separation of subjects from predicates, the negative, hypothetic and disjunctive judgments, are purely human habits. The ether, as Lord Salisbury said, is only a noun for the verb to undulate; and many of our theological ideas are admitted, even by those who call them "true," to be humanistic in like degree.

I fancy that these changes in the current notions of truth are what originally gave the impulse to Messrs. Dewey's and Schiller's views. The suspicion is in the air nowadays that the superiority of one of our formulas to another may not consist so much in its literal "objectivity," as in subjective qualities like its usefulness, its "elegance" or its congruity with our residual beliefs. Yielding to these suspicions, and generalizing, we fall into something like the humanistic state of mind. Truth we conceive to mean everywhere, not duplication, but addition; not the constructing of inner copies of already complete realities, but rather the collaborating with realities so as to bring about a clearer result. Obviously this state of mind is at first full of vagueness and ambiguity. "Collaborating" is a vague term; it must at any rate cover conceptions and logical arrangements. "Clearer" is vaguer still. Truth must bring clear thoughts, as well as clear the way to action. "Reality" is the vaguest term of all. The only way to test such a programme at all is to apply it to the various types of truth, in the hope of reaching an account that shall be more precise. Any hypothesis that forces such a review upon one has one great merit, even if in the end it prove invalid: it gets us better acquainted with the total subject. To give the theory plenty of "rope" and see if it hangs itself eventually is better tactics than to choke it off at the outset by abstract accusations of self-contradiction. I think therefore that a decided effort at sympathetic mental play with humanism is the provisional attitude to be recommended to the reader.

When I find myself playing sympathetically with humanism, something like what follows is what I end by conceiving it to mean.

Experience is a process that continually gives us new material to digest. We handle this intellectually by the mass of beliefs of which we find ourselves already possessed, assimilating, rejecting, or rearranging in different degrees. Some of the apperceiving ideas are recent acquisitions of our own, but most of them are common-sense traditions of the race. There is probably not a common-sense tradition, of all those which we now live by, that was not in the first instance a genuine discovery, an inductive generalization like those more recent ones of the atom, of inertia, of energy, of reflex action, or of fitness to survive. The notions of one Time and of one Space as single continuous receptacles; the distinction between thoughts and things, matter and mind; between permanent subjects and changing attributes; the conception of classes with sub-classes within them; the separation of fortuitous from regularly caused connections; surely all these were once definite conquests made at historic dates by our ancestors in their attempts to get the chaos of their crude individual experiences into a more shareable and manageable shape. They proved of such sovereign use as *denkmittel* that they are now a part of the very structure of our mind. We cannot play fast and loose with them. No experience can upset them. On the contrary, they apperceive every experience and assign it to its place.

To what effect? That we may the better forsee the course of our experiences, communicate with one another, and steer our lives by rule. Also that we may have a cleaner, clearer, more inclusive mental view.

The greatest common-sense achievement, after the discovery of one Time and one Space, is probably the concept of permanently existing things. When a rattle first drops out of the hand of a baby, he does not look to see where it has gone. Non-perception he accepts as annihilation until he finds a better belief. That our perceptions mean *beings,* rattles that are there whether we hold them in our hands or not, becomes an interpretation so luminous of what happens to us that, once employed, it never gets forgotten. It applies with equal felicity to things and persons, to the objective and to the ejective realm. However a Berkeley, a Mill, or a Cornelius may criticise it, it *works;* and in practical life we never think of "going back" upon it, or reading our incoming experiences in any other terms. We may, indeed, speculatively imagine a state of "pure" experience before the hypothesis of permanent objects behind its flux had been framed; and we can play with the idea that some primeval genius might have struck into a different hypothesis. But we cannot positively imagine today what the different hypothesis could have been, for the category of trans-perceptual reality is now one of the foundations of our life. Our thoughts must still employ it if they are to possess reasonableness and truth.

This notion of a *first* in the shape of a most chaotic pure experience which sets us questions, of a *second* in the way of fundamental categories, long ago wrought into the structure of our consciousness and practically irreversible, which define the general frame within which answers must fall, and of a *third* which gives the detail of the answers in the shapes most congruous with all our present needs, is, as I take it, the essence of the humanistic conception. It represents experience in its pristine purity to be now so enveloped in predicates historically worked out that we can think of it as little more than an *Other*, of a *That*, which the mind, in Mr. Bradley's phrase, "encounters," and to whose stimulating presence we respond by ways of thinking which we call "true" in proportion as they facilitate our mental or physical activities and bring us outer power and inner peace. But whether the Other, the universal *That*, has itself any definite inner structure, or whether, if it have any, the structure resembles any of our predicated *whats*, this is a question which humanism leaves untouched. For us, at any rate, it insists, reality is an accumulation of our own intellectual inventions, and the struggle for "truth" in our progressive dealings with it is always a struggle to work in new nouns and adjectives while altering as little as possible the old.

It is hard to see why either Mr. Bradley's own logic or his metaphysics should oblige him to quarrel with this conception. He might consistently adopt it *verbatim et literatim*, if he would, and simply throw his peculiar absolute round it, following in this the good example of Professor Royce. Bergson in France, and his disciples, Wilbois the physicist and Leroy are thoroughgoing humanists in the sense defined. Professor Milhaud also appears to be one; and the great Poincaré misses it by only the breadth of a hair. In Germany the name of Simmel offers itself as that of a humanist of the most radical sort. Mach and his school, and Hertz and Ostwald must be classed as humanists. The view is in the atmosphere and must be patiently discussed.

The best way to discuss it would be to see what the alternative might be. What is it indeed? Its critics make no explicit statement, Professor Royce being the only one so far who has formulated anything definite. The first service of humanism to philosophy accordingly seems to be that it will probably oblige those who dislike it to search their own hearts and heads. It will force analysis to the front and make it the order of the day. At present the lazy tradition that truth is *adæquatio intellectûs et rei* seems all there is to contradict it with. Mr. Bradley's only suggestion is that true thought "must correspond to a determinate being which it cannot be said to make," and obviously that sheds no new light. What is the meaning of the word to "correspond"? Where is the "being"?

What sort of things are "determinations," and what is meant in this particular case by "not to make"?

Humanism proceeds immediately to refine upon the looseness of these epithets. We correspond in *some* way with anything with which we enter into any relations at all. If it be a thing, we may produce an exact copy of it, or we may simply feel it as an existent in a certain place. If it be a demand, we may obey it without knowing anything more about it than its push. If it be a proposition, we may agree by not contradicting it, by letting it pass. If it be a relation between things, we may act on the first thing so as to bring ourselves out where the second will be. If it be something inaccessible, we may substitute a hypothetical object for it, which, having the same consequences, will cipher out for us real results. In a general way we may simply *add our thought to it;* and if it *suffers the addition,* and the whole situation harmoniously prolongs and enriches itself, the thought will pass for true.

As for the whereabouts of the beings thus corresponded to, although they may be outside of the present thought as well as in it, humanism sees no ground for saying they are outside of finite experience itself. Pragmatically, their reality means that we submit to them, take account of them, whether we like to or not, but this we must perpetually do with experiences other than our own. The whole system of what the present experience must correspond to "adequately" may be continuous with the present experience itself. Reality, so taken as experience other than the present, might be either the legacy of past experience or the content of experience to come. Its determinations for *us* are in any case the adjectives which our acts of judging fit to it, and those are essentially humanistic things.

To say that our thought does not "make" this reality means pragmatically that if our own particular thought were annihilated the reality would still be there in some shape, though possibly it might be a shape that would lack something that our thought supplies. That reality is "independent" means that there is something in every experience that escapes our arbitrary control. If it be a sensible experience it coerces our attention; if a sequence, we cannot invert it; if we compare two terms we can come to only one result. There is a push, an urgency, within our very experience, against which we are on the whole powerless, and which drives us in a

direction that is the destiny of our belief. That this drift of
experience itself is in the last resort due to something independent of all possible experience may or may not be true.
There may or may not be an extra-experiential *ding an sich*
that keeps the ball rolling, or an "absolute" that lies eternally
behind all the successive determinations which human thought
has made. But within our experience *itself*, at any rate,
humanism says, some determinations show themselves as
being independent of others; some questions, if we ever ask
them, can only be answered in one way; some beings, if we
ever suppose them, must be supposed to have existed previously to the supposing; some relations, if they exist ever,
must exist as long as their terms exist.

Truth thus means, according to humanism, the relation of
less fixed parts of experience (predicates) to other relatively
more fixed parts (subjects); and we are not required to seek
it in a relation of experience as such to anything beyond itself.
We can stay at home, for our behavior as experients is
hemmed in on every side. The forces both of advance and of
resistance are exerted by our own objects, and the notion
of truth as something opposed to waywardness or license
inevitably grows up solipsistically inside of every human life.

So obvious is all this that a common charge against the
humanistic authors "makes me tired." "How can a Deweyite
discriminate sincerity from bluff?" was a question asked at a
philosophic meeting where I reported on Dewey's *Studies*.
"How can the mere² pragmatist feel any duty to think truly?"
is the objection urged by Professor Royce. Mr. Bradley in
turn says that if a humanist understands his own doctrine, "he
must hold any idea, however mad, to be the truth, if any
one will have it so." And Professor Taylor describes pragmatism as believing anything one pleases and calling it truth.

Such a shallow sense of the conditions under which men's
thinking actually goes on seems to me most surprising. These
critics appear to suppose that, if left to itself, the rudderless
raft of our experience must be ready to drift anywhere or
nowhere. Even tho there were compasses on board, they
seem to say, there would be no pole for them to point to.
There must be absolute sailing-directions, they insist, decreed
from outside, and an independent chart of the voyage added
to the "mere" voyage itself, if we are ever to make a port.

But is it not obvious that even tho there be such absolute sailing-directions in the shape of pre-human standards of truth that we *ought* to follow, the only guarantee that we shall in fact follow them must lie in our human equipment. The "ought" would be a *brutum fulmen* unless there were a felt grain inside of our experience that conspired. As a matter of fact the devoutest believers in absolute standards must admit that men fail to obey them. Waywardness is here, in spite of the eternal prohibitions, and the existence of any amount of reality *ante rem* is no warrant against unlimited error *in rebus* being incurred. The only *real* guarantee we have against licentious thinking is the circumpressure of experience itself, which gets us sick of concrete errors, whether there be a trans-empirical reality or not. How does the partisan of absolute reality know what this orders him to think? He cannot get direct sight of the absolute; and he has no means of guessing what it wants of him except by following the humanistic clues. The only truth that he himself will ever practically *accept* will be that to which his finite experiences lead him of themselves. The state of mind which shudders at the idea of a lot of experiences left to themselves, and that augurs protection from the sheer name of an absolute, as if, however inoperative, that might still stand for a sort of ghostly security, is like the mood of those good people who, whenever they hear of a social tendency that is damnable, begin to redden and to puff, and say "Parliament or Congress ought to make a law against it," as if an impotent decree would give relief.

All the *sanctions* of a law of truth lie in the very texture of experience. Absolute or no absolute, the concrete truth *for us* will always be that way of thinking in which our various experiences most profitably combine.

And yet, the opponent obstinately urges, your humanist will always have a greater liberty to play fast and loose with truth than will your believer in an independent realm of reality that makes the standard rigid. If by this latter believer he means a man who pretends to know the standard and who fulminates it, the humanist will doubtless prove more flexible; but no more flexible than the absolutist himself if the latter follows (as fortunately our present-day absolutists do follow) empirical methods of inquiry in concrete affairs. To consider hypotheses is surely always better than to dogmatize *ins blaue hinein.*

Nevertheless this probable flexibility of temper in him has been used to convict the humanist of sin. Believing as he does, that truth lies *in rebus,* and is at every moment our own line of most propitious reaction, he stands forever debarred, as I have heard a learned colleague say, from trying to convert opponents, for does not their view, being *their* most propitious momentary reaction, already fill the bill? Only the believer in the *ante-rem* brand of truth can on this theory seek to make converts without self-stultification. But can there be self-stultification in urging any account whatever of truth? Can the definition ever contradict the deed? "Truth is what I feel like saying"—suppose that to be the definition. "Well, I feel like saying that, and I want you to feel like saying it, and shall continue to say it until I get you to agree." Where is there any contradiction? Whatever truth may be said to be, that is the kind of truth which the saying can be held to carry. The *temper* which a saying may comport is an extra-logical matter. It may indeed be hotter in some individual absolutist than in a humanist, but it need not be so in another. And the humanist, for his part, is perfectly consistent in compassing sea and land to make one proselyte, if his nature be enthusiastic enough.

"But how *can* you be enthusiastic over any view of things which you know to have been partly made by yourself, and which is liable to alter during the next minute? How is any heroic devotion to the ideal of truth possible under such paltry conditions?"

This is just another of those objections by which the anti-humanists show their own comparatively slack hold on the realities of the situation. If they would only follow the pragmatic method and ask: "What is truth *known-as?* What does its existence stand for in the way of concrete goods?"— they would see that the name of it is the *inbegriff* of almost everything that is valuable in our lives. The true is the opposite of whatever is instable, of whatever is practically disappointing, of whatever is useless, of whatever is lying and unreliable, of whatever is unverifiable and unsupported, of whatever is inconsistent and contradictory, of whatever is artificial and eccentric, of whatever is unreal in the sense of being of no practical account. Here are pragmatic reasons with a vengeance why we should turn to truth—truth saves us from a world of that complexion. What wonder that its very name awakens loyal feeling! In particular what wonder that all little provisional fool's paradises of belief should appear contemptible in comparison with its bare pursuit! When absolutists reject humanism because they feel it to be untrue, that means that the whole habit of their mental needs is wedded already to a different view of reality, in comparison with which the humanistic world seems but the whim of a few irresponsible youths. Their own subjective apperceiving mass is what speaks here in the name of the eternal natures and bids them reject our humanism—as they apprehend it. Just so with us humanists, when we condemn all noble, clean-cut, fixed, eternal, rational, temple-like systems of philosophy. These contradict the *dramatic temperament* of nature, as our dealings with nature and our habits of thinking have so far brought us to conceive it. They seem oddly personal and artificial, even when not bureaucratic and professional in an absurd degree. We turn from them to the great unpent and unstayed wilderness of truth as we feel it to be constituted, with as good a conscience as rationalists are moved by when they turn from our wilderness into their neater and cleaner intellectual abodes.[4]

This is surely enough to show that the humanist does not ignore the character of objectivity and independence in truth. Let me turn next to what his opponents mean when they say that to be true, our thoughts must "correspond."

The vulgar notion of correspondence here is that the thoughts must *copy* the reality—cognitio fit per *assimilationem* cogniti et cognoscentis; and philosophy, without having ever fairly sat down to the question, seems to have instinctively accepted this idea: propositions are held true if they copy the eternal thought; terms are held true if they copy extramental realities. Implicitly, I think that the copy-theory has animated most of the criticisms that have been made on humanism.

A priori, however, it is not self-evident that the sole business of our mind with realities should be to copy them. Let my reader suppose himself to constitute for a time all the reality there is in the universe, and then to receive the announcement that another being is to be created who shall know him truly. How will he represent the knowing in advance? What will he hope it to be? I doubt extremely whether it could ever occur to him to fancy it as a mere copying. Of what use to him would an imperfect second edition of himself in the newcomer's interior be? It would seem pure waste of a propitious opportunity. The demand would more probably be for something absolutely new. The reader would conceive the knowing humanistically, "the new-comer," he would say, "must *take account of my presence by reacting on it in such a way that good would accrue to us both.* If copying be requisite to that end, let there be copying; otherwise not." The essence in any case would not be the copying, but the enrichment of the previous world.

I read the other day, in a book of Professor Eucken's, a phrase, *"Die erhöhung des vorgefundenen daseins,"* which seems to be pertinent here. Why may not thought's mission be to increase and elevate, rather than simply to imitate and reduplicate, existence? No one who has read Lotze can fail to remember his striking comment on the ordinary view of the secondary qualities of matter, which brands them as "illusory" because they copy nothing in the thing. The notion of a world complete in itself, to which thought comes as a passive mirror, adding nothing to fact, Lotze says is irrational. Rather is thought itself a most momentous part of fact, and the whole mission of the pre-existing and insufficient world of matter may simply be to provoke thought to produce its far more precious supplement.

"Knowing," in short, may, for aught we can see beforehand to the contrary, be *only one way of getting into fruitful relations with reality,* whether copying be one of the relations or not.

It is easy to see from what special type of knowing the copy-theory arose. In our dealings with natural phenomena the great point is to be able to foretell. Foretelling, according to such a writer as Spencer, is the whole meaning of intelligence. When Spencer's "law of intelligence" says that inner and outer relations must "correspond," it means that the distribution of terms in our inner time-scheme and space-scheme must be an exact copy of the distribution in real time and space of the real terms. In strict theory the mental terms themselves need not answer to the real terms in the sense of severally copying them, symbolic mental terms being enough, if only the real dates and places be copied. But in our ordinary life the mental terms are images and the real ones are sensations, and the images so often copy the sensations, that we easily take copying of terms as well as of relations to be the natural significance of knowing. Meanwhile much, even of this common descriptive truth, is couched in verbal symbols. If our symbols *fit* the world, in the sense of determining our expectations rightly, they may even be the better for not copying its terms.

It seems obvious that the pragmatic account of all this routine of phenomenal knowledge is accurate. Truth here is a relation, not of our ideas to non-human realities, but of conceptual parts of our experience to sensational parts. Those thoughts are true which guide us to *beneficial interaction* with sensible particulars as they occur, whether they copy these in advance or not.

From the frequency of copying in the knowledge of phenomenal fact, copying has been supposed to be the essence of truth in matters rational also. Geometry and logic, it has been supposed, must copy archetypal thoughts in the Creator. But in these abstract spheres there is no need of assuming archetypes. The mind is free to carve so many figures out of space, to make so many numerical collections, to frame so many classes and series, and it can analyze and compare so endlessly, that the very superabundance of the resulting ideas makes us doubt the "objective" pre-existence of their models. It would be plainly wrong to suppose a God whose thought consecrated rectangular but not polar co-ordinates, or Jevons's notation but not Boole's. Yet if, on the other hand, we assume God to have thought in advance of every *possible* flight of human fancy in these directions, his mind becomes too much like a Hindoo idol with three heads, eight arms and six breasts, too much made up of superfoetation and redundancy for us to wish to copy it, and the whole notion of copying tends to evaporate from these sciences. Their objects can be better interpreted as being created step by step by men, as fast as they successively conceive them.

If now it be asked how, if triangles, squares, square roots, genera, and the like, are but improvised human "artefacts," their properties and relations can be so promptly known to be "eternal," the humanistic answer is easy. If triangles and genera are of our own production we can keep them invariant. We can make them "timeless" by expressly decreeing that on *the things we mean* time shall exert no altering effect, that they are intentionally and it may be fictitiously abstracted from every corrupting real associate and condition. But relations between invariant objects will themselves be invariant. Such relations cannot be happenings, for by hypothesis nothing shall happen to the objects. I have tried to show in the last chapter of my *Principles of Psychology*[5] that they can only be relations of comparison. No one so far seems to have noticed my suggestion, and I am too ignorant of the development of mathematics to feel very confident of my own view. But if it were correct it would solve the difficulty perfectly. Relations of comparison are matters of direct inspection. As soon as mental objects are mentally compared, they are perceived to be either like or unlike. But once the same, always the same, once different, always different, under these timeless conditions. Which is as much as to say that truths concerning these man-made objects are necessary and eternal. We can change our conclusions only by changing our data first.

The whole fabric of the *a priori* sciences can thus be treated as a man-made product. As Locke long ago pointed out, these sciences have no immediate connection with fact. Only *if* a fact can be humanized by being identified with any of these ideal objects, is what was true of the objects now true also of the facts. The truth itself meanwhile was originally a copy of nothing; it was only a relation directly perceived to obtain between two artificial mental things.[6]

We may now glance at some special types of knowing, so as to see better whether the humanistic account fits. On the mathematical and logical types we need not enlarge further, nor need we return at much length to the case of our descriptive knowledge of the course of nature. So far as this involves anticipation, tho that *may* mean copying, it need, as we saw, mean little more than "getting ready" in advance. But with many distant and future objects, our practical relations are to the last degree potential and remote. In no sense can we now get ready for the arrest of the earth's revolution by the tidal brake, for instance; and with the past, tho we suppose ourselves to know it truly, we have no practical relations at all. It is obvious that, altho interests strictly practical have been the original starting-point of our search for true phenomenal descriptions, yet an intrinsic interest in the bare describing function has grown up. We wish accounts that shall be true, whether they bring collateral profit or not. The primitive function has developed its demand for mere exercise. This theoretic curiosity seems to be the characteristically human *differentia*, and humanism recognizes its enormous scope. A true idea now means not only one that prepares us for an actual perception. It means also one that might prepare us for a merely possible perception, or one that, if spoken, would suggest possible perceptions to others, or suggest actual perceptions which the speaker cannot share. The *ensemble* of perceptions thus thought of as either actual or possible form a system which it is obviously advantageous to us to get into a stable and consistent shape; and here it is that the common-sense notion of permanent beings finds triumphant use. Beings acting outside of the thinker explain, not only his actual perceptions, past and future, but his possible perceptions and those of every one else. Accordingly they gratify our theoretic need in a supremely beautiful way. We pass from our immediate actual through them into the foreign and the potential, and back again into the future actual, accounting for innumerable particulars by a single cause. As in those circular panoramas, where a real foreground of dirt, grass, bushes, rocks and a broken-down cannon is enveloped by a canvas picture of sky and earth and of a raging battle, continuing the foreground so cunningly that the spectator can detect no joint; so these conceptual objects, added to our present perceptual reality, fuse with it into the whole universe of our belief. In spite of all berkeleyan criticism, we do not doubt that they are really there. Tho our discovery of any one of them may only date from now, we unhesitatingly say that it not only *is*, but *was* there, if, by so saying, the past appears connected more consistently with what we feel the present to be. This is historic truth. Moses wrote the Pentateuch, we think, because if he didn't, all our religious habits will have to be undone. Julius Caesar was real, or we can never listen to history again. Trilobites were once alive, or all our thought about the strata is at sea. Radium, discovered only yesterday, must always have existed, or its analogy with other natural elements, which are permanent, fails. In all this, it is but one portion of our beliefs reacting on another so as to yield the most satisfactory total state of mind. That state of mind, we say, sees truth, and the content of its deliverances we believe.

Of course, if you take the satisfactoriness concretely, as something felt by you now, and if, by truth, you mean truth taken abstractly and verified in the long run, you cannot make them equate, for it is notorious that the temporarily satisfactory is often false. Yet at each and every concrete moment, truth for each man is what that man "troweth" at that moment with the maximum of satisfaction to himself; and similarly, abstract truth, truth verified by the long run, and abstract satisfactoriness, long-run satisfactoriness, coincide. If, in short, we compare concrete with concrete and abstract with abstract, the true and the satisfactory do mean the same thing. I suspect that a certain muddling of matters hereabouts is what makes the general philosophic public so impervious to humanism's claims.

The fundamental fact about our experience is that it is a process of change. For the "trower" at any moment, truth, like the visible area round a man walking in a fog, or like what George Eliot calls "the wall of dark seen by small fishes' eyes that pierce a span in the wide Ocean," is an objective field which the next moment enlarges and of which it is the critic, and which then either suffers alteration or is continued unchanged. The critic sees both the first trower's truth and his own truth, compares them with each other, and verifies or confutes. *His* field of view is the reality independent of that earlier trower's thinking with which that thinking ought to correspond. But the critic is himself only a trower; and if the whole process of experience should terminate at that instant, there would be no otherwise known independent reality with which *his* thought might be compared.

The immediate in experience is always provisionally in this situation. The humanism, for instance, which I see and try so hard to defend, is the completest truth attained from my point of view up to date. But, owing to the fact that all experience is a process, no point of view can ever be *the* last one. Every one is insufficient and off its balance, and responsible to later points of view than itself. You, occupying some of these later points in your own person, and believing in the reality of others, will not agree that my point of view sees truth positive, truth timeless, truth that counts, unless they verify and confirm what it sees.

You generalize this by saying that any opinion, however satisfactory, can count positively and absolutely as true only so far as it agrees with a standard beyond itself; and if you then forget that this standard perpetually grows up endogenously inside the web of the experiences, you may carelessly go on to say that what distributively holds of each experience, holds also collectively of all experience, and that experience as such and in its totality owes whatever truth it may be possessed-of to its correspondence with absolute realities outside of its own being. This evidently is the popular and traditional position. From the fact that finite experiences must draw support from one another, philosophers pass to the notion that experience *überhaupt* must need an absolute support. The denial of such a notion by humanism lies probably at the root of most of the dislike which it incurs.

But is this not the globe, the elephant and the tortoise over again? Must not something end by supporting itself? Humanism is willing to let finite experience be self-supporting. Somewhere being must immediately breast nonentity. Why may not the advancing front of experience, carrying its immanent satisfactions and dissatisfactions, cut against the black inane as the luminous orb of the moon cuts the caerulean abyss? Why should anywhere the world be absolutely fixed and finished? And if reality genuinely grows, why may it not grow in these very determinations which here and now are made?

In point of fact it actually seems to grow by our mental determinations, be these never so "true." Take the "Great Bear" or "Dipper" constellation in the heavens. We call it by that name, we count the stars and call them seven, we say they were seven before they were counted, and we say that whether any one had ever noted the fact or not, the dim resemblance to a long-tailed (or long-necked?) animal was always truly there. But what do we mean by this projection into past eternity of recent human ways of thinking? Did an "absolute" thinker actually do the counting, tell off the stars upon his standing number-tally, and make the bear-comparison, silly as the latter is? Were they explicitly seven, explicitly bear-like, before the human witness came? Surely nothing in the truth of the attributions drives us to think this. They were only implicitly or virtually what we call them, and we human witnesses first explicated them and made them "real." A fact virtually pre-exists when every condition of its realization save one is already there. In this case the condition lacking is the act of the counting and comparing mind. But the stars (once the mind considers them) themselves dictate the result. The counting in no wise modifies their previous nature, and, they being what and where they are, the count cannot fall out differently. It could then *always* be made. *Never* could the number seven be questioned, *if the question once were raised.*

We have here a quasi-paradox. Undeniably something comes by the counting that was not there before. And yet that something was *always true.* In one sense you create it, and in another sense you *find* it. You have to treat your count as being true beforehand, the moment you come to treat the matter at all.

Our stellar attributes must always be called true, then; yet none the less are they genuine additions made by our intellect to the world of fact. Not additions of consciousness only, but additions of "content." They copy nothing that pre-existed, yet they agree with what pre-existed, fit it, amplify it, relate and connect it with a "wain," a number-tally, or what not, and build it out. It seems to me that humanism is the only theory that builds this case out in the good direction, and this case stands for innumerable other kinds of cases. In all such cases, odd as it may sound, our judgment may actually be said to retroact and to enrich the past.

Our judgments at any rate change the character of *future* reality by the acts to which they lead. Where these acts are acts expressive of trust—trust, *e.g.*, that a man is honest, that our health is good enough, or that we can make a successful effort—which acts may be a needed antecedent of the trusted things becoming true, Professor Taylor says[7] that our trust is at any rate *untrue when it is made, i.e.*, before the action; and I seem to remember that he disposes of anything like a faith in the general excellence of the universe (making the faithful person's part in it at any rate more excellent) as a "lie in the soul." But the pathos of this expression should not blind us to the complication of the facts. I doubt whether Professor Taylor would himself be in favor of practically handling trusters of these kinds as liars. Future and present really mix in such emergencies, and one can always escape lies in them by using hypothetic forms. But Mr. Taylor's attitude suggests such absurd possibilities of practice that it seems to me to illustrate beautifully how self-stultifying the conception of a truth that shall merely register a standing fixture may become. Theoretic truth, truth of passive copying, sought in the sole interests of copying as such, not because copying is *good for something*, but because copying ought *schlechthin* to be, seems, if you look at it coldly, to be an almost preposterous ideal. Why should the universe, existing in itself, also exist in copies? How *can* it be copied in the solidity of its objective fulness? And even if it could, what would the motive be? "Even the hairs of your head are numbered." Doubtless they are, virtually; but why, as an absolute proposition, *ought* the number to become copied and known? Surely knowing is only one way of interacting with reality and adding to its effect.

The opponent here will ask: "Has not the knowing of truth any substantive value on its own account, apart from the collateral advantages it may bring? And if you allow theoretic satisfactions to exist at all, do they not crowd the collateral satisfactions out of house and home, and must not pragmatism go into bankruptcy, if she admits them at all?" The destructive force of such talk disappears as soon as we use words concretely instead of abstractly, and ask, in our quality of good pragmatists, just what the famous theoretic needs are known as and in what the intellectual satisfactions consist.

Are they not all mere matters of *consistency*—and emphatically *not* of consistency between an absolute reality and the mind's copies of it, but of actually felt consistency among judgments, objects, and habits of reacting, in the mind's own experienceable world? And are not both our need of such consistency and our pleasure in it conceivable as outcomes of the natural fact that we are beings that do develop mental *habits*—habit itself proving adaptively beneficial in an environment where the same objects, or the same kinds of objects, recur and follow "law"? If this were so, what would have come first would have been the collateral profits of habit as such, and the theoretic life would have grown up in aid of these. In point of fact, this seems to have been the probable case. At life's origin, any present perception may have been "true"—if such a word could then be applicable. Later, when reactions became organized, the reactions became "true" whenever expectation was fulfilled by them. Otherwise they were "false" or "mistaken" reactions. But the same class of objects needs the same kind of reaction, so the impulse to react consistently must gradually have been established, and a disappointment felt whenever the results frustrated expectation. Here is a perfectly plausible germ for all our higher consistencies. Nowadays, if an object claims from us a reaction of the kind habitually accorded only to the opposite class of objects, our mental machinery refuses to run smoothly. The situation is intellectually unsatisfactory.

Theoretic truth thus falls *within* the mind, being the accord of some of its processes and objects with other processes and objects—"accord" consisting here in well-definable relations. So long as the satisfaction of feeling such an accord is denied us, whatever collateral profits may seem to inure from what we believe in are but as dust in the balance—provided always that we are highly organized intellectually, which the majority of us are not. The amount of accord which satisfies most men and women is merely the absence of violent clash between their usual thoughts and statements and the limited sphere of sense perceptions in which their lives are cast. The theoretic truth that most of us think we "ought" to attain to is thus the possession of a set of predicates that do not explicitly contradict their subjects. We preserve it as often as not by leaving other predicates and subjects out.

In some men theory is a passion, just as music is in others. The form of inner consistency is pursued far beyond the line at which collateral profits stop. Such men systematize and classify and schematize and make synoptical tables and invent ideal objects for the pure love of unifying. Too often the results, glowing with "truth" for the inventors, seem pathetically personal and artificial to bystanders. Which is as much as to say that the purely theoretic criterion of truth can leave us in the lurch as easily as any other criterion, and that the absolutists, for all their pretensions, are "in the same boat" concretely with those whom they attack.

I am well aware that this paper has been rambling in the extreme. But the whole subject is inductive, and sharp logic is hardly yet in order. My great trammel has been the non-existence of any definitely stated alternative on my opponents' part. It may conduce to clearness if I recapitulate, in closing, what I conceive the main points of humanism to be. They are these:

1. An experience, perceptual or conceptual, must conform to reality in order to be true.

2. By "reality" humanism means nothing more than the other conceptual or perceptual experiences with which a given present experience may find itself in point of fact mixed up.[8]

3. By "conforming," humanism means taking account-of in such a way as to gain any intellectually and practically satisfactory result.

4. To "take account-of" and to be "satisfactory" are terms that admit of no definition, so many are the ways in which these requirements can practically be worked out.

5. Vaguely and in general, we take account of a reality by *preserving* it in as unmodified a form as possible. But, to be then satisfactory, it must not contradict other realities outside of it which claim also to be preserved. That we must preserve all the experience we can and minimize contradiction in what we preserve, is about all that can be said in advance.

6. The truth which the conforming experience embodies may be a positive addition to the previous reality, and later judgments may have to conform to *it*. Yet, virtually at least, it may have been true previously. Pragmatically, virtual and actual truth mean the same thing: the possibility of only one answer, *when once the question is raised.*

THE WILL TO BELIEVE

and other essays

AUTHOR'S PREFACE TO
THE WILL TO BELIEVE
AND OTHER ESSAYS

At most of our American Colleges there are Clubs formed by the students devoted to particular branches of learning; and these clubs have the laudable custom of inviting once or twice a year some maturer scholar to address them, the occasion often being made a public one. I have from time to time accepted such invitations, and afterwards had my discourse printed in one or other of the Reviews. It has seemed to me that these addresses might now be worthy of collection in a volume, as they shed explanatory light upon each other, and taken together express a tolerably definite philosophic attitude in a very untechnical way.

Were I obliged to give a short name to the attitude in question, I should call it that of *radical empiricism*, in spite of the fact that such brief nicknames are nowhere more misleading than in philosophy. I say "empiricism," because it is contented to regard its most assured conclusions concerning matters of fact as hypotheses liable to modification in the course of future experience; and I say "radical," because it treats the doctrine of monism itself as an hypothesis, and, unlike so much of the half-way empiricism that is current under the name of positivism or agnosticism or scientific naturalism, it does not dogmatically affirm monism as something with which all experience has got to square. The difference between monism and pluralism is perhaps the most pregnant of all the differences in philosophy. *Primâ facie* the world is a pluralism; as we find it, its unity seems to be that of any collection; and our higher thinking consists chiefly of an effort to redeem it from that first crude form. Postulating more unity than the first experiences yield, we also discover more. But absolute unity, in spite of brilliant dashes in its

188 • THE WILL TO BELIEVE

direction, still remains undiscovered, still remains a *Grenzbe-griff.* "Ever not quite" must be the rationalistic philosopher's last confession concerning it. After all that reason can do has been done, there still remains the opacity of the finite facts as merely given, with most of their peculiarities mutually unmediated and unexplained. To the very last, there are the various "points of view" which the philosopher must distinguish in discussing the world; and what is inwardly clear from one point remains a bare externality and datum to the other. The negative, the alogical, is never wholly banished. Something—"call it fate, chance, freedom, spontaneity, the devil, what you will"—is still wrong and other and outside and unincluded, from *your* point of view, even though you be the greatest of philosophers. Something is always mere fact and *givenness;* and there may be in the whole universe no one point of view extant from which this would not be found to be the case. "Reason," as a gifted writer says, "is but one item in the mystery; and behind the proudest consciousness that ever reigned, reason and wonder blushed face to face. The inevitable stales, while doubt and hope are sisters. Not unfortunately the universe is wild—game-flavored as a hawk's wing. Nature is miracle all; the same returns not save to bring the different. The slow round of the engraver's lathe gains but the breadth of a hair, but the difference is distributed back over the whole curve, never an instant true—ever not quite." [1]

This is pluralism, somewhat rhapsodically expressed. He who takes for his hypothesis the notion that it is the permanent form of the world is what I call a radical empiricist. For him the crudity of experience remains an eternal element thereof. There is no possible point of view from which the world can appear an absolutely single fact. Real possibilities, real indeterminations, real beginnings, real ends, real evil, real crises, catastrophes, and escapes, a real God, and a real moral life, just as common-sense conceives these things, may remain in empiricism as conceptions which that philosophy gives up the attempt either to "overcome" or to reinterpret in monistic form.

Many of my professionally trained *confrères* will smile at the irrationalism of this view, and at the artlessness of my essays in point of technical form. But they should be taken as illustrations of the radically empiricist attitude rather than as argumentations for its validity. That admits meanwhile of being argued in as technical a shape as any one can desire, and possibly I may be spared to do later a share of that work. Meanwhile these essays seem to light up with a certain dramatic reality the attitude itself, and make it visible alongside of the higher and lower dogmatisms between which in the pages of philosophic history it has generally remained eclipsed from sight.

The first four essays are largely concerned with defending the legitimacy of religious faith. To some rationalizing readers such advocacy will seem a sad misuse of one's professional position. Mankind, they will say, is only too prone to follow faith unreasoningly, and needs no preaching nor encouragement in that direction. I quite agree that what mankind at large most lacks is criticism and caution, not faith. Its cardinal weakness is to let belief follow recklessly upon lively conception, especially when the conception has instinctive liking at its back. I admit, then, that were I addressing the Salvation Army or a miscellaneous popular crowd it would be a misuse of opportunity to preach the liberty of believing as I have in these pages preached it. What such audiences most need is that their faiths should be broken up and ventilated, that the northwest wind of science should get into them and blow their sickliness and barbarism away. But academic audiences, fed already on science, have a very different need. Paralysis of their native capacity for faith and timorous *abulia* in the religious field are their special forms of mental weakness, brought about by the notion, carefully instilled, that there is something called scientific evidence by waiting upon which they shall escape all danger of shipwreck in regard to truth. But there is really no scientific or other method by which men can steer safely between the opposite dangers of believing too little or of believing too much. To face such dangers is apparently our duty, and to hit the right channel between them is the measure of our wisdom as men. It does not follow, because recklessness may be a vice in soldiers, that courage ought never to be preached to them. What *should* be preached is courage weighted with responsibility, such courage as the Nelsons and Washingtons never failed to show after they had taken everything into account that might tell against their success, and made every provision to minimize disaster in case they met defeat. I do not think that any one can accuse me of preaching reckless faith. I have preached the right of the individual to indulge his personal faith at his personal risk. I have discussed the kinds of risk; I have contended that none of us escape all of them; and I have only pleaded that it is better to face them open-eyed than to act as if we did not know them to be there.

After all, tho, you will say, Why such an ado about a matter concerning which, however we may theoretically differ, we all practically agree? In this age of toleration, no scientist will ever try actively to interfere with our religious faith, provided we enjoy it quietly with our friends and do not make a public nuisance of it in the market-place. But it is just on this matter of the market-place that I think the utility of such essays as mine may turn. If religious hypotheses about the universe be in order at all, then the active faiths of individuals in them, freely expressing themselves in life, are the experimental tests by which they are verified, and the only means by which their truth or falsehood can be wrought out. The truest scientific hypothesis is that which, as we say, "works" best; and it can be no otherwise with religious hypotheses. Religious history proves that one hypothesis after another has worked ill, has crumbled at contact with a widening knowledge of the world, and has lapsed from the minds of men. Some articles of faith, however, have maintained themselves through every vicissitude, and possess even more vitality today than ever before: it is for the "science of religions" to tell us just which hypotheses these are. Meanwhile the freest competition of the various faiths with one another, and their openest application to life by their several champions, are the most favorable conditions under which the survival of the fittest can proceed. They ought therefore not to lie hid each under its bushel, indulged-in quietly with friends. They ought to live in publicity, vying with each other; and it seems to me that (the régime of tolerance once granted, and a fair field shown) the scientist has nothing to fear for his own interests from the liveliest possible state of fermentation in the religious world of his time. Those faiths will best stand the test which adopt also his hypotheses, and make them integral elements of their own. He should welcome therefore every species of religious agitation and discussion, so long as he is willing to allow that some religious hypothesis *may* be true. Of course there are plenty of scientists who would deny that dogmatically, maintaining that science has already ruled all possible religious hypotheses out of court. Such scientists ought, I agree, to aim at imposing privacy on religious faiths, the public manifestation of which could only be a nuisance in their eyes. With all such scientists, as well as with their allies outside of science, my quarrel openly lies; and I hope that my book may do something to persuade the reader of their crudity, and range him on my side. Religious fermentation is always a symptom of the intellectual vigor of a society; and it is only when they forget that they are hypotheses and put on rationalistic and authoritative pretensions, that our faiths do harm. The most interesting and valuable things about a man are his ideals and over-beliefs. The same is true of nations and historic epochs; and the excesses of which the particular individuals and epochs are guilty are compensated in the total, and become profitable to mankind in the long run. . . .

HARVARD UNIVERSITY
CAMBRIDGE, MASSACHUSETTS
December, 1896

THE WILL TO BELIEVE [1]

In the recently published Life by Leslie Stephen of his brother, Fitz-James, there is an account of a school to which the latter went when he was a boy. The teacher, a certain Mr. Guest, used to converse with his pupils in this wise: "Gurney, what is the difference between justification and sanctification?—Stephen, prove the omnipotence of God!" etc. In the midst of our Harvard freethinking and indifference we are prone to imagine that here at your good old orthodox College conversation continues to be somewhat upon this order; and to show you that we at Harvard have not lost all interest in these vital subjects, I have brought with me tonight something like a sermon on justification by faith to read to you —I mean an essay in justification *of* faith, a defence of our right to adopt a believing attitude in religious matters, in spite of the fact that our merely logical intellect may not have been coerced. "The Will to Believe," accordingly, is the title of my paper.

I have long defended to my own students the lawfulness of voluntarily adopted faith; but as soon as they have got well imbued with the logical spirit, they have as a rule refused to admit my contention to be lawful philosophically, even though in point of fact they were personally all the time chock-full of some faith or other themselves. I am all the while, however, so profoundly convinced that my own position is correct, that your invitation has seemed to me a good occasion to make my statements more clear. Perhaps your minds will be more open than those with which I have hitherto had to deal. I will be as little technical as I can, though I must begin by setting up some technical distinctions that will help us in the end.

I

LET us give the name of *hypothesis* to anything that may be proposed to our belief; and just as the electricians speak of live and dead wires, let us speak of any hypothesis as either *live* or *dead*. A live hypothesis is one which appeals as a real possibility to him to whom it is proposed. If I ask you to believe in the Mahdi, the notion makes no electric connection with your nature—it refuses to scintillate with any credibility at all. As an hypothesis it is completely dead. To an Arab, however (even if he be not one of the Mahdi's followers), the hypothesis is among the mind's possibilities: it is alive. This shows that deadness and liveness in an hypothesis are not intrinsic properties, but relations to the individual thinker. They are measured by his willingness to act. The maximum of liveness in an hypothesis means willingness to act irrevocably. Practically, that means belief; but there is some believing tendency wherever there is willingness to act at all.

Next, let us call the decision between two hypotheses an *option*. Options may be of several kinds. They may be— 1, *living* or *dead;* 2, *forced* or *avoidable;* 3, *momentous* or *trivial;* and for our purposes we may call an option a *genuine* option when it is of the forced, living, and momentous kind.

1. A living option is one in which both hypotheses are live ones. If I say to you: "Be a theosophist or be a Mohammedan," it is probably a dead option, because for you neither hypothesis is likely to be alive. But if I say: "Be an agnostic or be a Christian," it is otherwise: trained as you are, each hypothesis makes some appeal, however small, to your belief.

2. Next, if I say to you: "Choose between going out with your umbrella or without it," I do not offer you a genuine option, for it is not forced. You can easily avoid it by not going out at all. Similarly, if I say, "Either love me or hate me," "Either call my theory true or call it false," your option is avoidable. You may remain indifferent to me, neither loving nor hating, and you may decline to offer any judgment as to my theory. But if I say, "Either accept this truth or go without it," I put on you a forced option, for there is no standing place outside of the alternative. Every dilemma based on a complete logical disjunction, with no possibility of not choosing, is an option of this forced kind.

3. Finally, if I were Dr. Nansen and proposed to you to

join my North Pole expedition, your option would be momentous; for this would probably be your only similar opportunity, and your choice now would either exclude you from the North Pole sort of immortality altogether or put at least the chance of it into your hands. He who refuses to embrace a unique opportunity loses the prize as surely as if he tried and failed. *Per contra*, the option is trivial when the opportunity is not unique, when the stake is insignificant, or when the decision is reversible if it later prove unwise. Such trivial options abound in the scientific life. A chemist finds an hypothesis live enough to spend a year in its verification: he believes in it to that extent. But if his experiments prove inconclusive either way, he is quit for his loss of time, no vital harm being done.

It will facilitate our discussion if we keep all these distinctions well in mind.

II

THE next matter to consider is the actual psychology of human opinion. When we look at certain facts, it seems as if our passional and volitional nature lay at the root of all our convictions. When we look at others, it seems as if they could do nothing when the intellect had once said its say. Let us take the latter facts up first.

Does it not seem preposterous on the very face of it to talk of our opinions being modifiable at will? Can our will either help or hinder our intellect in its perceptions of truth? Can we, by just willing it, believe that Abraham Lincoln's existence is a myth, and that the portraits of him in McClure's Magazine are all of some one else? Can we, by any effort of our will, or by any strength of wish that it were true, believe ourselves well and about when we are roaring with rheumatism in bed, or feel certain that the sum of the two one-dollar bills in our pocket must be a hundred dollars? We can *say* any of these things, but we are absolutely impotent to believe them; and of just such things is the whole fabric of the truths that we do believe in made up—matters of fact, immediate or remote, as Hume said, and relations between ideas, which are either there or not there for us if we see them so, and which if not there cannot be put there by any action of our own.

In Pascal's Thoughts there is a celebrated passage known in literature as Pascal's wager. In it he tries to force us into Christianity by reasoning as if our concern with truth resembled our concern with the stakes in a game of chance. Translated freely his words are these: You must either believe or not believe that God is—which will you do? Your human reason cannot say. A game is going on between you and the nature of things which at the day of judgment will bring out either heads or tails. Weigh what your gains and your losses would be if you should stake all you have on heads, or God's existence: if you win in such case, you gain eternal beatitude; if you lose, you lose nothing at all. If there were an infinity of chances, and only one for God in this wager, still you ought to stake your all on God; for though you surely risk a finite loss by this procedure, any finite loss is reasonable, even a certain one is reasonable, if there is but the possibility of infinite gain. Go, then, and take holy water, and have masses said; belief will come and stupefy your scruples— *Cela vous fera croire et vous abêtira.* Why should you not? At bottom, what have you to lose?

You probably feel that when religious faith expresses itself thus, in the language of the gaming-table, it is put to its last trumps. Surely Pascal's own personal belief in masses and holy water had far other springs; and this celebrated page of his is but an argument for others, a last desperate snatch at a weapon against the hardness of the unbelieving heart. We feel that a faith in masses and holy water adopted wilfully after such a mechanical calculation would lack the inner soul of faith's reality; and if we were ourselves in the place of the Deity, we should probably take particular pleasure in cutting off believers of this pattern from their infinite reward. It is evident that unless there be some pre-existing tendency to believe in masses and holy water, the option offered to the will by Pascal is not a living option. Certainly no Turk ever took to masses and holy water on its account; and even to us Protestants these means of salvation seem such foregone impossibilities that Pascal's logic, invoked for them specifically, leaves us unmoved. As well might the Mahdi write to us, saying, "I am the Expected One whom God has created in his effulgence. You shall be infinitely happy if you confess me; otherwise you shall be cut off from the light of the sun. Weigh, then, your infinite gain if I am genuine against your finite sacrifice if I am not!" His logic would be that of Pascal; but he would vainly use it on us, for the hypothesis he offers us is dead. No tendency to act on it exists in us to any degree.

The talk of believing by our volition seems, then, from one point of view, simply silly. From another point of view it is worse than silly, it is vile. When one turns to the magnificent edifice of the physical sciences, and sees how it was reared; what thousands of disinterested moral lives of men lie buried in its mere foundations; what patience and postponement, what choking down of preference, what submission to the icy laws of outer fact are wrought into its very stones and mortar; how absolutely impersonal it stands in its vast augustness—then how besotted and contemptible seems every little sentimentalist who comes blowing his voluntary smoke-wreaths, and pretending to decide things from out of his private dream! Can we wonder if those bred in the rugged and manly school of science should feel like spewing such subjectivism out of their mouths? The whole system of loyalties which grow up in the schools of science go dead against its toleration; so that it is only natural that those who have caught the scientific fever should pass over to the opposite extreme, and write sometimes as if the incorruptibly truthful intellect ought positively to prefer bitterness and unacceptableness to the heart in its cup.

> It fortifies my soul to know
> That, though I perish, Truth is so—

sings Clough, while Huxley exclaims: "My only consolation lies in the reflection that, however bad our posterity may become, so far as they hold by the plain rule of not pretending to believe what they have no reason to believe, because it may be to their advantage so to pretend [the word "pretend" is surely here redundant], they will not have reached the lowest depth of immorality." And that delicious *enfant terrible* Clifford writes: "Belief is desecrated when given to unproved and unquestioned statements for the solace and private pleasure of the believer. . . . Whoso would deserve well of his fellows in this matter will guard the purity of his belief with a very fanaticism of jealous care, lest at any time it should rest on an unworthy object, and catch a stain which can never be wiped away. . . . If [a] belief has been accepted on insufficient evidence [even though the belief be true, as Clifford on the same page explains] the pleasure is a stolen one. . . . It is sinful because it is stolen in defiance of our duty to mankind. That duty is to guard ourselves from such beliefs as from a pestilence which may shortly master our own body and then spread to the rest of the town. . . . It is wrong always, everywhere, and for every one, to believe anything upon insufficient evidence."

III

ALL this strikes one as healthy, even when expressed, as by Clifford, with somewhat too much of robustious pathos in the voice. Free-will and simple wishing do seem, in the matter of our credences, to be only fifth wheels to the coach. Yet if any one should thereupon assume that intellectual insight is what remains after wish and will and sentimental preference have taken wing, or that pure reason is what then settles our opinions, he would fly quite as directly in the teeth of the facts.

It is only our already dead hypotheses that our willing nature is unable to bring to life again. But what has made them dead for us is for the most part a previous action of our willing nature of an antagonistic kind. When I say "willing nature," I do not mean only such deliberate volitions as may have set up habits of belief that we cannot now escape from, I mean all such factors of belief as fear and hope, prejudice and passion, imitation and partisanship, the circumpressure of our caste and set. As a matter of fact we find ourselves believing, we hardly know how or why. Mr. Balfour gives the name of "authority" to all those influences, born of the intellectual climate, that make hypotheses possible or impossible for us, alive or dead. Here in this room, we all of us believe in molecules and the conservation of energy, in democracy and necessary progress, in Protestant Christianity and the duty of fighting for "the doctrine of the immortal Monroe," all for no reasons worthy of the name. We see into these matters with no more inner clearness, and probably with much less, than any disbeliever in them might possess. His unconventionality would probably have some grounds to show for its conclusions; but for us, not insight, but the *prestige* of the opinions, is what makes the spark shoot from them and light up our sleeping magazines of faith. Our reason is quite satisfied, in nine hundred and ninety-nine cases out of every thousand of us, if it can find a few arguments that will do to recite in case our credulity is criticised by some one else. Our faith is faith in some one else's faith, and in the greatest matters this is most the case. Our belief in truth itself, for instance, that there is a truth, and that our minds and it are made for each other—what is it but a passionate affirmation of desire, in which our social system backs us up? We want to have a truth; we want to believe that our experiments and studies and discussions must put us in a continually better and better position towards it; and on this line we agree to fight out our thinking lives. But if a pyrrhonistic sceptic asks us *how we know* all this, can our logic find a reply? No! certainly it cannot. It is just one volition against another, we willing to go in for life upon a trust or assumption which he, for his part, does not care to make.²

As a rule we disbelieve all facts and theories for which we have no use. Clifford's cosmic emotions find no use for Christian feelings. Huxley belabors the bishops because there is no use for sacerdotalism in his scheme of life. Newman, on the contrary, goes over to Romanism, and finds all sorts of reasons good for staying there, because a priestly system is for him an organic need and delight. Why do so few "scientists" even look at the evidence for telepathy, so called? Because they think, as a leading biologist, now dead, once said to me, that even if such a thing were true, scientists ought to band together to keep it suppressed and concealed. It would undo the uniformity of Nature and all sorts of other things without which scientists cannot carry on their pursuits. But if this very man had been shown something which as a scientist he might *do* with telepathy, he might not only have examined the evidence, but even have found it good enough. This very law which the logicians would impose upon us— if I may give the name of logicians to those who would rule out our willing nature here—is based on nothing but their own natural wish to exclude all elements for which they, in their professional quality of logicians, can find no use.

Evidently, then, our non-intellectual nature does influence our convictions. There are passional tendencies and volitions which run before and others which come after belief, and it is only the latter that are too late for the fair; and they are not too late when the previous passional work has been already in their own direction. Pascal's argument, instead of being powerless, then seems a regular clincher, and is the last stroke needed to make our faith in masses and holy water complete. The state of things is evidently far from simple; and pure insight and logic, whatever they might do ideally, are not the only things that really do produce our creeds.

IV

OUR next duty, having recognized this mixed-up state of affairs, is to ask whether it be simply reprehensible and pathological, or whether, on the contrary, we must treat it as a normal element in making up our minds. The thesis I defend is, briefly stated, this: *Our passional nature not only lawfully may, but must, decide an option between propositions, whenever it is a genuine option that cannot by its nature be decided on intellectual grounds; for to say, under such circumstances, "Do not decide, but leave the question open," is itself a passional decision—just like deciding yes or no—and is attended with the same risk of losing the truth.* The thesis thus abstractly expressed will, I trust, soon become quite clear. But I must first indulge in a bit more of preliminary work.

V

IT WILL be observed that for the purposes of this discussion we are on "dogmatic" ground—ground, I mean, which leaves systematic philosophical scepticism altogether out of account. The postulate that there is truth, and that it is the destiny of our minds to attain it, we are deliberately resolving to make, though the sceptic will not make it. We part company with him, therefore, absolutely, at this point. But the faith that truth exists, and that our minds can find it, may be held in two ways. We may talk of the *empiricist* way and of the *absolutist* way of believing in truth. The absolutists in this matter say that we not only can attain to knowing truth, but we can *know when* we have attained to knowing it; while the empiricists think that although we may attain it, we cannot infallibly know when. To *know* is one thing, and to know for certain *that* we know is another. One may hold to the first being possible without the second; hence the empiricists and the absolutists, although neither of them is a sceptic in the usual philosophic sense of the term, show very different degrees of dogmatism in their lives.

If we look at the history of opinions, we see that the empiricist tendency has largely prevailed in science, while in philosophy the absolutist tendency has had everything its own way. The characteristic sort of happiness, indeed, which philosophies yield has mainly consisted in the conviction felt by each successive school or system that by it bottom-certitude had been attained. "Other philosophies are collections of opinions, mostly false; *my* philosophy gives standing-ground forever"—who does not recognize in this the keynote of every system worthy of the name? A system, to be a system at all, must come as a *closed* system, reversible in this or that detail, perchance, but in its essential features never!

Scholastic orthodoxy, to which one must always go when one wishes to find perfectly clear statement, has beautifully elaborated this absolutist conviction in a doctrine which it calls that of "objective evidence." If, for example, I am unable to doubt that I now exist before you, that two is less than three, or that if all men are mortal then I am mortal too, it is because these things illumine my intellect irresistibly. The final ground of this objective evidence possessed by certain propositions is the *adæquatio intellectûs nostri cum rê.* The certitude it brings involves an *aptitudinem ad extorquendum certum assensum* on the part of the truth envisaged, and on the side of the subject a *quietem in cognitione,* when once the object is mentally received, that leaves no possibility of doubt behind; and in the whole transaction nothing operates but the *entitas ipsa* of the object and the *entitas ipsa* of the mind. We slouchy modern thinkers dislike to talk in Latin, indeed, we dislike to talk in set terms at all; but at bottom our own state of mind is very much like this whenever we uncritically abandon ourselves: You believe in objective evidence, and I do. Of some things we feel that we are certain: we know, and we know that we do know. There is something that gives a click inside of us, a bell that strikes twelve, when the hands of our mental clock have swept the dial and meet over the meridian hour. The greatest empiricists among us are only empiricists on reflection: when left to their instincts, they dogmatize like infallible popes. When the

Cliffords tell us how sinful it is to be Christians on such "insufficient evidence," insufficiency is really the last thing they have in mind. For them the evidence is absolutely sufficient, only it makes the other way. They believe so completely in an anti-christian order of the universe that there is no living option: Christianity is a dead hypothesis from the start.

VI

But now, since we are all such absolutists by instinct, what in our quality of students of philosophy ought we to do about the fact? Shall we espouse and indorse it? Or shall we treat it as a weakness of our nature from which we must free ourselves, if we can?

I sincerely believe that the latter course is the only one we can follow as reflective men. Objective evidence and certitude are doubtless very fine ideals to play with, but where on this moonlit and dream-visited planet are they found? I am, therefore, myself a complete empiricist so far as my theory of human knowledge goes. I live, to be sure, by the practical faith that we must go on experiencing and thinking over our experience, for only thus can our opinions grow more true; but to hold any one of them—I absolutely do not care which —as if it never could be reinterpretable or corrigible, I believe to be a tremendously mistaken attitude, and I think that the whole history of philosophy will bear me out. There is but one indefectibly certain truth, and that is the truth that pyrrhonistic scepticism itself leaves standing—the truth that the present phenomenon of consciousness exists. That, however, is the bare starting-point of knowledge, the mere admission of a stuff to be philosophized about. The various philosophies are but so many attempts at expressing what this stuff really is. And if we repair to our libraries what disagreement do we discover! Where is a certainly true answer found? Apart from abstract propositions of comparison (such as two and two are the same as four), propositions which tell us nothing by themselves about concrete reality, we find no proposition ever regarded by any one as evidently certain that has not either been called a falsehood, or at least had its truth sincerely questioned by some one else. The transcending of the axioms of geometry, not in play but in earnest, by certain of our contemporaries (as Zöllner and Charles H.

Hinton), and the rejection of the whole Aristotelian logic by the Hegelians, are striking instances in point.

No concrete test of what is really true has ever been agreed upon. Some make the criterion external to the moment of perception, putting it either in revelation, the *consensus gentium*, the instincts of the heart, or the systematized experience of the race. Others make the perceptive moment its own test— Descartes, for instance, with his clear and distinct ideas guaranteed by the veracity of God; Reid with his "common-sense;" and Kant with his forms of synthetic judgment *a priori*. The inconceivability of the opposite; the capacity to be verified by sense; the possession of complete organic unity or self-relation, realized when a thing is its own other—are standards which, in turn, have been used. The much lauded objective evidence is never triumphantly there; it is a mere aspiration or *Grenzbegriff*, marking the infinitely remote ideal of our thinking life. To claim that certain truths now possess it, is simply to say that when you think them true and they *are* true, then their evidence is objective, otherwise it is not. But practically one's conviction that the evidence one goes by is of the real objective brand, is only one more subjective opinion added to the lot. For what a contradictory array of opinions have objective evidence and absolute certitude been claimed! The world is rational through and through—its existence is an ultimate brute fact; there is a personal God—a personal God is inconceivable; there is an extra-mental physical world immediately known—the mind can only know its own ideas; a moral imperative exists—obligation is only the resultant of desires; a permanent spiritual principle is in every one—there are only shifting states of mind; there is an endless chain of causes—there is an absolute first cause; an eternal necessity—a freedom; a purpose—no purpose; a primal One —a primal Many; a universal continuity—an essential discontinuity in things; an infinity—no infinity. There is this—there is that; there is indeed nothing which some one has not thought absolutely true, while his neighbor deemed it absolutely false; and not an absolutist among them seems ever to have considered that the trouble may all the time be essential, and that the intellect, even with truth directly in its grasp, may have no infallible signal for knowing whether it be truth or no. When, indeed, one remembers that the most striking practical application to life of the doctrine of objective certitude has been the conscientious labors of the Holy Office of the Inquisition, one feels less tempted than ever to lend the doctrine a respectful ear.

But please observe, now, that when as empiricists we give up the doctrine of objective certitude, we do not thereby give up the quest or hope of truth itself. We still pin our faith on its existence, and still believe that we gain an ever better position towards it by systematically continuing to roll up experiences and think. Our great difference from the scholastic lies in the way we face. The strength of his system lies in the principles, the origin, the *terminus a quo* of his thought; for us the strength is in the outcome, the upshot, the *terminus ad quem*. Not where it comes from but what it leads to is to decide. It matters not to an empiricist from what quarter an hypothesis may come to him: he may have acquired it by fair means or by foul; passion may have whispered or accident suggested it; but if the total drift of thinking continues to confirm it, that is what he means by its being true.

VII

ONE more point, small but important, and our preliminaries are done. There are two ways of looking at our duty in the matter of opinion—ways entirely different, and yet ways about whose difference the theory of knowledge seems hitherto to have shown very little concern. *We must know the truth; and we must avoid error*—these are our first and great commandments as would-be knowers; but they are not two ways of stating an identical commandment, they are two separable laws. Although it may indeed happen that when we believe the truth A, we escape as an incidental consequence from believing the falsehood B, it hardly ever happens that by merely disbelieving B we necessarily believe A. We may in escaping B fall into believing other falsehoods, C or D, just as bad as B; or we may escape B by not believing anything at all, not even A.

Believe truth! Shun error!—these, we see, are two materially different laws; and by choosing between them we may end by coloring differently our whole intellectual life. We may regard the chase for truth as paramount, and the avoidance of error as secondary; or we may, on the other hand, treat the avoidance of error as more imperative, and let truth take its chance. Clifford, in the instructive passage which I have quoted, exhorts us to the latter course. Believe nothing, he tells us, keep your mind in suspense forever, rather than by closing it on insufficient evidence incur the awful risk of believing lies. You, on the other hand, may think that the risk of being in error is a very small matter when compared with the blessings of real knowledge, and be ready to be duped many times in your investigation rather than postpone indefinitely the chance of guessing true. I myself find it impossible to go with Clifford. We must remember that these feelings of our duty about either truth or error are in any case only expressions of our passional life. Biologically considered, our minds are as ready to grind out falsehood as veracity, and he who says, "Better go without belief forever than believe a lie;" merely shows his own preponderant private horror of becoming a dupe. He may be critical of many of his desires and fears, but this fear he slavishly obeys. He cannot imagine any one questioning its binding force. For my own part, I have also a horror of being duped; but I can believe that worse things than being duped may happen to a man in this world: so Clifford's exhortation has to my ears a thoroughly fantastic sound. It is like a general informing his soldiers that it is better to keep out of battle forever than to risk a single wound. Not so are victories either over enemies or over nature gained. Our errors are surely not such awfully solemn things. In a world where we are so certain to incur them in spite of all our caution, a certain lightness of heart seems healthier than this excessive nervousness on their behalf. At any rate, it seems the fittest thing for the empiricist philosopher.

VIII

AND now, after all this introduction, let us go straight at our question. I have said, and now repeat it, that not only as a matter of fact do we find our passional nature influencing us in our opinions, but that there are some options between opinions in which this influence must be regarded both as an inevitable and as a lawful determinant of our choice.

I fear here that some of you my hearers will begin to scent danger, and lend an inhospitable ear. Two first steps of passion you have indeed had to admit as necessary—we must think so as to avoid dupery, and we must think so as to gain truth; but the surest path to those ideal consummations, you will probably consider, is from now onwards to take no further passional step.

Well, of course, I agree as far as the facts will allow. Wherever the option between losing truth and gaining it is not momentous, we can throw the chance of *gaining truth* away, and at any rate save ourselves from any chance of *believing falsehood*, by not making up our minds at all till objective evidence has come. In scientific questions, this is almost always the case; and even in human affairs in general, the need of acting is seldom so urgent that a false belief to act on is better than no belief at all. Law courts, indeed, have to decide on the best evidence attainable for the moment, because a judge's duty is to make law as well as to ascertain it, and (as a learned judge once said to me) few cases are worth spending much time over: the great thing is to have them decided on *any* acceptable principle, and got out of the way. But in our dealings with objective nature we obviously are recorders, not makers, of the truth; and decisions for the mere sake of deciding promptly and getting on to the next business would be wholly out of place. Throughout the breadth of physical nature facts are what they are quite independently of us, and seldom is there any such hurry about them that the risks of being duped by believing a premature theory need be faced. The questions here are always trivial options, the hypotheses are hardly living (at any rate not living for us spectators), the choice between believing truth or falsehood is seldom forced. The attitude of sceptical balance is therefore the absolutely wise one if we would escape mistakes. What difference, indeed, does it make to most of us whether we have or have not a theory of the Röntgen rays, whether we believe or not in mind-stuff, or have a conviction about the causality of conscious states? It makes no difference. Such options are not forced on us. On every account it is better not to make them, but still keep weighing reasons *pro et contra* with an indifferent hand.

I speak, of course, here of the purely judging mind. For purposes of discovery such indifference is to be less highly recommended, and science would be far less advanced than she is if the passionate desires of individuals to get their own faiths confirmed had been kept out of the game. See for example the sagacity which Spencer and Weismann now display. On the other hand, if you want an absolute duffer in an investigation, you must, after all, take the man who has no interest whatever in its results: he is the warranted incapable, the positive fool. The most useful investigator, because the most sensitive observer, is always he whose eager interest in one side of the question is balanced by an equally keen nervousness lest he become deceived.[3] Science has organized this nervousness into a regular *technique*, her so-called method of verification; and she has fallen so deeply in love with the method that one may even say she has ceased to care for truth by itself at all. It is only truth as technically verified that interests her. The truth of truths might come in merely affirmative form, and she would decline to touch it. Such truth as that, she might repeat with Clifford, would be stolen in defiance of her duty to mankind. Human passions, however, are stronger than technical rules. *"Le cœur a ses raisons,"* as Pascal says, *"que la raison ne connaît pas;"* and however indifferent to all but the bare rules of the game the umpire, the abstract intellect, may be, the concrete players who furnish him the materials to judge of are usually, each one of them, in love with some pet "live hypothesis" of his own. Let us agree, however, that wherever there is no forced option, the dispassionately judicial intellect with no pet hypothesis, saving us, as it does, from dupery at any rate, ought to be our ideal.

The question next arises: Are there not somewhere forced options in our speculative questions, and can we (as men who may be interested at least as much in positively gaining truth as in merely escaping dupery) always wait with impunity till the coercive evidence shall have arrived? It seems *a priori* improbable that the truth should be so nicely adjusted to our needs and powers as that. In the great boarding-house of nature, the cakes and the butter and the syrup seldom come out so even and leave the plates so clean. Indeed, we should view them with scientific suspicion if they did.

IX

Moral questions immediately present themselves as questions whose solution cannot wait for sensible proof. A moral question is a question not of what sensibly exists, but of what is good, or would be good if it did exist. Science can tell us what exists; but to compare the *worths*, both of what exists and of what does not exist, we must consult not science, but what Pascal calls our heart. Science herself consults her heart when she lays it down that the infinite ascertainment of fact and correction of false belief are the supreme goods for man. Challenge the statement, and science can only repeat it oracularly, or else prove it by showing that such ascertainment and correction bring man all sorts of other goods which man's heart in turn declares. The question of having moral beliefs at all or not having them is decided by our will. Are our moral preferences true or false, or are they only odd biological phenomena, making things good or bad for *us*, but in themselves indifferent? How can your pure intellect decide? If your heart does not *want* a world of moral reality, your head will assuredly never make you believe in one. Mephistophelian scepticism, indeed, will satisfy the head's play-instincts much better than any rigorous idealism can. Some men (even at the student age) are so naturally cool-hearted that the moralistic hypothesis never has for them any pungent life, and in their supercilious presence the hot young moralist always feels strangely ill at ease. The appearance of knowingness is on their side, of *naïveté* and gullibility on his. Yet, in the inarticulate heart of him, he clings to it that he is not a dupe, and that there is a realm in which (as Emerson says) all their wit and intellectual superiority is no better than the cunning of a fox. Moral scepticism can no more be refuted or proved by logic than intellectual scepticism can. When we stick to it that there *is* truth (be it of either kind), we do so with our whole nature, and resolve to stand or fall by the results. The sceptic with his whole nature adopts the doubting attitude; but which of us is the wiser, Omniscience only knows.

Turn now from these wide questions of good to a certain class of questions of fact, questions concerning personal relations, states of mind between one man and another. *Do you like me or not?*—for example. Whether you do or not depends, in countless instances, on whether I meet you half-way, am willing to assume that you must like me, and show you trust and expectation. The previous faith on my part in your liking's existence is in such cases what makes your liking come. But if I stand aloof, and refuse to budge an inch until I have objective evidence, until you shall have done something apt, as the absolutists say, *ad extorquendum assensum meum*, ten to one your liking never comes. How many women's hearts are vanquished by the mere sanguine insistence of some man that they *must* love him! he will not consent to the hypothesis that they cannot. The desire for a certain kind of truth here brings about that special truth's existence; and so it is in innumerable cases of other sorts. Who gains promotions, boons, appointments, but the man in whose life they are seen to play the part of live hypotheses, who discounts them, sacrifices other things for their sake before they have come, and takes risks for them in advance? His faith acts on the powers above him as a claim, and creates its own verification.

A social organism of any sort whatever, large or small, is what it is because each member proceeds to his own duty with a trust that the other members will simultaneously do theirs. Wherever a desired result is achieved by the co-operation of many independent persons, its existence as a fact is a pure consequence of the precursive faith in one another of those immediately concerned. A government, an army, a commercial system, a ship, a college, an athletic team, all exist on this condition, without which not only is nothing achieved, but nothing is even attempted. A whole train of passengers (individually brave enough) will be looted by a few highwaymen, simply because the latter can count on one another, while each passenger fears that if he makes a movement of resistance, he will be shot before any one else backs him up. If we believed that the whole car-full would rise at once with us, we should each severally rise, and train-robbing would never even be attempted. There are, then, cases where a fact cannot come at all unless a preliminary faith exists in its coming. *And where faith in a fact can help create the fact,* that would be an insane logic which should say that faith running ahead of scientific evidence is the "lowest kind of immorality" into which a thinking being can fall. Yet such is the logic by which our scientific absolutists pretend to regulate our lives!

X

IN TRUTHS dependent on our personal action, then, faith based on desire is certainly a lawful and possibly an indispensable thing.

But now, it will be said, these are all childish human cases, and have nothing to do with great cosmical matters, like the question of religious faith. Let us then pass on to that. Religions differ so much in their accidents that in discussing the religious question we must make it very generic and broad. What then do we now mean by the religious hypothesis? Science says things are; morality says some things are better than other things; and religion says essentially two things.

First, she says that the best things are the more eternal things, the overlapping things, the things in the universe that throw the last stone, so to speak, and say the final word. "Perfection is eternal"—this phrase of Charles Secrétan seems a good way of putting this first affirmation of religion, an affirmation which obviously cannot yet be verified scientifically at all.

The second affirmation of religion is that we are better off even now if we believe her first affirmation to be true.

Now, let us consider what the logical elements of this situation are *in case the religious hypothesis in both its branches be really true.* (Of course, we must admit that possibility at the outset. If we are to discuss the question at all, it must involve a living option. If for any of you religion be a hypothesis that cannot, by any living possibility be true, then you need go no farther. I speak to the "saving remnant" alone.) So proceeding, we see, first that religion offers itself as a *momentous* option. We are supposed to gain, even now, by our belief, and to lose by our nonbelief, a certain vital good. Secondly, religion is a *forced* option, so far as that good goes. We cannot escape the issue by remaining sceptical and waiting for more light, because, although we do avoid error in that way *if religion be untrue,* we lose the good, *if it be true,* just as certainly as if we positively chose to disbelieve. It is as if a man should hesitate indefinitely to ask a certain woman to marry him because he was not perfectly sure that she would prove an angel after he brought her home. Would he not cut himself off from that particular angel-possibility as decisively as if he went and married some one else? Scepticism, then, is not avoidance of option; it is option of a certain particular kind of risk. *Better risk loss of truth than chance of error*— that is your faith-vetoer's exact position. He is actively playing his stake as much as the believer is; he is backing the field against the religious hypothesis, just as the believer is backing the religious hypothesis against the field. To preach scepticism to us as a duty until "sufficient evidence" for religion be found, is tantamount therefore to telling us, when in presence of the religious hypothesis, that to yield to our fear of its being error is wiser and better than to yield to our hope that it may be true. It is not intellect against all passions, then; it is only intellect with one passion laying down its law. And by what, forsooth, is the supreme wisdom of this passion warranted? Dupery for dupery, what proof is there that dupery through hope is so much worse than dupery through fear? I, for one, can see no proof; and I simply refuse obedience to the scientist's command to imitate his kind of option, in a case where my own stake is important enough to give me the right to choose my own form of risk. If religion be true and the evidence for it be still insufficient, I do not wish, by putting your extinguisher upon my nature (which feels to me as if it had after all some business in this matter), to forfeit my sole chance in life of getting upon the winning side—that chance depending, of course, on my willingness to run the risk of acting as if my passional need of taking the world religiously might be prophetic and right.

All this is on the supposition that it really may be prophetic and right, and that, even to us who are discussing the matter, religion is a live hypothesis which may be true. Now, to most of us religion comes in a still further way that makes a veto on our active faith even more illogical. The more perfect and more eternal aspect of the universe is represented in our religions as having personal form. The universe is no longer a mere *It* to us, but a *Thou*, if we are religious; and any relation that may be possible from person to person might be possible here. For instance, although in one sense we are passive portions of the universe, in another we show a curious autonomy, as if we were small active centres on our own account. We feel, too, as if the appeal of religion to us were made to our own active good-will, as if evidence might be forever withheld from us unless we met the hypothesis half-way. To take a trivial illustration: just as a man who in a company of gentlemen made no advances, asked a warrant for every concession, and believed no one's word without proof, would cut himself off by such churlishness from all the social rewards that a more trusting spirit would earn—so here, one who should shut himself up in snarling logicality and try to make the gods extort his recognition willy-nilly, or not get it at all, might cut himself off forever from his only opportunity of making the gods' acquaintance. This feeling, forced on us we know not whence, that by obstinately believing that there are gods (although not to do so would be so easy both for our logic and our life) we are doing the universe the deepest service we can, seems part of the living essence of the religious hypothesis. If the hypothesis *were* true in all its parts, including this one, then pure intellectualism, with its veto on our making willing advances, would be an absurdity; and some participation of our sympathetic nature would be logically required. I, therefore, for one, cannot see my way to accepting the agnostic rules for truth-seeking, or wilfully agree to keep my willing nature out of the game. I cannot do so for this plain reason, that *a rule of thinking which would absolutely prevent me from acknowledging certain kinds of truth if those kinds of truth were really there, would be an irrational rule*. That for me is the long and short of the formal logic of the situation, no matter what the kinds of truth might materially be.

I confess I do not see how this logic can be escaped. But sad experience makes me fear that some of you may still shrink from radically saying with me, *in abstracto*, that we have the right to believe at our own risk any hypothesis that is live enough to tempt our will. I suspect, however, that if this is so, it is because you have got away from the abstract logical point of view altogether, and are thinking (perhaps without realizing it) of some particular religious hypothesis which for you is dead. The freedom to "believe what we will" you apply to the case of some patent superstition; and the faith you think of is the faith defined by the schoolboy when he said, "Faith is when you believe something that you know ain't true." I can only repeat that this is misapprehension. *In concreto*, the freedom to believe can only cover living options which the intellect of the individual cannot by itself resolve; and living options never seem absurdities to him who has them to consider. When I look at the religious question as it really puts itself to concrete men, and when I think of all the possibilities which both practically and theoretically it involves, then this command that we shall put a stopper on our heart, instincts, and courage, and *wait*—acting of course meanwhile more or less as if religion were *not* true '—till doomsday, or till such time as our intellect and senses working together may have raked in evidence enough—this command, I say, seems to me the queerest idol ever manufactured in the philosophic cave. Were we scholastic absolutists, there might be more excuse. If we had an infallible intellect with its objective certitudes, we might feel ourselves disloyal to such a perfect organ of knowledge in not trusting to it exclusively, in not waiting for its releasing word. But if we are empiricists, if we believe that no bell in us tolls to let us know for certain when truth is in our grasp, then it seems a piece of idle fantasticality to preach so solemnly our duty of waiting for the bell. Indeed we *may* wait if we will—I hope you do not think that I am denying that—but if we do so, we do so at our peril as much as if we believed. In either case we *act*, taking our life in our hands. No one of us ought to issue vetoes to the other, nor should we bandy words of abuse. We ought, on the contrary, delicately and profoundly to respect one another's mental freedom: then only shall we bring about the intellectual republic; then only shall we have that spirit of inner tolerance without which all our outer tolerance is soulless, and which is empiricism's glory; then only shall we live and let live, in speculative as well as in practical things.

I began by a reference to Fitz-James Stephen; let me end by a quotation from him. "What do you think of yourself? What do you think of the world? . . . These are questions with which all must deal as it seems good to them. They are riddles of the Sphinx, and in some way or other we must deal with them. . . . In all important transactions of life we have to take a leap in the dark. . . . If we decide to leave the riddles unanswered, that is a choice; if we waver in our answer, that, too, is a choice: but whatever choice we make, we make it at our peril. If a man chooses to turn his back altogether on God and the future, no one can prevent him; no one can show beyond reasonable doubt that he is mistaken. If a man thinks otherwise and acts as he thinks, I do not see that any one can prove that *he* is mistaken. Each must act as he thinks best; and if he is wrong, so much the worse for him. We stand on a mountain pass in the midst of whirling snow and blinding mist, through which we get glimpses now and then of paths which may be deceptive. If we take the wrong road we shall be dashed to pieces. We do not certainly know whether there is any right one. What must we do? 'Be strong and of a good courage.' Act for the best, hope for the best, and take what comes. . . . If death ends all, we cannot meet death better." [5]

THE MORAL PHILOSOPHER
AND THE MORAL LIFE [1]

The main purpose of this paper is to show that there is
no such thing possible as an ethical philosophy dogmatically
made up in advance. We all help to determine the content
of ethical philosophy so far as we contribute to the race's moral
life. In other words, there can be no final truth in ethics any
more than in physics, until the last man has had his experience
and said his say. In the one case as in the other, however, the
hypotheses which we now make while waiting, and the acts
to which they prompt us, are among the indispensable conditions which determine what that "say" shall be.

First of all, what is the position of him who seeks an ethical
philosophy? To begin with, he must be distinguished from all
those who are satisfied to be ethical sceptics. He *will* not be
a sceptic; therefore so far from ethical scepticism being one
possible fruit of ethical philosophizing, it can only be regarded as that residual alternative to all philosophy which
from the outset menaces every would-be philosopher who may
give up the quest discouraged, and renounce his original aim.
That aim is to find an account of the moral relations that
obtain among things, which will weave them into the unity
of a stable system, and make of the world what one may call
a genuine universe from the ethical point of view. So far as
the world resists reduction to the form of unity, so far as
ethical propositions seem unstable, so far does the philosopher
fail of his ideal. The subject-matter of his study is the ideals
he finds existing in the world; the purpose which guides him
is this ideal of his own, of getting them into a certain form.
This ideal is thus a factor in ethical philosophy whose legitimate presence must never be overlooked; it is a positive contribution which the philosopher himself necessarily makes to

the problem. But it is his only positive contribution. At the outset of his inquiry he ought to have no other ideals. Were he interested peculiarly in the triumph of any one kind of good, he would *pro tanto* cease to be a judicial investigator, and become an advocate for some limited element of the case.

There are three questions in ethics which must be kept apart. Let them be called respectively the *psychological* question, the *metaphysical* question, and the *casuistic* question. The psychological question asks after the historical *origin* of our moral ideas and judgments; the metaphysical question asks what the very *meaning* of the words "good," "ill," and "obligation" are; the casuistic question asks what is the *measure* of the various goods and ills which men recognize, so that the philosopher may settle the true order of human obligations.

I

THE psychological question is for most disputants the only question. When your ordinary doctor of divinity has proved to his own satisfaction that an altogether unique faculty called "conscience" must be postulated to tell us what is right and what is wrong; or when your popular-science enthusiast has proclaimed that "apriorism" is an exploded superstition, and that our moral judgments have gradually resulted from the teaching of the environment, each of these persons thinks that ethics is settled and nothing more is to be said. The familiar pair of names, Intuitionist and Evolutionist, so commonly used now to connote all possible differences in ethical opinion, really refer to the psychological question alone. The discussion of this question hinges so much upon particular details that it is impossible to enter upon it at all within the limits of this paper. I will therefore only express dogmatically my own belief, which is this—that the Benthams, the Mills, and the Bains have done a lasting service in taking so many of our human ideals and showing how they must have arisen from the association with acts of simple bodily pleasures and reliefs from pain. Association with many remote pleasures will unquestionably make a thing significant of goodness in our minds; and the more vaguely the goodness is conceived of, the more mysterious will its source appear to be. But it is surely impossible to explain all our sentiments and preferences in this simple way. The more minutely psychology studies human nature, the more clearly it finds there traces of secondary affections, relating the impressions of the environment with one another and with our impulses in quite different ways from those mere associations of coexistence and succession which are practically all that pure empiricism can admit. Take the love of drunkenness; take bashfulness, the terror of high places, the tendency to sea-sickness, to faint at the sight of blood, the susceptibility to musical sounds; take the emotion of the comical, the passion for poetry, for mathematics, or for metaphysics—no one of these things can be wholly explained by either association or utility. They go with other things that can be so explained, no doubt; and some of them are prophetic of future utilities, since there is nothing in us for which some use may not be found. But their origin is in incidental complications to our cerebral structure, a structure whose original features arose with no reference to the perception of such discords and harmonies as these.

Well, a vast number of our moral perceptions also are certainly of this secondary and brain-born kind. They deal with directly felt fitnesses between things, and often fly in the teeth of all the prepossessions of habit and presumptions of utility. The moment you get beyond the coarser and more commonplace moral maxims, the Decalogues and Poor Richard's Almanacs, you fall into schemes and positions which to the eye of common-sense are fantastic and overstrained. The sense for abstract justice which some persons have is as eccentric a variation, from the natural-history point of view, as is the passion for music or for the higher philosophical consistencies which consumes the soul of others. The feeling of the inward dignity of certain spiritual attitudes, as peace, serenity, simplicity, veracity; and of the essential vulgarity of others, as querulousness, anxiety, egoistic fussiness, etc.— are quite inexplicable except by an innate preference of the more ideal attitude for its own pure sake. The nobler thing *tastes* better, and that is all that we can say. "Experience" of consequences may truly teach us what things are *wicked*, but what have consequences to do with what is *mean* and *vulgar?* If a man has shot his wife's paramour, by reason of what subtile repugnancy in things is it that we are so disgusted when we hear that the wife and the husband have made it up and are living comfortably together again? Or if the hypothesis were offered us of a world in which Messrs. Fourier's and Bellamy's and Morris's utopias should all be outdone, and millions kept permanently happy on the one simple condition that a certain lost soul on the far-off edge of things should lead a life of lonely torture, what except a specifical and independent sort of emotion can it be which would make us immediately feel, even though an impulse arose within us to clutch at the happiness so offered, how hideous a thing would be its enjoyment when deliberately accepted as the fruit of such a bargain? To what, once more, but subtle brain-born feelings of discord can be due all these recent protests against the entire race-tradition of retributive justice?—I refer to Tolstoï with his ideas of nonresistance, to Mr. Bellamy with his substitution of oblivion for repentance (in his novel of Dr. Heidenhain's Process), to M. Guyau with his radical condemnation of the punitive ideal. All these subtleties of the moral sensibility go as much beyond what can be ciphered out from the "laws of association" as the delicacies of sentiment possible between a pair of young lovers go beyond such precepts of the "etiquette to be observed during engagement" as are printed in manuals of social form.

No! Purely inward forces are certainly at work here. All the higher, more penetrating ideals are revolutionary. They present themselves far less in the guise of effects of past experience than in that of probable causes of future experience, factors to which the environment and the lessons it has so far taught us must learn to bend.

This is all I can say of the psychological question now. In the last chapter of a recent work [2] I have sought to prove in a general way the existence, in our thought, of relations which do not merely repeat the couplings of experience. Our ideals have certainly many sources. They are not all explicable as signifying corporeal pleasures to be gained, and pains to be escaped. And for having so constantly perceived this psychological fact, we must applaud the intuitionist school. Whether or not such applause must be extended to that school's other characteristics will appear as we take up the following questions.

The next one in order is the metaphysical question, of what we mean by the words "obligation," "good," and "ill."

II

FIRST of all, it appears that such words can have no application or relevancy in a world in which no sentient life exists. Imagine an absolutely material world, containing only physical and chemical facts, and existing from eternity without a God, without even an interested spectator: would there be any sense in saying of that world that one of its states is better than another? Or if there were two such worlds possible, would there be any rhyme or reason in calling one good and the other bad—good or bad positively, I mean, and apart from the fact that one might relate itself better than the other to the philosopher's private interests? But we must leave these private interests out of the account, for the philosopher is a mental fact, and we are asking whether goods and evils and obligations exist in physical facts *per se*. Surely there is no *status* for good and evil to exist in, in a purely insentient world. How can one physical fact, considered simply as a physical fact, be "better" than another? Betterness is not a physical relation. In its mere material capacity, a thing can no more be good or bad than it can be pleasant or painful. Good for what? Good for the production of another physical fact, do you say? But what in a purely physical universe demands the production of that other fact? Physical facts simply *are* or are *not;* and neither when present or absent, can they be supposed to make demands. If they do, they can only do so by having desires; and then they have ceased to be purely physical facts, and have become facts of conscious sensibility. Goodness, badness, and obligation must be *realized* somewhere in order really to exist; and the first step in ethical philosophy is to see that no merely inorganic "nature of things" can realize them. Neither moral relations nor the moral law can swing *in vacuo*. Their only habitat can be a mind which feels them; and no world composed of merely physical facts can possibly be a world to which ethical propositions apply.

The moment one sentient being, however, is made a part of the universe, there is a chance for goods and evils really to exist. Moral relations now have their *status*, in that being's consciousness. So far as he feels anything to be good, he *makes* it good. It *is* good, for him; and being good for him, is absolutely good, for he is the sole creator of values in that universe, and outside of his opinion things have no moral character at all.

In such a universe as that it would of course be absurd to raise the question of whether the solitary thinker's judgments of good and ill are true or not. Truth supposes a standard outside of the thinker to which he must conform; but here the thinker is a sort of divinity, subject to no higher judge. Let us call the supposed universe which he inhabits a *moral solitude*. In such a moral solitude it is clear that there can be no outward obligation, and that the only trouble the god-like thinker is liable to have will be over the consistency of his own several ideals with one another. Some of these will no doubt be more pungent and appealing than the rest, their goodness will have a profounder, more penetrating taste; they will return to haunt him with more obstinate regrets if violated. So the thinker will have to order his life with them as its chief determinants, or else remain inwardly discordant and unhappy. Into whatever equilibrium he may settle, though, and however he may straighten out his system, it will be a right system; for beyond the facts of his own sub-jectivity there is nothing moral in the world.

If now we introduce a second thinker with his likes and dislikes into the universe, the ethical situation becomes much more complex, and several possibilities are immediately seen to obtain.

One of these is that the thinkers may ignore each other's attitude about good and evil altogether, and each continue to indulge his own preferences, indifferent to what the other may feel or do. In such a case we have a world with twice as much of the ethical quality in it as our moral solitude, only it is without ethical unity. The same object is good or bad there, according as you measure it by the view which this one or that one of the thinkers takes. Nor can you find any possible ground in such a world for saying that one thinker's opinion is more correct than the other's, or that either has the truer moral sense. Such a world, in short, is not a moral universe but a moral dualism. Not only is there no single point of view within it from which the values of things can be unequivocally judged, but there is not even a demand for such a point of view, since the two thinkers are supposed to be indifferent to each other's thoughts and acts. Multiply the thinkers into a pluralism, and we find realized for us in the ethical sphere something like that world which the antique sceptics conceived of—in which individual minds are the measures of all things, and in which no one "objective" truth, but only a multitude of "subjective" opinions, can be found.

But this is the kind of world with which the philosopher, so long as he holds to the hope of a philosophy, will not put up. Among the various ideals represented, there must be, he thinks, some which have the more truth or authority; and to these the others *ought* to yield, so that system and subordination may reign. Here in the word "ought" the notion of *obligation* comes emphatically into view, and the next thing in order must be to make its meaning clear.

Since the outcome of the discussion so far has been to show us that nothing can be good or right except so far as some consciousness feels it to be good or thinks it to be right, we perceive on the very threshold that the real superiority and authority which are postulated by the philosopher to reside in some of the opinions, and the really inferior character which he supposes must belong to others, cannot be explained by any abstract moral "nature of things" existing antecedently to the concrete thinkers themselves with their ideals. Like the positive attributes good and bad, the comparative ones better and worse must be *realized* in order to be real. If one ideal judgment be objectively better than another, that betterness must be made flesh by being lodged concretely in some -one's actual perception. It cannot float in the atmosphere, for it is not a sort of meteorological phenomenon, like the aurora borealis or the zodiacal light. Its *esse* is *percipi,* like the *esse* of the ideals themselves between which it obtains. The philosopher, therefore, who seeks to know which ideal ought to have supreme weight and which one ought to be subordinated, must trace the *ought* itself to the *de facto* constitution of some existing consciousness, behind which, as one of the data of the universe, he as a purely ethical philosopher is unable to go. This consciousness must make the one ideal right by feeling it to be right, the other wrong by feeling it to be wrong. But now what particular consciousness in the universe *can* enjoy this prerogative of obliging others to conform to a rule which it lays down?

If one of the thinkers were obviously divine, while all the rest were human, there would probably be no practical dispute about the matter. The divine thought would be the model, to which the others should conform. But still the theoretic question would remain, What is the ground of the obligation, even here?

In our first essays at answering this question, there is an inevitable tendency to slip into an assumption which ordinary men follow when they are disputing with one another about questions of good and bad. They imagine an abstract moral order in which the objective truth resides; and each tries to prove that this pre-existing order is more accurately reflected in his own ideas than in those of his adversary. It is because one disputant is backed by this overarching abstract order that we think the other should submit. Even so, when it is a question no longer of two finite thinkers, but of God and ourselves—we follow our usual habit, and imagine a sort of *de jure* relation, which antedates and overarches the mere facts, and would make it right that we should conform our thoughts to God's thoughts, even though he made no claim to that effect, and though we preferred *de facto* to go on thinking for ourselves.

But the moment we take a steady look at the question, *we see not only that without a claim actually made by some concrete person there can be no obligation, but that there is some obligation wherever there is a claim.* Claim and obligation are, in fact, coextensive terms; they cover each other exactly. Our ordinary attitude of regarding ourselves as subject to an overarching system of moral relations, true "in themselves," is therefore either an out-and-out superstition, or else it must be treated as a merely provisional abstraction from that real Thinker in whose actual demand upon us to think as he does our obligation must be ultimately based. In a theistic-ethical philosophy that thinker in question is, of course, the Deity to whom the existence of the universe is due.

I know well how hard it is for those who are accustomed to what I have called the superstitious view, to realize that every *de facto* claim creates in so far forth an obligation. We inveterately think that something which we call the "validity" of the claim is what gives to it its obligatory character, and that this validity is something outside of the claim's mere existence as a matter of fact. It rains down upon the claim, we think, from some sublime dimension of being, which the moral law inhabits, much as upon the steel of the compass-needle the influence of the Pole rains down from out of the starry heavens. But again, how can such an inorganic abstract character of imperativeness, additional to the imperativeness which is in the concrete claim itself, *exist?* Take any demand, however slight, which any creature, however weak, may make. Ought it not, for its own sole sake, to be satisfied? If not, prove why not. The only possible kind of proof you could adduce would be the exhibition of another creature who should make a demand that ran the other way. The only possible reason there can be why any phenomenon ought to exist is that such a phenomenon actually is desired. Any desire is imperative to the extent of its amount; it *makes* itself valid by the fact that it exists at all. Some desires, truly enough, are small desires; they are put forward by insignificant persons, and we customarily make light of the obligations which they bring. But the fact that such personal demands as these impose small obligations does not keep the largest obligations from being personal demands.

If we must talk impersonally, to be sure we can say that "the universe" requires, exacts, or makes obligatory such or such an action, whenever it expresses itself through the desires of such or such a creature. But it is better not to talk about the universe in this personified way, unless we believe in a universal or divine consciousness which actually exists. If there be such a consciousness, then its demands carry the most of obligation simply because they are the greatest in amount. But it is even then not *abstractly* right that we should respect them. It is only *concretely* right, or right after the fact, and by virtue of the fact, that they are actually made. Suppose we do not respect them, as seems largely to be the case in this queer world. That ought not to be, we say; that is wrong. But in what way is this fact of wrongness made more acceptable or intelligible when we imagine it to consist rather in the laceration of an *à priori* ideal order than in the disappointment of a living personal God? Do we, perhaps, think that we cover God and protect him and make his impotence over us less ultimate, when we back him up with this *à priori* blanket from which he may draw some warmth of further appeal? But the only force of appeal to *us*, which either a living God or an abstract ideal order can wield, is found in the "everlasting ruby vaults" of our own human hearts, as they happen to beat responsive and not irresponsive to the claim. So far as they do feel it when made by a living consciousness, it is life answering to life. A claim thus livingly acknowledged is acknowledged with a solidity and fulness which no thought of an "ideal" backing can render more complete; while if, on the other hand, the heart's response is withheld, the stubborn phenomenon is there of an impotence in the claims which the universe embodies, which no talk about an eternal nature of things can gloze over or dispel. An ineffective *à priori* order is as impotent a thing as an ineffective God; and in the eye of philosophy, it is as hard a thing to explain.

We may now consider that what we distinguished as the metaphysical question in ethical philosophy is sufficiently answered, and that we have learned what the words "good," "bad," and "obligation" severally mean. They mean no absolute natures, independent of personal support. They are objects of feeling and desire, which have no foothold or anchorage in Being, apart from the existence of actually living minds.

Wherever such minds exist, with judgments of good and ill, and demands upon one another, there is an ethical world in its essential features. Were all other things, gods and men and starry heavens, blotted out from this universe, and were there left but one rock with two loving souls upon it, that rock would have as thoroughly moral a constitution as any possible world which the eternities and immensities could harbor. It would be a tragic constitution, because the rock's inhabitants would die. But while they lived, there would be real good things and real bad things in the universe; there would be obligations, claims, and expectations; obediences, refusals, and disappointments; compunctions and longings for harmony to come again, and inward peace of conscience when it was restored; there would, in short, be a moral life, whose active energy would have no limit but the intensity of interest in each other with which the hero and heroine might be endowed.

We, on this terrestrial globe, so far as the visible facts go, are just like the inhabitants of such a rock. Whether a God exist, or whether no God exist, in yon blue heaven above us bent, we form at any rate an ethical republic here below. And the first reflection which this leads to is that ethics have as genuine and real a foothold in a universe where the highest consciousness is human, as in a universe where there is a God as well. "The religion of humanity" affords a basis for ethics as well as theism does. Whether the purely human system can gratify the philosopher's demand as well as the other is a different question, which we ourselves must answer ere we close.

III

THE last fundamental question in Ethics was, it will be remembered, the *casuistic* question. Here we are, in a world where the existence of a divine thinker has been and perhaps always will be doubted by some of the lookers-on, and where, in spite of the presence of a large number of ideals in which human beings agree, there are a mass of others about which no general consensus obtains. It is hardly necessary to present a literary picture of this, for the facts are too well known. The wars of the flesh and the spirit in each man, the concupiscences of different individuals pursuing the same unshareable material or social prizes, the ideals which contrast so according to races, circumstances, temperaments, philosophical beliefs, etc. —all form a maze of apparently inextricable confusion with no obvious Ariadne's thread to lead one out. Yet the philosopher, just because he is a philosopher, adds his own peculiar ideal to the confusion (with which if he were willing to be a sceptic he would be passably content), and insists that over all these individual opinions there is a *system of truth* which he can discover if he only takes sufficient pains.

We stand ourselves at present in the place of that philosopher, and must not fail to realize all the features that the situation comports. In the first place we will not be sceptics; we hold to it that there is a truth to be ascertained. But in the second place we have just gained the insight that that truth cannot be a self-proclaiming set of laws, or an abstract "moral reason," but can only exist in act, or in the shape of an opinion held by some thinker really to be found. There is, however, no visible thinker invested with authority. Shall we then simply proclaim our own ideals as the lawgiving ones? No; for if we are true philosophers we must throw our own spontaneous ideals, even the dearest, impartially in with that total mass of ideals which are fairly to be judged. But how then can we as philosophers ever find a test; how avoid complete moral scepticism on the one hand, and on the other escape bringing a wayward personal standard of our own along with us, on which we simply pin our faith?

The dilemma is a hard one, nor does it grow a bit more easy as we revolve it in our minds. The entire undertaking of the philosopher obliges him to seek an impartial test. That test, however, must be incarnated in the demand of some actually existent person; and how can he pick out the person save by an act in which his own sympathies and prepossessions are implied?

One method indeed presents itself, and has as a matter of history been taken by the more serious ethical schools. If the heap of things demanded proved on inspection less chaotic than at first they seemed, if they furnished their own relative test and measure, then the casuistic problem would be solved. If it were found that all goods *quâ* goods contained a common essence, then the amount of this essence involved in any one good would show its rank in the scale of goodness, and order could be quickly made; for this essence would be *the* good upon which all thinkers were agreed, the relatively objective and universal good that the philosopher seeks. Even his own private ideals would be measured by their share of it, and find their rightful place among the rest.

Various essences of good have thus been found and proposed as bases of the ethical system. Thus, to be a mean between two extremes; to be recognized by a special intuitive faculty; to make the agent happy for the moment; to make others as well as him happy in the long run; to add to his perfection or dignity; to harm no one; to follow from reason or flow from universal law; to be in accordance with the will of God; to promote the survival of the human species on this planet—are so many tests, each of which has been maintained by somebody to constitute the essence of all good things or actions so far as they are good.

No one of the measures that have been actually proposed has, however, given general satisfaction. Some are obviously not universally present in all cases, *e.g.*, the character of harming no one, or that of following a universal law; for the best course is often cruel; and many acts are reckoned good on the sole condition that they be exceptions, and serve not as examples of a universal law. Other characters, such as following the will of God, are unascertainable and vague. Others again, like survival, are quite indeterminate in their consequences, and leave us in the lurch where we most need their help: a philosopher of the Sioux Nation, for example, will be certain to use the survival-criterion in a very different way from ourselves. The best, on the whole, of these marks and measures of goodness seems to be the capacity to bring happiness. But in order not to break down fatally, this test must be taken to cover innumerable acts and impulses that never *aim* at happiness; so that, after all, in seeking for a universal principle we inevitably are carried onward to the *most* universal principle—that *the essence of good is simply to satisfy demand.* The demand may be for anything under the sun. There is really no more ground for supposing that all our demands can be accounted for by one universal underlying kind of motive than there is ground for supposing that all physical phenomena are cases of a single law. The elementary forces in ethics are probably as plural as those of physics are. The various ideals have no common character apart from the fact that they are ideals. No single abstract principle can be so used as to yield to the philosopher anything like a scientifically accurate and genuinely useful casuistic scale.

A look at another peculiarity of the ethical universe, as we find it, will still further show us the philosopher's perplexities. As a purely theoretic problem, namely, the casuistic question would hardly ever come up at all. If the ethical philosopher were only asking after the best *imaginable* system of goods he would indeed have an easy task; for all demands as such are *primâ facie* respectable, and the best simply imaginary world be one in which *every* demand was gratified as soon as made. Such a world would, however, have to have a physical constitution entirely different from that of the one which we inhabit. It would need not only a space, but a time, of n-dimensions, to include all the acts and experiences incompatible with one another here below, which would then go on in conjunction, such as spending our money, yet growing rich; taking our holiday, yet getting ahead with our work; shooting and fishing, yet doing no hurt to the beasts; gaining no end of experience, yet keeping our youthful freshness of heart; and the like. There can be no question that such a system of things, however brought about, would be the absolutely ideal system; and that if a philosopher could create universes *a priori,* and provide all the mechanical conditions, that is the sort of universe which he should unhesitatingly create.

But this world of ours is made on an entirely different pattern, and the casuistic question here is most tragically practical. The actually possible in this world is vastly narrower than all that is demanded; and there is always a *pinch* between the ideal and the actual which can only be got through by leaving part of the ideal behind. There is hardly a good which we can imagine except as competing for the possession of the same bit of space and time with some other imagined good. Every end of desire that presents itself appears exclusive of some other end of desire. Shall a man drink and smoke, *or* keep his nerves in condition?—he cannot do both. Shall he follow his fancy for Amelia, *or* for Henrietta?—both cannot be the choice of his heart. Shall he have the dear old Republican party, *or* a spirit of unsophistication in public affairs?—he cannot have both, etc. So that the ethical philosopher's demand for the right scale of subordination in ideals is the fruit of an altogether practical need. Some part of the ideal must be butchered, and he needs to know which part. It is a tragic situation, and no mere speculative conundrum, with which he has to deal.

Now *we* are blinded to the real difficulty of the philosopher's task by the fact that we are born into a society whose ideals are largely ordered already. If we follow the ideal which is conventionally highest, the others which we butcher either die and do not return to haunt us; or if they come back and accuse us of murder, every one applauds us for turning to them a deaf ear. In other words, our environment encourages us not to be philosophers but partisans. The philosopher, however, cannot, so long as he clings to his own ideal of objectivity, rule out any ideal from being heard. He is confident, and rightly confident, that the simple taking counsel of his own intuitive preferences would be certain to end in a mutilation of the fulness of the truth. The poet Heine is said to have written "Bunsen" in the place of "Gott" in his copy of that author's work entitled *God in History,* so as to make it read *Bunsen in der Geschichte.* Now, with no disrespect to the good and learned Baron, is it not safe to say that any single philosopher, however wide his sympathies, must be just such a Bunsen in der Geschichte of the moral world, so soon as he attempts to put his own ideas of order into that howling mob of desires, each struggling to get breathing-room for the ideal to which it clings? The very best of men must not only be insensible, but be ludicrously and peculiarly insensible, to many goods. As a militant, fighting free-handed that the goods to which he *is* sensible may not be submerged and lost from out of life, the philosopher, like every other human being, is in a natural position. But think of Zeno and of Epicurus, think of Calvin and of Paley, think of Kant and Schopenhauer, of Herbert Spencer and John Henry Newman, no longer as one-sided champions of special ideals, but as schoolmasters deciding what all must think—and what more grotesque topic could a satirist wish for on which to exercise his pen? The fabled attempt of Mrs. Partington to arrest the rising tide of the North Atlantic with her broom was a reasonable spectacle compared with their effort to substitute the content of their clean-shaven systems for that exuberant mass of goods with which all human nature is in travail, and groaning to bring to the light of day. Think, furthermore, of such individual moralists, no longer as mere schoolmasters, but as pontiffs armed with the temporal power, and having authority in every concrete case of conflict to order which good shall be butchered and which shall be suffered to survive, and the notion really turns one pale. All one's slumbering revolutionary instincts waken at the thought of any single moralist wielding such powers of life and death. Better chaos forever than an order based on any closet-philosopher's rule, even though he were the most enlightened possible member of his tribe. No! if the philosopher is to keep his judicial position, he must never become one of the parties to the fray.

What can he do, then, it will now be asked, except to fall back on scepticism and give up the notion of being a philosopher at all?

But do we not already see a perfectly definite path of escape which is open to him just because he is a philosopher, and not the champion of one particular ideal? Since everything which is demanded is by that fact a good, must not the guiding principle for ethical philosophy (since all demands conjointly cannot be satisfied in this poor world) be simply to satisfy at all times *as many demands as we can?* That act must be the best act accordingly, which makes for the *best whole*, in the sense of awakening the least sum of dissatisfactions. In the casuistic scale, therefore, those ideals must be written highest which *prevail at the least cost,* or by whose realization the least possible number of other ideals are destroyed. Since victory and defeat there must be, the victory to be philosophically prayed for is that of the more inclusive side, of the side which even in the hour of triumph will to some degree do justice to the ideals in which the vanquished party's interests lay. The course of history is nothing but the story of men's struggles from generation to generation to find the more and more inclusive order. *Invent some manner* of realizing your own ideals which will also satisfy the alien demands— that and that only is the path of peace! Following this path, society has shaken itself into one sort of relative equilibrium after another by a series of social discoveries quite analogous to those of science. Polyandry and polygamy and slavery, private warfare and liberty to kill, judicial torture and arbitrary royal power have slowly succumbed to actually aroused complaints; and though some one's ideals are unquestionably the worse off for each improvement, yet a vastly greater total number of them find shelter in our civilized society than in the older savage ways. So far then, and up to date, the casuistic scale is made for the philosopher already far better than he can ever make it for himself. An experiment of the most searching kind has proved that the laws and usages of the land are what yield the maximum of satisfaction to the thinkers taken all together. The presumption in cases of conflict must always be in favor of the conventionally recognized good. The philosopher must be a conservative, and in the construction of his casuistic scale must put the things most in accordance with the customs of the community on top.

And yet if he be a true philosopher he must see that there is nothing final in any actually given equilibrium of human ideals, but that, as our present laws and customs have fought and conquered other past ones, so they will in their turn be overthrown by any newly discovered order which will hush up the complaints that they still give rise to, without producing others louder still. "Rules are made for man, not man for rules,"—that one sentence is enough to immortalize Green's Prolegomena to Ethics. And although a man always risks much when he breaks away from established rules and strives to realize a larger ideal whole than they permit, yet the philosopher must allow that it is at all times open to any one to make the experiment, provided he fear not to stake his life and character upon the throw. The pinch is always here. Pent in under every system of moral rules are innumerable persons whom it weighs upon, and goods which it represses; and these are always rumbling and grumbling in the background, and ready for any issue by which they may get free. See the abuses which the institution of private property covers, so that even to-day it is shamelessly asserted among us that one of the prime functions of the national government is to help the adroiter citizens to grow rich. See the unnamed and unnamable sorrows which the tyranny, on the whole so beneficent, of the marriage-institution brings to so many, both of the married and the unwed. See the wholesale loss of opportunity under our *régime* of so-called equality and industrialism, with the drummer and the counter-jumper in the saddle, for so many faculties and graces which could flourish in the feudal world. See our kindliness for the humble and the outcast, how it wars with that stern weeding-out which until now has been the condition of every perfection in the breed. See everywhere the struggle and the squeeze; and everlastingly the problem how to make them less. The anarchists, nihilists, and free-lovers; the free-silverites, socialists, and single-tax men; the free-traders and civil-service reformers; the prohibitionists and anti-vivisectionists; the radical darwinians with their idea of the suppression of the weak—these and all the conservative sentiments of society arrayed against them, are simply deciding through actual experiment by what sort of conduct the maximum amount of good can be gained and kept in this world. These experiments are to be judged, not *a priori,* but by actual finding, after the fact of their making, how much more outcry or how much appeasement comes about. What closet-solutions can possibly anticipate the result of trials made on such a scale? Or what can any superficial theorist's judgment be worth, in a world where every one of hundreds of ideals has its special champion already provided in the shape of some genius expressly born to feel it, and to fight to death in its behalf? The pure philosopher can only follow the windings of the spectacle, confident that the line of least resistance will always be towards the richer and the more inclusive arrangement, and that by one tack after another some approach to the kingdom of heaven is incessantly made.

IV

ALL this amounts to saying that, so far as the casuistic question goes, ethical science is just like physical science, and instead of being deducible all at once from abstract principles, must simply bide its time, and be ready to revise its conclusions from day to day. The presumption of course, in both sciences, always is that the vulgarly accepted opinions are true, and the right casuistic order that which public opinion believes in; and surely it would be folly quite as great, in most of us, to strike out independently and to aim at originality in ethics as in physics. Every now and then, however, some one is born with the right to be original, and his revolutionary thought or action may bear prosperous fruit. He may replace old "laws of nature" by better ones; he may, by breaking old moral rules in a certain place, bring in a total condition of things more ideal than would have followed had the rules been kept.

On the whole, then, we must conclude that no philosophy of ethics is possible in the old-fashioned absolute sense of the term. Everywhere the ethical philosopher must wait on facts. The thinkers who create the ideals come he knows not whence, their sensibilities are evolved he knows not how; and the question as to which of two conflicting ideals will give the best universe then and there, can be answered by him only through the aid of the experience of other men. I said some time ago, in treating of the "first" question, that the intuitional moralists deserve credit for keeping most clearly to the psychological facts. They do much to spoil this merit on the whole, however, by mixing with it that dogmatic temper which, by absolute distinctions and unconditional "thou shalt nots," changes a growing, elastic, and continuous life into a superstitious system of relics and dead bones. In point of fact, there are no absolute evils, and there are no non-moral goods; and the *highest* ethical life—however few may be called to bear its burdens—consists at all times in the breaking of rules which have grown too narrow for the actual case. There is but one unconditional commandment, which is that we should seek incessantly, with fear and trembling, so to vote and to act as to bring about the very largest total universe of good which we can see. Abstract rules indeed can help; but they help the less in proportion as our intuitions are more piercing, and our vocation is the stronger for the moral life. For every real dilemma is in literal strictness a unique situation; and the exact combination of ideals realized and ideals disappointed which each decision creates is always a universe without a precedent, and for which no adequate previous rule exists. The philosopher, then, *quâ* philosopher, is no better able to determine the best universe in the concrete emergency than other men. He sees, indeed, somewhat better than most men what the question always is, not a question of this good or that good simply taken, but of the two total universes with which these goods respectively belong. He knows that he must vote always for the richer universe, for the good which seems most organizable, most fit to enter into complex combinations, most apt to be a member of a more inclusive whole. But which particular universe this is he cannot know for certain in advance; he only knows that if he makes a bad mistake the cries of the wounded will soon inform him of the fact. In all this the philosopher is just like the rest of us non-philosophers, so far as we are just and sympathetic instinctively, and so far as we are open to the voice of complaint. His function is in fact indistinguishable from that of the best kind of statesman at the present day. His books upon ethics, therefore, so far as they truly touch the moral life, must more and more ally themselves with a literature which is confessedly tentative and suggestive rather than dogmatic, I mean with novels and dramas of the deeper sort, with sermons, with books on statecraft and philanthropy and social and economical reform. Treated in this way ethical treatises may be voluminous and luminous as well; but they never can be *final*, except in their abstractest and vaguest features; and they must more and more abandon the old-fashioned, clear-cut, and would-be "scientific" form.

V

THE chief of all the reasons why concrete ethics cannot be final is that they have to wait on metaphysical and theological beliefs. I said some time back that real ethical relations existed in a purely human world. They would exist even in what we called a moral solitude if the thinker had various ideals which took hold of him in turn. His self of one day would make demands on his self of another; and some of the demands might be urgent and tyrannical, while others were gentle and easily put aside. We call the tyrannical demands *imperatives*. If we ignore these we do not hear the last of it. The good which we have wounded returns to plague us with interminable crops of consequential damages, compunctions and regrets. Obligation can thus exist inside a single thinker's consciousness; and perfect peace can abide with him only so far as he lives according to some sort of a casuistic scale which keeps his more imperative goods on top. It is the nature of these goods to be cruel to their rivals. Nothing shall avail when weighed in the balance against them. They call out all the mercilessness in our disposition, and do not easily forgive us if we are so soft-hearted as to shrink from sacrifice in their behalf.

The deepest difference, practically, in the moral life of man is the difference between the easy-going and the strenuous mood. When in the easy-going mood the shrinking from present ill is our ruling consideration. The strenuous mood, on the contrary, makes us quite indifferent to present ill, if only the greater ideal be attained. The capacity for the strenuous mood probably lies slumbering in every man, but it has more difficulty in some than in others in waking up. It needs the wilder passions to arouse it, the big fears, loves, and indignations; or else the deeply penetrating appeal of some one of the higher fidelities, like justice, truth, or freedom. Strong relief is a necessity of its vision; and a world where all the mountains are brought down and all the valleys are exalted is no congenial place for its habitation. This is why in a solitary thinker this mood might slumber on forever without waking. His various ideals, known to him to be mere preferences of his own, are too nearly of the same denominational value: he can play fast or loose with them at will. This too is why, in a merely human world without a God, the appeal to our moral energy falls short of its maximal stimulating power. Life, to be sure, is even in such a world a genuinely ethical symphony; but it is played in the compass of a couple of poor octaves, and the infinite scale of values fails to open up. Many of us, indeed, like Sir James Stephen in those eloquent *Essays by a Barrister*, would openly laugh at the very idea of the strenuous mood being awakened in us by those claims of remote posterity which constitute the last appeal of the religion of humanity. We do not love these men of the future keenly enough; and we love them perhaps the less the more we hear of their evolutionized perfection, their high average longevity and education, their freedom from war and crime, their relative immunity from pain and zymotic disease, and all their other negative superiorities. This is all too finite, we say; we see too well the vacuum beyond. It lacks the note of infinitude and mystery, and may all be dealt with in the don't-care mood. No need of agonizing ourselves or making others agonize for these good creatures just at present.

When, however, we believe that a God is there, and that he is one of the claimants, the infinite perspective opens out. The scale of the symphony is incalculably prolonged. The more imperative ideals now begin to speak with an altogether new objectivity and significance, and to utter the penetrating, shattering, tragically challenging note of appeal. They ring out like the call of Victor Hugo's alpine eagle, *"qui parle au précipice et que le gouffre entend,"* and the strenuous mood awakens at the sound. It saith among the trumpets, ha, ha! it smelleth the battle afar off, the thunder of the captains and the shouting. Its blood is up; and cruelty to the lesser claims, so far from being a deterrent element, does but add to the stern joy with which it leaps to answer to the greater. All through history, in the periodical conflicts of puritanism with the don't-care temper, we see the antagonism of the strenuous and genial moods, and the contrast between the ethics of infinite and mysterious obligation from on high, and those of prudence and the satisfaction of merely finite need.

The capacity of the strenuous mood lies so deep down among our natural human possibilities that even if there were no metaphysical or traditional grounds for believing in a God, men would postulate one simply as a pretext for living hard, and getting out of the game of existence its keenest possibilities of zest. Our attitude towards concrete evils is entirely different in a world where we believe there are none but finite demanders, from what it is in one where we joyously face tragedy for an infinite demander's sake. Every sort of energy and endurance, of courage and capacity for handling life's evils, is set free in those who have religious faith. For this reason the strenuous type of character will on the battle-field of human history always outwear the easy-going type, and religion will drive irreligion to the wall.

It would seem, too—and this is my final conclusion—that

the stable and systematic moral universe for which the ethical philosopher asks is fully possible only in a world where there is a divine thinker with all-enveloping demands. If such a thinker existed, his way of subordinating the demands to one another would be the finally valid casuistic scale; his claims would be the most appealing; his ideal universe would be the most inclusive realizable whole. If he now exist, then actualized in his thought already must be that ethical philosophy which we seek as the pattern which our own must evermore approach.³ In the interests of our own ideal of systematically unified moral truth, therefore, we, as would-be philosophers, must postulate a divine thinker, and pray for the victory of the religious cause. Meanwhile, exactly what the thought of the infinite thinker may be is hidden from us even were we sure of his existence; so that our postulation of him after all serves only to let loose in us the strenuous mood. But this is what it does in all men, even those who have no interest in philosophy. The ethical philosopher, therefore, whenever he ventures to say which course of action is the best, is on no essentially different level from the common man. "See, I have set before thee this day life and good, and death and evil; therefore, choose life that thou and thy seed may live"—when this challenge comes to us, it is simply our total character and personal genius that are on trial; and if we invoke any so-called philosophy, our choice and use of that also are but revelations of our personal aptitude or incapacity for moral life. From this unsparing practical ordeal no professor's lectures and no array of books can save us. The solving word, for the learned and the unlearned man alike, lies in the last resort in the dumb willingnesses and un-willingnesses of their interior characters, and nowhere else. It is not in heaven, neither is it beyond the sea; but the word is very nigh unto thee, in thy mouth and in thy heart, that thou mayest do it.

THE GOSPEL OF
RELAXATION

I wish in the following hour to take certain psychological doctrines and show their practical applications to mental hygiene—to the hygiene of our American life more particularly. Our people, especially in academic circles, are turning towards psychology nowadays with great expectations; and, if psychology is to justify them, it must be by showing fruits in the pedagogic and therapeutic lines.

The reader may possibly have heard of a peculiar theory of the emotions, commonly referred to in psychological literature as the Lange-James theory. According to this theory, our emotions are mainly due to those organic stirrings that are aroused in us in a reflex way by the stimulus of the exciting object or situation. An emotion of fear, for example, or surprise, is not a direct effect of the object's presence on the mind, but an effect of that still earlier effect, the bodily commotion which the object suddenly excites; so that, were this bodily commotion suppressed, we should not so much *feel* fear as call the situation fearful; we should not feel surprise, but coldly recognize that the object was indeed astonishing. One enthusiast has even gone so far as to say that when we feel sorry it is because we weep, when we feel afraid it is because we run away, and not conversely. Some of you may perhaps be acquainted with the paradoxical formula. Now, whatever exaggeration may possibly lurk in this account of our emotions (and I doubt myself whether the exaggeration be very great), it is certain that the main core of it is true, and that the mere giving way to tears, for example, or to the outward expression of an anger-fit, will result for the moment in making the inner grief or anger more acutely felt. There is, accordingly, no better known or more generally useful precept in the moral training of youth, or in one's personal self-discipline, than that which bids us pay primary attention to what we do and express, and not to care too much for what we feel. If we only check a cowardly impulse in time, for example, or if we only *don't* strike the blow or rip out with the complaining or insulting word that we shall regret as long as we live, as long as we live, our feelings themselves will presently be the calmer and better, with no particular guidance from us on their own account. Action seems to follow feeling, but really action and feeling go together; and by regulating the action, which is under the more direct control of the will, we can indirectly regulate the feeling, which is not.

Thus the sovereign voluntary path to cheerfulness, if our spontaneous cheerfulness be lost, is to sit up cheerfully, to look round cheerfully, and to act and speak as if cheerfulness were already there. If such conduct does not make you soon feel cheerful, nothing else on that occasion can. So to feel brave, act as if we *were* brave, use all our will to that end, and a courage-fit will very likely replace the fit of fear. Again, in order to feel kindly toward a person to whom we have been inimical, the only way is more or less deliberately to smile, to make sympathetic inquiries, and to force ourselves to say genial things. One hearty laugh together will bring enemies into a closer communion of heart than hours spent on both sides in inward wrestling with the mental demon of uncharitable feeling. To wrestle with a bad feeling only pins our attention on it, and keeps it still fastened in the mind: whereas, if we act as if from some better feeling, the old bad feeling soon folds its tent like an Arab, and silently steals away.

The best manuals of religious devotion accordingly reiterate the maxim that we must let our feelings go, and pay no regard to them whatever. In an admirable and widely successful little book called *The Christian's Secret of a Happy Life*, by Mrs. Hannah Whitall Smith, I find this lesson on almost every page. *Act* faithfully, and you really have faith, no matter how cold and even how dubious you may feel. "It is your purpose God looks at," writes Mrs. Smith, "not your feelings about that purpose; and your purpose, or will, is therefore the only thing you need attend to. . . . Let your emotions come or let them go, just as God pleases, and make no account of them either way. . . . They really have nothing to do with the matter. They are not the indicators of your spiritual state, but are merely the indicators of your temperament or of your present physical condition."

But you all know these facts already, so I need no longer press them on your attention. From our acts and from our attitudes ceaseless inpouring currents of sensation come, which help to determine from moment to moment what our inner states shall be: that is a fundamental law of psychology which I will therefore proceed to assume.

A Viennese neurologist of considerable reputation has recently written about the *Binnenleben*, as he terms it, or buried life of human beings. No doctor, this writer says, can get into really profitable relations with a nervous patient until he gets some sense of what the patient's *Binnenleben* is, of the sort of unuttered inner atmosphere in which his consciousness dwells alone with the secrets of its prison-house. This inner personal tone is what we can't communicate or describe articulately to others; but the wraith and ghost of it, so to speak, are often what our friends and intimates feel as our most characteristic quality. In the unhealthy-minded, apart from all sorts of old regrets, ambitions checked by shames and aspirations obstructed by timidities, it consists mainly of bodily discomforts not distinctly localized by the sufferer, but breeding a general self-mistrust and sense that things are not as they should be with him. Half the thirst for alchohol that exists in the world exists simply because alchohol acts as a temporary anæsthetic and effacer to all these morbid feelings that never ought to be in a human being at all. In the healthy-minded, on the contrary, there are no fears or shames to discover; and the sensations that pour in from the organism only help to swell the general vital sense of security and readiness for anything that may turn up.

Consider, for example, the effects of a well-toned *motor-apparatus*, nervous and muscular, on our general personal self-consciousness, the sense of elasticity and efficiency that results. They tell us that in Norway the life of the women has lately been entirely revolutionized by the new order of muscular feelings with which the use of the *ski,* or long snow-shoes, as a sport for both sexes, has made the women acquainted. Fifteen years ago the Norwegian women were even more than the women of other lands votaries of the old-fashioned ideal of femininity, "the domestic angel," the "gentle and refining influence" sort of thing. Now these sedentary fireside tabbycats of Norway have been trained, they say, by the snow-shoes into lithe and audacious creatures, for whom no night is too dark or height too giddy, and who are not only saying good-bye to the traditional feminine pallor and delicacy of constitution, but actually taking the lead in every educational and social reform. I cannot but think that the tennis and tramping and skating habits and the bicycle-craze which are so rapidly extending among our dear sisters and daughters in this country are going also to lead to a sounder and heartier moral tone, which will send its tonic breath through all our American life.

I hope that here in America more and more the ideal of the well-trained and vigorous body will be maintained neck by neck with that of the well-trained and vigorous mind as the two coequal halves of the higher education for men and women alike. The strength of the British Empire lies in the strength of character of the individual Englishman, taken all alone by himself. And that strength, I am persuaded, is perennially nourished and kept up by nothing so much as by the national worship, in which all classes meet, of athletic outdoor life and sport.

I recollect, years ago, reading a certain work by an American doctor on hygiene and the laws of life and the type of future humanity. I have forgotten its author's name and its title, but I remember well an awful prophecy that it contained about the future of our muscular system. Human perfection, the writer said, means ability to cope with the environment; but the environment will more and more require mental power from us, and less and less will ask for bare brute strength. Wars will cease, machines will do all our heavy work, man will become more and more a mere director of nature's energies, and less and less an exerter of energy on his own account. So that, if the *homo sapiens* of the future can only digest his food and think, what need will he have of well-developed muscles at all? And why, pursued this writer, should we not even now be satisfied with a more delicate and intellectual type of beauty than that which pleased our ancestors? Nay, I have heard a fanciful friend make a still further advance in this "new-man" direction. With our future food, he says, itself prepared in liquid form from the chemical elements of the atmosphere, pepsinated or half-digested in advance, and sucked up through a glass tube from a tin can, what need shall we have of teeth, or stomachs even? They may go, along with our muscles and our physical courage, while, challenging ever more and more our proper admiration, will grow the gigantic domes of our crania, arching over our spectacled eyes, and animating our flexible little lips to those floods of learned and ingenious talk which will constitute our most congenial occupation.

I am sure that your flesh creeps at this apocalyptic vision. Mine certainly did so; and I cannot believe that our muscular vigor will ever be a superfluity. Even if the day ever dawns in which it will not be needed for fighting the old heavy battles against Nature, it will still always be needed to furnish the background of sanity, serenity, and cheerfulness to life, to give moral elasticity to our disposition, to round off the wiry edge of our fretfulness, and make us good-humored and easy of approach. Weakness is too apt to be what the doctors call irritable weakness. And that blessed internal peace and confidence, that *acquiescentia in seipso*, as Spinoza used to call it, that wells up from every part of the body of a muscularly well-trained human being, and soaks the indwelling soul of him with satisfaction, is, quite apart from every consideration of its mechanical utility, an element of spiritual hygiene of supreme significance.

And now let me go a step deeper into mental hygiene, and try to enlist your insight and sympathy in a cause which I believe is one of paramount patriotic importance to us Yankees. Many years ago a Scottish medical man, Dr. Clouston, a mad-doctor as they call him there, or what we should call an asylum physician (the most eminent one in Scotland), visited this country, and said something that has remained in my memory ever since. "You Americans," he said, "wear too much expression on your faces. You are living like an army with all its reserves engaged in action. The duller countenances of the British population betoken a better scheme of life. They suggest stores of reserved nervous force to fall back upon, if any occasion should arise that requires it. This inexcitability, this presence at all times of power not used, I regard," continued Dr. Clouston, "as the great safeguard of our British people. The other thing in you gives me a sense of insecurity, and you ought somehow to tone yourselves down. You really do carry too much expression, you take too intensely the trivial moments of life."

Now Dr. Clouston is a trained reader of the secrets of the soul as expressed upon the countenance, and the observation of his which I quote seems to me to mean a great deal. And all Americans who stay in Europe long enough to get accustomed to the spirit that reigns and expresses itself there, so unexcitable as compared with ours, make a similar observation when they return to their native shores. They find a wild-eyed look upon their compatriot's faces, either of too desperate eagerness and anxiety or of too intense responsiveness and good-will. It is hard to say whether the men or the women show it most. It is true that we do not all feel about it as Dr. Clouston felt. Many of us, far from deploring it, admire it. We say: "What intelligence it shows! How different from the stolid cheeks, the codfish eyes, the slow, inanimate demeanor we have been seeing in the British Isles!" Intensity, rapidity, vivacity of appearance, are indeed with us something of a nationally accepted ideal; and the medical notion of "irritable weakness" is not the first thing suggested by them to our mind, as it was to Dr. Clouston's. In a weekly paper not very long ago I remember reading a story in which, after describing the beauty and interest of the heroine's personality, the author summed up her charms by saying that to all who looked upon her an impression as of "bottled lightning" was irresistibly conveyed.

Bottled lightning, in truth, is one of our American ideals, even of a young girl's character! Now it is most ungracious, and it may seem to some persons unpatriotic, to criticise in public the physical peculiarities of one's own people, of one's own family, so to speak. Besides, it may be said, and said with justice, that there are plenty of bottled-lightning temperaments in other countries, and plenty of phlegmatic temperaments here; and that, when all is said and done, the more or less of tension about which I am making such a fuss is a very small item in the sum total of a nation's life, and not worth solemn treatment at a time when agreeable rather than disagreeable things should be talked about. Well, in one sense the more or less of tension in our faces and in our unused muscles *is* a small thing: not much mechanical work is done by these contractions. But it is not always the material size of a thing that measures its importance: often it is its place and function. One of the most philosophical remarks I ever heard made was by an unlettered workman who was doing some repairs at my house many years ago. "There is very little difference between one man and another," he said, "when you go to the bottom of it. But what little there is, is very important." And the remark certainly applies to this case. The general over-contraction may be small when estimated in foot-pounds, but its importance is immense on account of its *effects on the over-contracted person's spiritual life*. This follows as a necessary consequence from the theory of our emotions to which I made reference at the beginning of this article. For by the sensations that so incessantly pour in from the over-tense excited body the over-tense and excited habit of mind is kept up; and the sultry, threatening, exhausting, thunderous inner atmosphere never quite clears away. If you never wholly give yourself up to the chair you sit in, but always keep your leg- and body-muscles half contracted for a rise; if you breathe eighteen or nineteen instead of sixteen times a minute, and never quite breathe out at that— what mental mood *can* you be in but one of inner panting and expectancy, and how can the future and its worries possibly forsake your mind? On the other hand, how can they gain admission to your mind if your brow be unruffled, your respiration calm and complete, and your muscles all relaxed?

Now what is the cause of this absence of repose, this bottled-lightning quality in us Americans? The explanation of it that is usually given is that it comes from the extreme dryness of our climate and the acrobatic performances of our thermometer, coupled with the extraordinary progressiveness of our life, the hard work, the railroad speed, the rapid success, and all the other things we know so well by heart. Well, our climate is certainly exciting, but hardly more so than that of many parts of Europe, where nevertheless no bottled-lightning girls are found. And the work done and the pace of life are as extreme in every great capital of Europe as they are here. To me both of these pretended causes are utterly insufficient to explain the facts.

To explain them, we must go not to physical geography, but to psychology and sociology. The latest chapter both in sociology and in psychology to be developed in a manner that approaches adequacy is the chapter on the imitative impulse. First Bagehot, then Tarde, then Royce and Baldwin here, have shown that invention and imitation, taken together, form, one may say, the entire warp and woof of human life, in so far as it is social. The American over-tension and jerkiness and breathlesness and intensity and agony of expression are primarily social, and only secondarily physiological, phenomena. They are *bad habits*, nothing more or less, bred of custom and example, born of the imitation of bad models and the cultivation of false personal ideals. How are idioms acquired, how do local peculiarities of phrase and accent come about? Through an accidental example set by some one, which struck the ears of others, and was quoted and copied till at last every one in the locality chimed in. Just so it is with national tricks of vocalization or intonation, with national manners, fashions of movement and gesture, and habitual expressions of face. We, here in America, through following a succession of pattern-setters whom it is now impossible to trace, and through influencing each other in a bad direction, have at last settled down collectively into what, for better or worse, is our own characteristic national type—a type with the production of which, so far as these habits go, the climate and conditions have had practically nothing at all to do.

This type, which we have thus reached by our imitativeness, we now have fixed upon us, for better or worse. Now no type can be *wholly* disadvantageous; but, so far as our type follows the bottled-lightning fashion, it cannot be wholly good. Dr. Clouston was certainly right in thinking that eagerness, breathlessness, and anxiety are not signs of strength: they are signs of weakness and of bad coordination. The even forehead, the slab-like cheek, the codfish eye, may be less interesting for the moment; but they are more promising signs than intense expression is of what we may expect of their possessor in the long run. Your dull, unhurried worker gets over a great deal of ground, because he never goes backwards or breaks down. Your intense, convulsive worker breaks down and has bad moods so often that you never know where he may be when you most need his help—he may be having one of his "bad days." We say that so many of our fellow-countrymen collapse, and have to be sent abroad to rest their nerves, because they work so hard. I suspect that this is an immense mistake. I suspect that neither the nature nor the amount of our work is accountable for the frequency and severity of our breakdowns, but that their cause lies rather in those absurd feelings of hurry and having no time, in that breathlessness and tension, that anxiety of feature and that solicitude for results, that lack of inner harmony and ease, in short, by which with us the work is so apt to be accompanied, and from which a European who should do the same work would nine times out of ten be free. These perfectly wanton and unnecessary tricks of inner attitude and outer manner in us, caught from the social atmosphere, kept up by tradition, and idealized by many as the admirable way of life, are the last straws that break the American camel's back, the final overflowers of our measure of wear and tear and fatigue.

The voice, for example, in a surprisingly large number of us has a tired and plaintive sound. Some of us are really tired (for I do not mean absolutely to deny that our climate has a tiring quality); but far more of us are not tired at all, or would not be tired at all unless we had got into a wretched trick of feeling tired, by following the prevalent habits of vocalization and expression. And if talking high and tired, and living excitedly and hurriedly, would only enable us to *do* more by the way, even while breaking us down in the end, it would be different. There would be some compensation, some excuse, for going on so. But the exact reverse is the case. It is your relaxed and easy worker, who is in no hurry, and quite thoughtless most of the while of consequences, who is your efficient worker; and tension and anxiety, and present and future, all mixed up together in our mind at once, are the surest drags upon steady progress and hindrances to our success. My colleague, Professor Münsterberg, an excellent observer, who came here recently, has written some notes on America to German papers. He says in substance that the appearance of unusual energy in America is superficial and illusory, being really due to nothing but the habits of jerkiness and bad co-ordination for which we have to thank the defective training of our people. I think myself that it is high time for old legends and traditional opinions to be changed; and that, if any one should begin to write about Yankee inefficiency and feebleness, and inability to do anything with time except to waste it, he would have a very pretty paradoxical little thesis to sustain, with a great many facts to quote, and a great deal of experience to appeal to in its proof.

Well, my friends, if our dear American character is weakened by all this over-tension—and I think, whatever reserves you may make, that you will agree as to the main facts—where does the remedy lie? It lies, of course, where lay the origins of the disease. If a vicious fashion and taste are to blame for the thing, the fashion and taste must be changed. And, though it is no small thing to inoculate seventy millions of people with new standards, yet, if there is to be any relief, that will have to be done. We must change ourselves from a race that admires jerk and snap for their own sakes, and looks down upon low voices and quiet ways as dull, to one that, on the contrary, has calm for its ideal, and for their own sakes loves harmony, dignity, and ease.

So we go back to the psychology of imitation again. There is only one way to improve ourselves, and that is by some of us setting an example which the others may pick up and imitate till the new fashion spreads from east to west. Some of us are in more favorable positions than others to set new fashions. Some are much more striking personally and imitable, so to speak. But no living person is sunk so low as not to be imitated by somebody. Thackeray somewhere says of the Irish nation that there never was an Irishman so poor that he didn't have a still poorer Irishman living at his expense; and, surely, there is no human being whose example doesn't work contagiously in *some* particular. The very idiots at our public institutions imitate each other's peculiarities. And, if you should individually achieve calmness and harmony in your own person, you may depend upon it that a wave of imitation will spread from you, as surely as the circles spread outward when a stone is dropped into a lake.

Fortunately, we shall not have to be absolute pioneers. Even now in New York they have formed a society for the improvement of our national vocalization, and one perceives its machinations already in the shape of various newspaper paragraphs intended to stir up dissatisfaction with the awful thing that it is. And, better still than that, because more radical and general, is the gospel of relaxation, as one may call it, preached by Miss Annie Payson Call of Boston, in her admirable little volume called *Power through Repose*, a book that ought to be in the hands of every teacher and student in America of either sex. You need only be followers, then, on a path already opened up by others. But of one thing be confident: others still will follow you.

And this brings me to one more application of psychology to practical life, to which I will call attention briefly, and then close. If one's example of easy and calm ways is to be effectively contagious, one feels by instinct that the less voluntarily one aims at getting imitated, the more unconscious one keeps in the matter, the more likely one is to succeed. *Become the imitable thing,* and you may then discharge your minds of all responsbility for the imitation. The laws of social nature will take care of that result. Now the psychological principle on which this precept reposes is a law of very deep and wide-spread importance in the conduct of our lives, and at the same time a law which we Americans most grievously neglect. Stated technically, the law is this: that *strong feeling about one's self tends to arrest the free association of one's objective ideas and motor processes.* We get the extreme example of this in the mental disease called melancholia.

A melancholic patient is filled through and through with intensely painful emotion about himself. He is threatened, he is guilty, he is doomed, he is annihilated, he is lost. His mind is fixed as if in a cramp on these feelings of his own situation, and in all the books on insanity you may read that the usual varied flow of his thoughts has ceased. His associative processes, to use the technical phrase, are inhibited; and his ideas stand stock-still, shut up to their one monotonous function of reiterating inwardly the fact of the man's desperate estate. And this inhibitive influence is not due to the mere fact that his emotion is *painful.* Joyous emotions about the self also stop the association of our ideas. A saint in ecstasy is as motionless and irresponsive and one-idea'd as a melancholiac. And, without going as far as ecstatic saints, we know how in every one a great or sudden pleasure may paralyze the flow of thought. Ask young people returning from a party or a spectacle, and all excited about it, what it was. "Oh, it was *fine!* it was *fine!* it was *fine!*" is all the information you are likely to receive until the excitement has calmed down. Probably every one of my hearers has been made temporarily half-idiotic by some great success or piece of good fortune. "*Good!* GOOD! GOOD!" is all we can at such times say to ourselves until we smile at our own very foolishness.

Now from all this we can draw an extremely practical

conclusion. If, namely, we wish our trains of ideation and volition to be copious and varied and effective, we must form the habit of freeing them from the inhibitive influence of reflection upon them, of egoistic preoccupation about their results. Such a habit, like other habits, can be formed. Prudence and duty and self-regard, emotions of ambition and emotions of anxiety, have, of course, a needful part to play in our lives. But confine them as far as possible to the occasions when you are making your general resolutions and deciding on your plans of campaign, and keep them out of the details. When once a decision is reached and execution is the order of the day, dismiss absolutely all responsibility and care about the outcome. *Unclamp,* in a word, your intellectual and practical machinery, and let it run free; and the service it will do you will be twice as good. Who are the scholars who get "rattled" in the recitation-room? Those who think of the possibilities of failure and feel the great importance of the act. Who are those who do recite well? Often those who are most indifferent. *Their* ideas reel themselves out of their memory of their own accord. Why do we hear the complaint so often that social life in New England is either less rich and expressive or more fatiguing than it is in some other parts of the world? To what is the fact, if fact it be, due unless to the over-active conscience of the people, afraid of either saying something too trivial and obvious, or something insincere, or something unworthy of one's interlocutor, or something in some way or other not adequate to the occasion? How can conversation possibly steer itself through such a sea of responsibilities and inhibitions as this? On the other hand, conversation does flourish and society is refreshing, and neither dull on the one hand nor exhausting from its effort on the other, wherever people forget their scruples and take the brakes off their hearts, and let their tongues wag as automatically and irresponsibly as they will.

They talk much in pedagogic circles today about the duty of the teacher to prepare for every lesson in advance. To some extent this is useful. But we Yankees are assuredly not those to whom such a general doctrine should be preached. We are only too careful as it is. The advice I should give to most teachers would be in the words of one who is herself an admirable teacher. Prepare yourself in the *subject so well that it shall be always on tap:* then in the class-room trust your spontaneity and fling away all further care.

My advice to students, especially to girl-students, would be somewhat similar. Just as a bicycle-chain may be too tight, so may one's carefulness and conscientiousness be so tense as to hinder the running of one's mind. Take, for example, periods when there are many successive days of examination impending. One ounce of good nervous tone in an examination is worth many pounds of anxious study for it in advance. If you want really to do your best in an examination, fling away the book the day before, say to yourself, "I won't waste another minute on this miserable thing, and I don't care an iota whether I succeed or not." Say this sincerely, and feel it; and go out and play, or go to bed and sleep, and I am sure the results next day will encourage you to use the method permanently. I have heard this advice given to a student by Miss Call, whose book on muscular relaxation I quoted a moment ago. In her later book, entitled *As a Matter of Course*, the gospel of moral relaxation, of dropping things from the mind, and not "caring" is preached with equal success. Not only our preachers, but our friends the theosophists and mind-curers of various religious sects are also harping on this string. And with the doctors, the Delsarteans, the various mind-curing sects, and such writers as Mr. Dresser, Prentice Mulford, Mr. Horace Fletcher, and Mr. Trine to help, and the whole band of school-teachers and magazine-readers chiming in, it really looks as if a good start might be made in the direction of changing our American mental habit into something more indifferent and strong.

Worry means always and invariably inhibition of associations and loss of effective power. Of course, the sovereign cure for worry is religious faith; and this, of course, you also know. The turbulent billows of the fretful surface leave the deep parts of the ocean undisturbed, and to him who has a hold on vaster and more permanent realities the hourly vicissitudes of his personal destiny seem relatively insignificant things. The really religious person is accordingly unshakable and full of equanimity, and calmly ready for any duty that the day may bring forth. This is charmingly illustrated by a little work with which I recently became acquainted, "The Practice of the Presence of God, the Best Ruler of a Holy Life, by Brother Lawrence, being Conversations and Letters of

Nicholas Herman of Lorraine, Translated from the French."[1]
I extract a few passages, the conversations being given in indirect discourse. Brother Lawrence was a Carmelite friar,
converted at Paris in 1666. "He said that he had been foot-
man to M. Fieubert, the Treasurer, and that he was a great
awkward fellow, who broke everything. That he had desired
to be received into a monastery, thinking that he would there
be made to smart for his awkwardness and the faults he
should commit, and so he should sacrifice to God his life,
with its pleasures; but that God had disappointed him, he
having met with nothing but satisfaction in that state. . . .

"That he had long been troubled in mind from a certain
belief that he should be damned; that all the men in the
world could not have persuaded him to the contrary; but
that he had thus reasoned with himself about it: *I engaged in
a religious life only for the love of God, and I have en-
deavored to act only for Him; whatever becomes of me,
whether I be lost or saved, I will always continue to act purely
for the love of God. I shall have this good at least, that till
death I shall have done all that is in me to love Him. . . .*
That since then he had passed his life in perfect liberty and
continual joy.

"That when an occasion of practising some virtue offered,
he addressed himself to God, saying, 'Lord, I cannot do this
unless thou enablest me'; and that then he received strength
more than sufficient. That, when he had failed in his duty,
he only confessed his fault, saying to God, 'I shall never do
otherwise, if You leave me to myself; it is You who must
hinder my failing, and mend what is amiss.' That after this
he gave himself no further uneasiness about it.

"That he had been lately sent into Burgundy to buy the
provision of wine for the society, which was a very unwelcome
task for him, because he had no turn for business, and because he was lame, and could not go about the boat but
by rolling himself over the casks. That, however, he gave
himself no uneasiness about it, nor about the purchase of the
wine. That he said to God, 'It was his business he was about,'
and that he afterward found it well performed. That he had
been sent into Auvergne, the year before, upon the same account; that he could not tell how the matter passed, but that
it proved very well.

"So, likewise, in his business in the kitchen (to which he

had naturally a great aversion), having accustomed himself to do everything there for the love of God, and with prayer upon all occasions, for his grace to do his work well, he had found everything easy during fifteen years that he had been employed there.

"That he was very well pleased with the post he was now in, but that he was as ready to quit that as the former, since he was always pleasing himself in every condition, by doing little things for the love of God.

"That the goodness of God assured him he would not forsake him utterly, and that he would give him strength to bear whatever evil he permitted to happen to him; and, therefore, that he feared nothing, and had no occasion to consult with anybody about his state. That, when he had attempted to do it, he had always come away more perplexed."

The simple-heartedness of the good Brother Lawrence, and the relaxation of all unnecessary solicitudes and anxieties in him, is a refreshing spectacle.

The need of feeling responsible all the livelong day has been preached long enough in our New England. Long enough exclusively, at any rate, and long enough to the female sex. What our girl-students and woman-teachers most need nowadays is not the exacerbation, but rather the toning-down of their moral tensions. Even now I fear that some one of my fair hearers may be making an undying resolve to become strenuously relaxed, cost what it will, for the remainder of her life. It is needless to say that that is not the way to do it. The way to do it, paradoxical as it may seem, is genuinely not to care whether you are doing it or not. Then, possibly, by the grace of God, you may all at once find that you *are* doing it, and, having learned what the trick feels like, you may (again by the grace of God) be enabled to go on.

And that something like this may be the happy experience of all my hearers is, in closing, my most earnest wish.

ON A CERTAIN BLINDNESS
IN HUMAN BEINGS

Our judgments concerning the worth of things, big or little, depend on the *feelings* the things arouse in us. Where we judge a thing to be precious in consequence of the *idea* we frame of it, this is only because the idea is itself associated already with a feeling. If we were radically feelingless, and if ideas were the only things our mind could entertain, we should lose all our likes and dislikes at a stroke, and be unable to point to any one situation or experience in life more valuable or significant than any other.

Now the blindness in human beings, of which this discourse will treat, is the blindness with which we all are afflicted in regard to the feelings of creatures and people different from ourselves.

We are practical beings, each of us with limited functions and duties to perform. Each is bound to feel intensely the importance of his own duties and the significance of the situations that call these forth. But this feeling is in each of us a vital secret, for sympathy with which we vainly look to others. The others are too much absorbed in their own vital secrets to take an interest in ours. Hence the stupidity and injustice of our opinions, so far as they deal with the significance of alien lives. Hence the falsity of our judgments, so far as they presume to decide in an absolute way on the value of other persons' conditions or ideals.

Take our dogs and ourselves, connected as we are by a tie more intimate than most ties in this world; and yet, outside of that tie of friendly fondness, how insensible, each of us, to all that makes life significant for the other!—we to the rapture of bones under hedges, or smells of trees and lamp-posts, they to the delights of literature and art. As you sit reading the most moving romance you ever fell upon, what sort of a judge is your fox-terrier of your behavior? With all his good will toward you, the nature of your conduct is absolutely excluded from his comprehension. To sit there like a senseless statue, when you might be taking him to walk and throwing sticks for him to catch! What queer disease is this that comes over you every day, of holding things and staring at them like that for hours together, paralyzed of motion and vacant of all conscious life? The African savages came nearer the truth; but they, too, missed it, when they gathered wonderingly round one of our American travellers who, in the interior, had just come into possession of a stray copy of the New York *Commercial Advertiser,* and was devouring it column by column. When he got through, they offered him a high price for the mysterious object; and, being asked for what they wanted it, they said: "For an eye medicine,"— that being the only reason they could conceive of for the protracted bath which he had given his eyes upon its surface.

The spectator's judgment is sure to miss the root of the matter, and to possess no truth. The subject judged knows a part of the world of reality which the judging spectator fails to see, knows more while the spectator knows less; and, wherever there is conflict of opinion and difference of vision, we are bound to believe that the truer side is the side that feels the more, and not the side that feels the less.

Let me take a personal example of the kind that befalls each one of us daily:

Some years ago, while journeying in the mountains of North Carolina, I passed by a large number of "coves," as they call them there, or heads of small valleys between the hills, which had been newly cleared and planted. The impression on my mind was one of unmitigated squalor. The settler had in every case cut down the more manageable trees, and left their charred stumps standing. The larger trees he had girdled and killed, in order that their foliage should not cast a shade. He had then built a log cabin, plastering its chinks with clay, and had set up a tall zigzag rail fence around the scene of his havoc, to keep the pigs and cattle out. Finally, he had irregularly planted the intervals between the stumps and trees with Indian corn, which grew among the chips; and there he dwelt with his wife and babes—an axe, a gun, a few utensils, and some pigs and chickens feeding in the woods, being the sum total of his possessions.

The forest had been destroyed; and what had "improved" it out of existence was hideous, a sort of ulcer, without a single element of artificial grace to make up for the loss of Nature's beauty. Ugly, indeed, seemed the life of the squatter, scudding, as the sailors say, under bare poles, beginning again away back where our first ancestors started, and by hardly a single item the better off for all the achievements of the intervening generations.

Talk about going back to nature!—I said to myself, oppressed by the dreariness, as I drove by. Talk of a country life for one's old age and for one's children! Never thus, with nothing but the bare ground and one's bare hands to fight the battle! Never, without the best spoils of culture woven in! The beauties and commodities gained by the centuries are sacred. They are our heritage and birthright. No modern person ought to be willing to live a day in such a state of rudimentariness and denudation.

Then I said to the mountaineer who was driving me, "What sort of people are they who have to make these new clearings?" "All of us," he replied. "Why, we ain't happy here, unless we are getting one of these coves under cultivation." I instantly felt that I had been losing the whole inward significance of the situation. Because to me the clearings spoke of naught but denudation, I thought that to those whose sturdy arms and obedient axes had made them they could tell no other story. But, when *they* looked on the hideous stumps, what they thought of was personal victory. The chips, the girdled trees, and the vile split rails spoke of honest sweat, persistent toil and final reward. The cabin was a warrant of safety for self and wife and babes. In short, the clearing, which to me was a mere ugly picture on the retina, was to them a symbol redolent with moral memories and sang a very pæan of duty, struggle, and success.

I had been as blind to the peculiar ideality of their conditions as they certainly would also have been to the ideality of mine, had they had a peep at my strange indoor academic ways of life at Cambridge.

Wherever a process of life communicates an eagerness to him who lives it, there the life becomes genuinely significant.

Sometimes the eagerness is more knit up with the motor activities, sometimes with the perceptions, sometimes with the imagination, sometimes with reflective thought. But, wherever it is found, there is the zest, the tingle, the excitement of reality; and there *is* "importance" in the only real and positive sense in which importance ever anywhere can be.

Robert Louis Stevenson has illustrated this by a case, drawn from the sphere of the imagination, in an essay which I really think deserves to become immortal, both for the truth of its matter and the excellence of its form.

"Toward the end of September," Stevenson writes, "when school-time was drawing near, and the nights were already black, we would begin to sally from our respective villas, each equipped with a tin bull's-eye lantern. The thing was so well known that it had worn a rut in the commerce of Great Britain; and the grocers, about the due time, began to garnish their windows with our particular brand of luminary. We wore them buckled to the waist upon a cricket belt, and over them, such was the rigor of the game, a buttoned top-coat. They smelled noisomely of blistered tin. They never burned aright, though they would always burn our fingers. Their use was naught, the pleasure of them merely fanciful, and yet a boy with a bull's-eye under his top-coat asked for nothing more. The fishermen used lanterns about their boats, and it was from them, I suppose, that we had got the hint; but theirs were not bull's-eyes, nor did we ever play at being fishermen. The police carried them at their belts, and we had plainly copied them in that; yet we did not pretend to be policemen. Burglars, indeed, we may have had some haunting thought of; and we had certainly an eye to past ages when lanterns were more common, and to certain story-books in which we had found them to figure very largely. But take it for all in all, the pleasure of the thing was substantive; and to be a boy with a bull's-eye under his top-coat was good enough for us.

"When two of these asses met, there would be an anxious 'Have you got your lantern?' and a gratified 'Yes!' That was the shibboleth, and very needful, too; for, as it was the rule to keep our glory contained, none could recognize a lantern-bearer unless (like the polecat) by the smell. Four or five would sometimes climb into the belly of a ten-man lugger, with nothing but the thwarts above them—for the cabin was usually locked—or chose out some hollow of the links where the wind might whistle overhead. Then the coats would be unbuttoned, and the bull's-eyes discovered; and in the chequering glimmer, under the huge, windy hall of the night, and cheered by a rich steam of toasting tinware, these fortunate young gentlemen would crouch together in the cold sand of the links, or on the scaly bilges of the fishing-boat, and delight them with inappropriate talk. Woe is me that I cannot give some specimens! . . . But the talk was but a condiment, and these gatherings themselves only accidents in the career of the lantern-bearer. The essence of this bliss was to walk by yourself in the black night, the slide shut, the topcoat buttoned, not a ray escaping, whether to conduct your footsteps or to make your glory public—a mere pillar of darkness in the dark; and all the while, deep down in the privacy of your fool's heart, to know you had a bull's-eye at your belt, and to exult and sing over the knowledge.

"It is said that a poet has died young in the breast of the most stolid. It may be contended rather that a (somewhat minor) bard in almost every case survives, and is the spice of life to his possessor. Justice is not done to the versatility and the unplumbed childishness of man's imagination. His life from without may seem but a rude mound of mud: there will be some golden chamber at the heart of it, in which he dwells delighted; and for as dark as his pathway seems to the observer, he will have some kind of bull's-eye at his belt.

. . . "There is one fable that touches very near the quick of life—the fable of the monk who passed into the woods, heard a bird break into song, hearkened for a trill or two, and found himself at his return a stranger at his convent gates; for he had been absent fifty years, and of all his comrades there survived but one to recognize him. It is not only in the woods that this enchanter carols, though perhaps he is native there. He sings in the most doleful places. The miser hears him and chuckles, and his days are moments. With no more apparatus than an evil-smelling lantern, I have evoked him on the naked links. All life that is not merely mechanical is spun out of two strands—seeking for that bird and hearing him. And it is just this that makes life so hard to value, and the delight of each so incommunicable. And it is just a knowledge of this, and a remembrance of those fortunate hours in which the bird *has* sung to *us*, that fills us with such wonder when we turn to the pages of the realist. There, to be sure, we find a picture of life in so far as it consists of mud and of old iron, cheap desires and cheap fears, that which we are ashamed to remember and that which we are careless whether we forget; but of the note of that time-devouring nightingale we hear no news.

. . . "Say that we came [in such a realistic romance] on some such business as that of my lantern-bearers on the links, and described the boys as very cold, spat upon by flurries of rain, and drearily surrounded, all of which they were; and their talk as silly and indecent, which it certainly was. To the eye of the observer they *are* wet and cold and drearily surrounded; but ask themselves, and they are in the heaven of a recondite pleasure, the ground of which is an ill-smelling lantern.

"For, to repeat, the ground of a man's joy is often hard to hit. It may hinge at times upon a mere accessory, like the lantern; it may reside in the mysterious inwards of psychology. . . . It has so little bond with externals . . . that it may even touch them not, and the man's true life, for which he consents to live, lie together in the field of fancy. . . . In such a case the poetry runs underground. The observer (poor soul, with his documents!) is all abroad. For to look at the man is but to court deception. We shall see the trunk from which he draws his nourishment; but he himself is above and abroad in the green dome of foliage, hummed through by winds and nested in by nightingales. And the true realism were that of the poets, to climb after him like a squirrel, and catch some glimpse of the heaven in which he lives. And the true realism, always and everywhere, is that of the poets: to find out where joy resides, and give it a voice far beyond singing.

"For to miss the joy is to miss all. In the joy of the actors lies the sense of any action. That is the explanation, that the excuse. To one who has not the secret of the lanterns the scene upon the links is meaningless. And hence the haunting and truly spectral unreality of realistic books. . . . In each we miss the personal poetry, the enchanted atmosphere, that rainbow work of fancy that clothes what is naked and seems to ennoble what is base; in each, life falls dead like dough, instead of soaring away like a balloon into the colors of the sunset; each is true, each inconceivable; for no man lives in the external truth among salts and acids, but in the warm, phantasmagoric chamber of his brain, with the painted windows and the storied wall." [1]

These paragraphs are the best thing I know in all Stevenson. "To miss the joy is to miss all." Indeed, it is. Yet we are but finite, and each one of us has some single specialized vocation of his own. And it seems as if energy in the service of its particular duties might be got only by hardening the heart toward everything unlike them. Our deadness toward all but one particular kind of joy would thus be the price we inevitably have to pay for being practical creatures. Only in some pitiful dreamer, some philosopher, poet, or romancer, or when the common practical man becomes a lover, does the hard externality give way, and a gleam of insight into the ejective world, as Clifford called it, the vast world of inner life beyond us, so different from that of outer seeming, illuminate our mind. Then the whole scheme of our customary values gets confounded, then our self is riven and its narrow interests fly to pieces, then a new centre and a new perspective must be found.

The change is well described by my colleague, Josiah Royce: "What, then, is our neighbor? Thou hast regarded his thought, his feeling, as somehow different from thine. Thou hast said, 'A pain in him is not like a pain in me, but something far easier to bear.' He seems to thee a little less living than thou; his life is dim, it is cold, it is a pale fire beside thy own burning desires. . . . So, dimly and by instinct hast thou lived with thy neighbor, and hast known him not, being blind. Thou hast made [of him] a thing, no Self at all. Have done with this illusion, and simply try to learn the truth. Pain is pain, joy is joy, everywhere, even as in thee. In all the songs of the forest birds; in all the cries of the wounded and dying, struggling in the captor's power; in the boundless sea where the myriads of water-creatures strive and die; amid all the countless hordes of savage men; in all sickness and sorrow; in all exultation and hope, everywhere, from the lowest to the noblest, the same conscious, burning, wilful life is found, endlessly manifold as the forms of the living creatures, unquenchable as the fires of the sun, real as these impulses that even now throb in thine own little selfish heart. Lift up thy eyes, behold that life, and then turn away, and forget it as

258 • THE WILL TO BELIEVE

thou canst; but, if thou hast *known* that, thou hast begun to
know thy duty." [2]

This higher vision of an inner significance in what, until
then, we had realized only in the dead external way, often
comes over a person suddenly; and, when it does so, it makes
an epoch in his history. As Emerson says, there is a depth in
those moments that constrains us to ascribe more reality to
them than to all other experiences. The passion of love will
shake one like an explosion, or some act will awaken a re-
morseful compunction that hangs like a cloud over all one's
later day.

This mystic sense of hidden meaning starts upon us often
from non-human natural things. I take this passage from
Obermann, a French novel that had some vogue in its day:
"Paris, March 7. It was dark and rather cold. I was gloomy,
and walked because I had nothing to do. I passed by some
flowers placed breast-high upon a wall. A jonquil in bloom was
there. It is the strongest expression of desire: it was the
first perfume of the year. I felt all the happiness destined for
man. This unutterable harmony of souls, the phantom of the
ideal world, arose in me complete. I never felt anything so
great or so instantaneous. I know not what shape, what analogy, what secret of relation it was that made me see in this
flower a limitless beauty. . . . I shall never enclose in a conception this power, this immensity that nothing will express;
this form that nothing will contain; this ideal of a better
world which one feels, but which it would seem that nature
has not made." [3]

Wordsworth and Shelley are similarly full of this sense of
a limitless significance in natural things. In Wordsworth it
was a somewhat austere and moral significance—a "lonely
cheer."

> To every natural form, rock, fruit, or flower,
> Even the loose stones that cover the highway,
> I gave a moral life: I saw them feel
> Or linked them to some feeling: the great mass
> Lay bedded in some quickening soul, and all
> That I beheld respired with inward meaning. [4]

"Authentic tidings of invisible things!" Just what this hidden presence in nature was, which Wordsworth so rapturously felt, and in the light of which he lived, tramping the hills for days together, the poet never could explain logically or in articulate conceptions. Yet to the reader who may himself have had gleaming moments of a similar sort the verses in which Wordsworth simply proclaims the fact of them come with a heart-satisfying authority:

> Magnificent
> The morning rose, in memorable pomp,
> Glorious as ere I had beheld. In front
> The sea lay laughing at a distance; near
> The solid mountains shone, bright as the clouds,
> Grain-tinctured, drenched in empyrean light;
> And in the meadows and the lower grounds
> Was all the sweetness of a common dawn,—
> Dews, vapors, and the melody of birds,
> And laborers going forth to till the fields.
>
> Ah! need I say, dear Friend, that to the brim
> My heart was full; I made no vows, but vows
> Were then made for me; bond unknown to me
> Was given, that I should be, else sinning greatly,
> A dedicated Spirit. On I walked,
> In thankless blessedness, which yet survives.[5]

As Wordsworth walked, filled with his strange inner joy, responsive thus to the secret life of nature round about him, his rural neighbors, tightly and narrowly intent upon their own affairs, their crops and lambs and fences, must have thought him a very insignificant and foolish personage. It surely never occurred to any one of them to wonder what was going on inside of *him* or what it might be worth. And yet that inner life of his carried the burden of a significance that has fed the souls of others, and fills them to this day with inner joy.

Richard Jeffries has written a remarkable autobiographic document entitled *The Story of my Heart*. It tells, in many pages, of the rapture with which in youth the sense of the life of nature filled him. On a certain hill-top he says:

"I was utterly alone with the sun and the earth. Lying down on the grass, I spoke in my soul to the earth, the sun, the air, and the distant sea, far beyond sight. . . . With all the intensity of feeling which exalted me, all the intense communion I held with the earth, the sun and sky, the stars hidden by the light, with the ocean—in no manner can the thrilling depth of these feelings be written—with these I prayed as if they were the keys of an instrument. . . . The great sun, burning with light, the strong earth—dear earth—the warm sky, the pure air, the thought of ocean, the inexpressible beauty of all filled me with a rapture, an ecstasy, an inflatus. With this inflatus, too, I prayed. . . . The prayer, this soul-emotion, was in itself, not for an object: it was a passion. I hid my face in the grass. I was wholly prostrated, I lost myself in the wrestle, I was rapt and carried away. . . . Had any shepherd accidentally seen me lying on the turf, he would only have thought I was resting a few minutes. I made no outward show. Who could have imagined the whirlwind of passion that was going on in me as I reclined there!" [*]

Surely, a worthless hour of life, when measured by the usual standards of commercial value. Yet in what other *kind* of value can the preciousness of any hour, made precious by any standard, consist, if it consist not in feelings of excited significance like these, engendered in some one, by what the hour contains?

Yet so blind and dead does the clamor of our own practical interests make us to all other things, that it seems almost as if it were necessary to become worthless as a practical being, if one is to hope to attain to any breadth of insight into the impersonal world of worths as such, to have any perception of life's meaning on a large objective scale. Only your mystic, your dreamer, or your insolvent tramp or loafer, can afford so sympathetic an occupation, an occupation which will change the usual standards of human value in the twinkling of an eye, giving to foolishness a place ahead of power, and laying low in a minute the distinctions which it takes a hardworking conventional man a lifetime to build up. You may be a prophet, at this rate; but you cannot be a worldly success.

Walt Whitman, for instance, is accounted by many of us a contemporary prophet. He abolishes the usual human distinctions, brings all conventionalisms into solution, and loves and celebrates hardly any human attributes save those elementary ones common to all members of the race. For this he becomes a sort of ideal tramp, a rider on omnibus-tops and ferryboats, and, considered either practically or academically, a worthless, unproductive being. His verses are but ejaculations—things mostly without subject or verb, a succession of interjections on an immense scale. He felt the human crowd as rapturously as Wordsworth felt the mountains, felt it as an overpoweringly significant presence, simply to absorb one's mind in which should be business sufficient and worthy to fill the days of a serious man. As he crosses Brooklyn ferry, this is what he feels:

Flood-tide below me! I watch you, face to face;
Clouds of the west! sun there half an hour high! I see you also face to face.
Crowds of men and women attired in the usual costumes! how curious you are to me!
On the ferry-boats, the hundreds and hundreds that cross, returning home, are more curious to me than you suppose;
And you that shall cross from shore to shore years hence, are more to me, and more in my meditations, than you might suppose.
Others will enter the gates of the ferry, and cross from shore to shore;
Others will watch the run of the flood-tide;
Others will see the shipping of Manhattan north and west, and the heights of Brooklyn to the south and east;
Others will see the islands large and small;
Fifty years hence, others will see them as they cross, the sun half an hour high.
A hundred years hence, or ever so many hundred years hence, others will see them,
Will enjoy the sunset, the pouring in of the flood-tide, the falling back to the sea of the ebb-tide.
It avails not, neither time or place—distance avails not.
Just as you feel when you look on the river and sky, so I felt;
Just as any of you is one of a living crowd, I was one of a crowd;
Just as you are refresh'd by the gladness of the river and the bright flow, I was refresh'd;
Just as you stand and lean on the rail, yet hurry with the swift current, I stood, yet was hurried;
Just as you look on the numberless masts of ships, and the thick-stemmed pipes of steamboats, I looked.

I too many and many a time cross'd the river, the sun half an
hour high;
I watched the Twelfth-month sea-gulls—I saw them high in
the air, with motionless wings, oscillating their bodies,
I saw how the glistening yellow lit up parts of their bodies,
and left the rest in strong shadow,
I saw the slow-wheeling circles, and the gradual edging
toward the south.
Saw the white sails of schooners and sloops, saw the ships
at anchor,
The sailors at work in the rigging, or out astride the spars;
The scalloped-edged waves in the twilight, the ladled cups,
the frolicsome crests and glistening;
The stretch afar growing dimmer and dimmer, the gray walls
of the granite store-houses by the docks;
On the neighboring shores, the fires from the foundry chim-
neys burning high . . . into the night,
Casting their flicker of black . . . into the clefts of streets.
These, and all else, were to me the same as they are to you.⁷

And so on, through the rest of a divinely beautiful poem.
And, if you wish to see what this hoary loafer considered the
most worthy way of profiting by life's heaven-sent opportunities, read the delicious volume of his letters to a young car-
conductor who had become his friend:

"New York, Oct. 9, 1868.
"*Dear Pete*, It is splendid here this forenoon—bright and
cool. I was out early taking a short walk by the river only two
squares from where I live. . . . Shall I tell you about [my life]
just to fill up? I generally spend the forenoon in my room
writing, etc., then take a bath fix up and go out about twelve
and loaf somewhere or call on someone down town or on
business, or perhaps if it is very pleasant and I feel like it
ride a trip with some driver friend on Broadway from 23rd
Street to Bowling Green, three miles each way. (Every day
I find I have plenty to do, every hour is occupied with something.) You know it is a never ending amusement and study
and recreation for me to ride a couple of hours on a pleasant
afternoon on a Broadway stage in this way. You see everything as you pass, a sort of living, endless panorama—shops
and splendid buildings and great windows: on the broad side-

walks crowds of women richly dressed continually passing, altogether different, superior in style and looks from any to be seen anywhere else—in fact a perfect stream of people—men too dressed in high style, and plenty of foreigners—and then in the streets the thick crowd of carriages, stages, carts, hotel and private coaches, and in fact all sorts of vehicles and many first class teams, mile after mile, and the splendor of such a great street and so many tall, ornamental, noble buildings many of them of white marble, and the gayety and motion on every side: you will not wonder how much attraction all this is on a fine day, to a great loafer like me, who enjoys so much seeing the busy world move by him, and exhibiting itself for his amusement, while he takes it easy and just looks on and observes." [8]

Truly a futile way of passing the time, some of you may say, and not altogether creditable to a grown-up man. And yet, from the deepest point of view, who knows the more of truth, and who knows the less—Whitman on his omnibus-top, full of the inner joy with which the spectacle inspires him, or you, full of the disdain which the futility of his occupation excites?

When your ordinary Brooklynite or New Yorker, leading a life replete with too much luxury, or tired and careworn about his personal affairs, crosses the ferry or goes up Broadway, *his* fancy does not thus "soar away into the colors of the sunset" as did Whitman's, nor does he inwardly realize at all the indisputable fact that this world never did anywhere or at any time contain more of essential divinity, or of eternal meaning, than is embodied in the fields of vision over which his eyes so carelessly pass. There is life; and there, a step away, is death. There is the only kind of beauty there ever was. There is the old human struggle and its fruits together. There is the text and the sermon, the real and the ideal in one. But to the jaded and unquickened eye it is all dead and common, pure vulgarism, flatness, and disgust. "Hech! it is a sad sight!" says Carlyle, walking at night with some one who appeals to him to note the splendor of the stars. And that very repetition of the scene to new generations of men in *secula seculorum*, that eternal recurrence of the common order, which so fills a Whitman with mystic satisfaction, is to a Schopenhauer, with the emotional anæsthesia, the feeling of "awful inner emptiness" from out of which he views it all, the chief ingredient of the tedium it instills. What is life on the largest scale, he asks, but the same recurrent inanities, the same dog barking, the same fly buzzing, forevermore? Yet of the kind of fibre of which such inanities consist is the material woven of all the excitements, joys, and meanings that ever were, or ever shall be, in this world.

To be rapt with satisfied attention, like Whitman, to the mere spectacle of the world's presence, is one way, and the most fundamental way, of confessing one's sense of its unfathomable significance and importance. But how can one attain to the feeling of the vital significance of an experience, if one have it not to begin with? There is no receipt which one can follow. Being a secret and a mystery, it often comes in mysteriously unexpected ways. It blossoms sometimes from out of the very grave wherein we imagined that our happiness was buried. Benvenuto Cellini, after a life all in the outer sunshine, made of adventures and artistic excitements, suddenly finds himself cast into a dungeon in the Castle of San Angelo. The place is horrible. Rats and wet and mould possess it. His leg is broken and his teeth fall out, apparently with scurvy. But his thoughts turn to God as they have never turned before. He gets a Bible, which he reads during the one hour in the twenty-four in which a wandering ray of daylight penetrates his cavern. He has religious visions. He sings psalms to himself, and composes hymns. And thinking, on the last day of July, of the festivities customary on the morrow in Rome, he says to himself: "All these past years I celebrated this holiday with the vanities of the world: from this year henceforward I will do it with the divinity of God. And then I said to myself, 'Oh, how much more happy I am for this present life of mine than for all those things remembered!' " [9]

But the great understander of these mysterious ebbs and flows is Tolstoï. They throb all through his novels. In his *War and Peace,* the hero, Peter, is supposed to be the richest man in the Russian empire. During the French invasion he is taken prisoner, and dragged through much of the retreat. Cold, vermin, hunger, and every form of misery assail him, the result being a revelation to him of the real scale of life's values. "Here only, and for the first time, he appreciated, because he was deprived of it, the happiness of eating when he was hungry, of drinking when he was thirsty, of sleeping when he was sleepy, and of talking when he felt the desire to exchange some words. . . . Later in life he always recurred with joy to this month of captivity, and never failed to speak with enthusiasm of the powerful and ineffaceable sensations, and especially of the moral calm which he had experienced at this epoch. When at daybreak, on the morrow of his imprisonment, he saw [I abridge here Tolstoï's description] the mountains with their wooded slopes disappearing in the grayish mist; when he felt the cool breeze caress him; when he saw the light drive away the vapors, and the sun rise majestically behind the clouds and cupolas, and the crosses, the dew, the distance, the river, sparkle in the splendid, cheerful rays—his heart overflowed with emotion. This emotion kept continually with him, and increased a hundred-fold as the difficulties of his situation grew graver. . . . He learnt that man is meant for happiness, and that this happiness is in him, in the satisfaction of the daily needs of existence, and that unhappiness is the fatal result, not of our need, but of our abundance. . . . When calm reigned in the camp, and the embers paled, and little by little went out, the full moon had reached the zenith. The woods and the fields roundabout lay clearly visible; and, beyond the inundation of light which filled them, the view plunged into the limitless horizon. Then Peter cast his eyes upon the firmament, filled at that hour with myriads of stars. 'All that is mine,' he thought. 'All that is in me, is me! And that is what they think they have taken prisoner! That is what they have shut up in a cabin!' So he smiled, and turned in to sleep among his comrades." [10]

The occasion and the experience, then, are nothing. It all depends on the capacity of the soul to be grasped, to have its life-currents absorbed by what is given. "Crossing a bare common," says Emerson, "in snow puddles, at twilight, under a clouded sky, without having in my thoughts any occurrence of special good fortune, I have enjoyed a perfect exhilaration. I am glad to the brink of fear."

Life is always worth living, if one have such responsive sensibilities. But we of the highly educated classes (so called) have most of us got far, far away from Nature. We are trained to seek the choice, the rare, the exquisite exclusively, and to overlook the common. We are stuffed with abstract conceptions, and glib with verbalities and verbosities; and in the culture of these higher functions the peculiar sources of joy connected with our simpler functions often dry up, and we grow stone-blind and insensible to life's more elementary and general goods and joys.

The remedy under such conditions is to descend to a more profound and primitive level. To be imprisoned or shipwrecked or forced into the army would permanently show the good of life to many an over-educated pessimist. Living in the open air and on the ground, the lop-sided beam of the balance slowly rises to the level line; and the over-sensibilities and insensibilities even themselves out. The good of all the artificial schemes and fevers fades and pales; and that of seeing, smelling, tasting, sleeping, and daring and doing with one's body, grows and grows. The savages and children of nature, to whom we deem ourselves so much superior, certainly are alive where we are often dead, along these lines; and, could they write as glibly as we do, they would read us impressive lectures on our impatience for improvement and on our blindness to the fundamental static goods of life. "Ah! my brother," said a chieftain to his white guest, "thou wilt never know the happiness of both thinking of nothing and doing nothing. This, next to sleep, is the most enchanting of all things. Thus we were before our birth, and thus we shall be after death. Thy people, . . . when they have finished reaping one field, they begin to plough another; and, if the day were not enough, I have seen them plough by moonlight. What is their life to ours,—the life that is as naught to them? Blind that they are, they lose it all! But we live in the present." [11]

The intense interest that life can assume when brought down to the non-thinking level, the level of pure sensorial perception, has been beautifully described by a man who *can* write,—Mr. W. H. Hudson, in his volume, *Idle Days in Patagonia*.

"I spent the greater part of one winter," says this admirable author, "at a point on the Rio Negro, seventy or eighty miles from the sea.

. . . "It was my custom to go out every morning on horseback with my gun and, followed by one dog, to ride away from the valley; and no sooner would I climb the terrace, and plunge into the gray, universal thicket, than I would find myself as completely alone as if five hundred instead of only five miles separated me from the valley and river. So wild and solitary and remote seemed that gray waste, stretching away into infinitude, a waste untrodden by man, and where the wild animals are so few that they have made no discoverable path in the wilderness of thorns. . . . Not once nor twice nor thrice, but day after day I returned to this solitude, going to it in the morning as if to attend a festival, and leaving it only when hunger and thirst and the westering sun compelled me. And yet I had no object in going,—no motive which could be put into words; for, although I carried a gun, there was nothing to shoot—the shooting was all left behind in the valley. . . . Sometimes I would pass a whole day without seeing one mammal, and perhaps not more than a dozen birds of any size. The weather at that time was cheerless, generally with a gray film of cloud spread over the sky, and a bleak wind, often cold enough to make my bridle-hand quite numb. . . . At a slow pace, which would have seemed intolerable under other circumstances, I would ride about for hours together at a stretch. On arriving at a hill, I would slowly ride to its summit, and stand there to survey the prospect. On every side it stretched away in great undulations, wild and irregular. How gray it all was! Hardly less so near at hand than on the haze-wrapped horizon where the hills were dim and the outline obscured by distance. Descending from my outlook, I would take up my aimless wanderings again, and visit other elevations to gaze on the same landscape from another point; and so on for hours. And at noon I would dismount, and sit or lie on my folded poncho for an hour or longer. One day in these rambles I discovered a small grove composed of twenty or thirty trees, growing at a convenient distance apart, that had evidently been resorted to by a herd of deer or other wild animals. This grove was on a hill differing in shape from other hills in its neighborhood; and, after a time, I made a point of finding and using it as a resting-place every day at noon. I did not ask myself why I made choice of that one spot, sometimes going out of my way to sit there, instead of sitting down under any one of the millions of trees and bushes on any other hillside. I thought nothing about it, but acted unconsciously. Only afterward it seemed to me that, after having rested there once, each time I wished to rest again, the wish came associated with the image of that particular clump of trees, with polished stems and clean bed of sand beneath; and in a short time I formed a habit of returning, animal like, to repose at that same spot.

"It was, perhaps, a mistake to say that I would sit down

and rest, since I was never tired; and yet, without being tired, that noon-day pause, during which I sat for an hour without moving, was strangely grateful. All day there would be no sound, not even the rustling of a leaf. One day, while *listening* to the silence, it occurred to my mind to wonder what the effect would be if I were to shout aloud. This seemed at the time a horrible suggestion, which almost made me shudder. But during those solitary days it was a rare thing for any thought to cross my mind. In the state of mind I was in, thought had become impossible. My state was one of *suspense* and *watchfulness;* yet I had no expectation of meeting an adventure, and felt as free from apprehension as I feel now while sitting in a room in London. The state seemed familiar rather than strange, and accompanied by a strong feeling of elation; and I did not know that something had come between me and my intellect until I returned to my former self—to thinking, and the old insipid existence [again].

"I had undoubtedly *gone back;* and that state of intense watchfulness or alertness, rather, with suspension of the higher intellectual faculties, represented the mental state of the pure savage. He thinks little, reasons little, having a surer guide in his [mere sensory perceptions]. He is in perfect harmony with nature, and is nearly on a level, mentally, with the wild animals he preys on, and which in their turn sometimes prey on him." [12]

For the spectator, such hours as Mr. Hudson writes of form a mere tale of emptiness, in which nothing happens, nothing is gained, and there is nothing to describe. They are meaningless and vacant tracts of time. To him who feels their inner secret, they tingle with an importance that unutterably vouches for itself. I am sorry for the boy or girl, or man or woman, who has never been touched by the spell of this mysterious sensorial life, with its irrationality, if so you like to call it, but its vigilance and its supreme felicity. The holidays of life are its most vitally significant portions, because they are, or at least should be, covered with just this kind of magically irresponsible spell.

And now what is the result of all these considerations and quotations? It is negative in one sense, but positive in another. It absolutely forbids us to be forward in pronouncing on the meaninglessness of forms of existence other than our own; and it commands us to tolerate, respect, and indulge those whom we see harmlessly interested and happy in their own ways, however unintelligible these may be to us. Hands off: neither the whole of truth nor the whole of good is revealed to any single observer, although each observer gains a partial superiority of insight from the peculiar position in which he stands. Even prisons and sick-rooms have their special revelations. It is enough to ask of each of us that he should be faithful to his own opportunities and make the most of his own blessings, without presuming to regulate the rest of the vast field.

WHAT MAKES A LIFE
SIGNIFICANT?

In my previous talk, "On a Certain Blindness," I tried to make you feel how soaked and shot-through life is with values and meanings which we fail to realize because of our external and insensible point of view. The meanings are there for the others, but they are not there for us. There lies more than a mere interest of curious speculation in understanding this. It has the most tremendous practical importance. I wish that I could convince you of it as I feel it myself. It is the basis of all our tolerance, social, religious, and political. The forgetting of it lies at the root of every stupid and sanguinary mistake that rulers over subject-peoples make. The first thing to learn in intercourse with others is non-interference with their own peculiar ways of being happy, provided those ways do not assume to interfere by violence with ours. No one has insight into all the ideals. No one should presume to judge them off-hand. The pretension to dogmatize about them in each other is the root of most human injustices and cruelties, and the trait in human character most likely to make the angels weep.

Every Jack sees in his own particular Jill charms and perfections to the enchantment of which we stolid onlookers are stone-cold. And which has the superior view of the absolute truth, he or we? Which has the more vital insight into the nature of Jill's existence, as a fact? Is he in excess, being in this matter a maniac? or are we in defect, being victims of a pathological anæsthesia as regards Jill's magical importance? Surely the latter; surely to Jack are the profounder truths revealed; surely poor Jill's palpitating little life-throbs *are* among the wonders of creation, *are* worthy of this sympathetic interest; and it is to our shame that the rest of us cannot feel like Jack. For Jack realizes Jill concretely, and we do not. He struggles toward a union with her inner life, divining her feelings, anticipating her desires, understanding her limits as manfully as he can, and yet inadequately, too; for he is also afflicted with some blindness, even here. Whilst we, dead clods that we are, do not even seek after these things, but are contented that that portion of eternal fact named Jill should be for us as if it were not. Jill, who knows her inner life, knows that Jack's way of taking it—so importantly—is the true and serious way; and she responds to the truth in him by taking him truly and seriously, too. May the ancient blindness never wrap its clouds about either of them again! Where would any of *us* be, were there no one willing to know us as we really are or ready to repay us for *our* insight by making recognizant return? We ought, all of us, to realize each other in this intense, pathetic, and important way.

If you say that this is absurd, and that we cannot be in love with everyone at once, I merely point out to you that, as a matter of fact, certain persons do exist with an enormous capacity for friendship and for taking delight in other people's lives; and that such persons know more of truth than if their hearts were not so big. The vice of ordinary Jack and Jill affection is not its intensity, but its exclusions and its jealousies. Leave those out, and you see that the ideal I am holding up before you, however impracticable today, yet contains nothing intrinsically absurd.

We have unquestionably a great cloud-bank of ancestral blindness weighing down upon us, only transiently riven here and there by fitful revelations of the truth. It is vain to hope for this state of things to alter much. Our inner secrets must remain for the most part impenetrable by others, for beings as essentially practical as we are are necessarily short of sight. But, if we cannot gain much positive insight into one another, cannot we at least use our sense of our own blindness to make us more cautious in going over the dark places? Cannot we escape some of those hideous ancestral intolerances and cruelties, and positive reversals of the truth?

For the remainder of this hour I invite you to seek with me some principle to make our tolerance less chaotic. And, as I began my previous lecture by a personal reminiscence, I am going to ask your indulgence for a similar bit of egotism now.

A few summers ago I spent a happy week at the famous

Assembly Grounds on the borders of Chautauqua Lake. The moment one treads that sacred enclosure, one feels one's self in an atmosphere of success. Sobriety and industry, intelligence and goodness, orderliness and ideality, prosperity and cheerfulness, pervade the air. It is a serious and studious picnic on a gigantic scale. Here you have a town of many thousands of inhabitants, beautifully laid out in the forest and drained, and equipped with means for satisfying all the necessary lower and most of the superfluous higher wants of man. You have a first-class college in full blast. You have magnificent music— a chorus of seven hundred voices, with possibly the most perfect open-air auditorium in the world. You have every sort of athletic exercise from sailing, rowing, swimming, bicycling, to the ball-field and the more artificial doings which the gymnasium affords. You have kindergartens and model secondary schools. You have general religious services and special clubhouses for the several sects. You have perpetually running soda-water fountains, and daily popular lectures by distinguished men. You have the best of company, and yet no effort. You have no zymotic diseases, no poverty, no drunkenness, no crime, no police. You have culture, you have kindness, you have cheapness, you have equality, you have the best fruits of what mankind has fought and bled and striven for under the name of civilization for centuries. You have, in short, a foretaste of what human society might be, were it all in the light, with no suffering and no dark corners.

I went in curiosity for a day. I stayed for a week, held spell-bound by the charm and ease of everything, by the middle-class paradise, without a sin, without a victim, without a blot, without a tear.

And yet what was my own astonishment, on emerging into the dark and wicked world again, to catch myself quite unexpectedly and involuntarily saying: "Ouf! what a relief! Now for something primordial and savage, even though it were as bad as an Armenian massacre, to set the balance straight again. This order is too tame, this culture too second-rate, this goodness too uninspiring. This human drama without a villain or a pang; this community so refined that ice-cream and soda-water is the utmost offering it can make to the brute animal in man; this city simmering in the tepid lakeside sun; this atrocious harmlessness of all things—I cannot abide with them. Let me take my chances again in the big outside worldly wilderness with all its sins and sufferings. There are the heights and depths, the precipices and the steep ideals, the gleams of the awful and the infinite; and there is more hope and help a thousand times than in this dead level and quintessence of every mediocrity."

Such was the sudden right-about-face performed for me by my lawless fancy! There had been spread before me the realization—on a small, sample scale of course—of all the ideals for which our civilization has been striving: security, intelligence, humanity, and order; and here was the instinctive hostile reaction, not of the natural man, but of a so-called cultivated man upon such a Utopia. There seemed thus to be a self-contradiction and paradox somewhere, which I, as a professor drawing a full salary, was in duty bound to unravel and explain, if I could.

So I meditated. And, first of all, I asked myself what the thing was that was so lacking in this Sabbatical city, and the lack of which kept one forever falling short of the higher sort of contentment. And I soon recognized that it was the element that gives to the wicked outer world all its moral style, expressiveness and picturesqueness—the element of precipitousness, so to call it, of strength and strenuousness, intensity and danger. What excites and interests the looker-on at life, what the romances and the statues celebrate and the grim civic monuments remind us of, is the everlasting battle of the powers of light with those of darkness; with heroism, reduced to its bare chance, yet ever and anon snatching victory from the jaws of death. But in this unspeakable Chautauqua there was no potentiality of death in sight anywhere, and no point of the compass visible from which danger might possibly appear. The ideal was so completely victorious already that no sign of any previous battle remained, the place just resting on its oars. But what our human emotions seem to require is the sight of the struggle going on. The moment the fruits are being merely eaten, things become ignoble. Sweat and effort, human nature strained to its uttermost and on the rack, yet getting through alive, and then turning its back on its success to pursue another more rare and arduous still—this is the sort of thing the presence of which inspires us, and the reality of which it seems to be the function of all the higher forms of literature and fine art to bring home to us and suggest. At Chautauqua there were no racks, even in the place's historical museum; and no sweat, except possibly the gentle moisture on the brow of some lecturer, or on the sides of some player in the ball-field.

Such absence of human nature *in extremis* anywhere seemed, then, a sufficient explanation for Chautauqua's flatness and lack of zest.

But was not this a paradox well calculated to fill one with dismay? It looks indeed, thought I, as if the romantic idealists with their pessimism about our civilization were, after all, quite right. An irremediable flatness is coming over the world. Bourgeoisie and mediocrity, church sociables and teachers' conventions, are taking the place of the old heights and depths and romantic chiaroscuro. And, to get human life in its wild intensity, we must in future turn more and more away from the actual, and forget it, if we can, in the romancer's or the poet's pages. The whole world, delightful and sinful as it may still appear for a moment to one just escaped from the Chautauquan enclosure, is nevertheless obeying more and more just those ideals that are sure to make of it in the end a mere Chautauqua Assembly on an enormous scale. *Was im Gesang soll leben muss im Leben untergehn.* Even now, in our own country, correctness, fairness, and compromise for every small advantage are crowding out all other qualities. The higher heroisms and the old rare flavors are passing out of life. [1]

With these thoughts in my mind, I was speeding with the train toward Buffalo, when, near that city, the sight of a workman doing something on the dizzy edge of a sky-scaling iron construction brought me to my senses very suddenly. And now I perceived, by a flash of insight, that I had been steeping myself in pure ancestral blindness, and looking at life with the eyes of a remote spectator. Wishing for heroism and the spectacle of human nature on the rack, I had never noticed the great fields of heroism lying around about me, I had failed to see it present and alive. I could only think of it as dead and embalmed, labelled and costumed, as it is in the pages of romance. And yet there it was before me in the daily lives of the laboring classes. Not in clanging fights and desperate marches only is heroism to be looked for, but on every railway bridge and fire-proof building that is going up today. On freight-trains, on the decks of vessels, in cattle-yards and mines, on lumber-rafts, among the firemen and the policemen, the demand for courage is incessant; and the supply never fails. There, every day of the year somewhere, is human nature *in extremis for you.* And wherever a scythe, an axe, a pick, or a shovel is wielded, you have it sweating and aching and with its powers of patient endurance racked to the utmost under the length of hours of the strain.

As I awoke to all this unidealized heroic life around me, the scales seemed to fall from my eyes; and a wave of sympathy greater than anything I had ever before felt with the common life of common men began to fill my soul. It began to seem as if virtue with horny hands and dirty skin were the only virtue genuine and vital enough to take account of. Every other virtue poses; none is absolutely unconscious and simple, and unexpectant of decoration or recognition, like this. These are our soldiers, thought I, these our sustainers, these the very parents of our life.

Many years ago, when in Vienna, I had had a similar feeling of awe and reverence in looking at the peasant-women, in from the country on their business at the market for the day. Old hags many of them were, dried and brown and wrinkled, kerchiefed and short-petticoated, with thick wool stockings on their bony shanks, stumping through the glittering thoroughfares, looking neither to the right nor the left, bent on duty, envying nothing, humble-hearted, remote; and yet at bottom, when you came to think of it, bearing the whole fabric of the splendors and corruptions of that city on their laborious backs. For where would any of it have been without their unremitting, unrewarded labor in the fields? And so with us: not to our generals and poets, I thought, but to the Italian and Hungarian laborers in the Subway, rather, ought the monuments of gratitude and reverence of a city like Boston to be reared.

If any of you have been readers of Tolstoï, you will see that I passed into a vein of feeling similar to his, with its abhorrence of all that conventionally passes for distinguished, and its exclusive deification of the bravery, patience, kindliness, and dumbness of the unconscious natural man.

Where now is *our* Tolstoï, I said, to bring the truth of all this home to our American bosoms, fill us with a better insight, and wean us away from that spurious literary romanticism on which our wretched culture—as it calls itself—is fed? Divinity lies all about us, and culture is too hide-bound to even suspect the fact. Could a Howells or a Kipling be enlisted in this mission? or are they still too deep in the ancestral blindness, and not humane enough for the inner joy and meaning of the laborer's existence to be really revealed? Must we wait for some one born and bred and living as a laborer himself, but who, by grace of Heaven, shall also find a literary voice?

And there I rested on that day, with a sense of widening of vision, and with what it is surely fair to call an increase of religious insight into life. In God's eyes the differences of social position, of intellect, of culture, of cleanliness, of dress, which different men exhibit, and all the other rarities and exceptions on which they so fantastically pin their pride, must be so small as practically quite to vanish; and all that should remain is the common fact that here we are, a countless multitude of vessels of life, each of us pent in to peculiar difficulties, with which we must severally struggle by using whatever of fortitude and goodness we can summon up. The exercise of the courage, patience, and kindness, must be the significant portion of the whole business; and the distinctions of position can only be a manner of diversifying the phenomenal surface upon which these underground virtues may manifest their effects. At this rate, the deepest human life is everywhere, is eternal. And, if any human attributes exist only in particular individuals, they must belong to the mere trapping and decoration of the surface-show.

Thus are men's lives levelled up as well as levelled down—levelled up in their common inner meaning, levelled down in their outer gloriousness and show. Yet always, we must confess, this levelling insight tends to be obscured again; and always the ancestral blindness returns and wraps us up, so that we end once more by thinking that creation can be for no other purpose than to develop remarkable situations and conventional distinctions and merits. And then always some new leveller in the shape of a religious prophet has to arise—the Buddha, the Christ, or some Saint Francis, some Rousseau or Tolstoï—to redispel our blindness. Yet, little by little, there comes some stable gain; for the world does get more humane, and the religion of democracy tends toward permanent increase.

This, as I said, became for a time my conviction, and gave me great content. I have put the matter into the form of a personal reminiscence, so that I might lead you into it more directly and completely, and so save time. But now I am going to discuss the rest of it with you in a more impersonal way.

Tolstoï's levelling philosophy began long before he had the crisis of melancholy commemorated in that wonderful document of his entitled 'My Confession,' which led the way to his more specifically religious works. In his masterpiece *War and Peace*—assuredly the greatest of human novels—the rôle of the spiritual hero is given to a poor little soldier named Karataïeff, so helpful, so cheerful, and so devout that, in spite of his ignorance and filthiness, the sight of him opens the heavens, which have been closed, to the mind of the principal character of the book; and his example evidently is meant by Tolstoï to let God into the world again for the reader. Poor little Karataïeff is taken prisoner by the French; and, when too exhausted by hardship and fever to march, is shot as other prisoners were in the famous retreat from Moscow. The last view one gets of him is his little figure leaning against a white birch-tree, and uncomplainingly awaiting the end.

"The more," writes Tolstoï in the work 'My Confession,' "the more I examined the life of these laboring folks, the more persuaded I became that they veritably have faith, and get from it alone the sense and the possibility of life. . . . Contrariwise to those of our own class, who protest against destiny and grow indignant at its rigor, these people receive maladies and misfortunes without revolt, without opposition, and with a firm and tranquil confidence that all had to be like that, could not be otherwise, and that it is all right so. . . . The more we live by our intellect, the less we understand the meaning of life. We see only a cruel jest in suffering and death, whereas these people live, suffer, and draw near to death with tranquillity, and oftener than not with joy. . . . There are enormous multitudes of them happy with the most perfect happiness, although deprived of what for us is the sole good of life. Those who understand life's meaning, and know how to live and die thus, are to be counted not by twos, threes, tens, but by hundreds, thousands, millions. They labor quietly, endure privations and pains, live and die, and throughout everything see the good without seeing the vanity. I had to love these people. The more I entered into their life, the more I loved them; and the more it became possible for me to live, too. It came about not only that the life of our society, of the learned and of the rich, disgusted me—more than that, it lost all semblance of meaning in my eyes. All our actions, our deliberations, our sciences, our arts, all appeared to me with a new significance. I understood that these things might be charming pastimes, but that one need seek in them no depth, whereas the life of the hardworking populace, of that multitude of human beings who really contribute to existence, appeared to me in its true light. I understood that there veritably is life, that the meaning which life there receives is the truth; and I accepted it." [2]

In a similar way does Stevenson appeal to our piety toward the elemental virtue of mankind.

"What a wonderful thing," he writes, [3] "is this Man! How surprising are his attributes! Poor soul, here for so little, cast among so many hardships, savagely surrounded, savagely descended, irremediably condemned to prey upon his fellow-lives—who should have blamed him, had he been of a piece with his destiny and a being merely barbarous? . . . [Yet] it matters not where we look, under what climate we observe him, in what stage of society, in what depth of ignorance, burdened with what erroneous morality; in ships at sea, a man inured to hardship and vile pleasures, his brightest hope a fiddle in a tavern, and a bedizened trull who sells herself to rob him, and he, for all that, simple, innocent, cheerful, kindly like a child, constant to toil, brave to drown, for others; . . . in the slums of cities, moving among indifferent millions to mechanical employments, without hope of change in the future, with scarce a pleasure in the present, and yet true to his virtues, honest up to his lights, kind to his neighbors, tempted perhaps in vain by the bright gin-palace, . . . often repaying the world's scorn with service, often standing firm upon a scruple; . . . everywhere some virtue cherished or affected, everywhere some decency of thought and courage, everywhere the ensign of man's ineffectual goodness—ah! if I could show you this! If I could show you these men and women all the world over, in every stage of history, under every abuse of error, under every circumstance of failure, without hope, without help, without thanks, still obscurely fighting the lost fight of virtue, still clinging to some rag of honor, the poor jewel of their souls."

All this is as true as it is splendid, and terribly do we need our Tolstoïs and Stevensons to keep our sense for it alive.

Yet you remember the Irishman who, when asked, "Is not one man as good as another?" replied, "Yes; and a great deal better, too!" Similarly (it seems to me) does Tolstoï over-correct our social prejudices, when he makes his love of the peasant so exclusive, and hardens his heart toward the educated man as absolutely as he does. Grant that at Chautauqua there was little moral effort, little sweat or muscular strain in view. Still, deep down in the souls of the participants we may be sure that something of the sort was hid, some inner stress, some vital virtue not found wanting when required. And, after all, the question recurs, and forces itself upon us. Is it so certain that the surroundings and circumstances of the virtue do make so little difference in the importance of the result? Is the functional utility, the worth to the universe of a certain definite amount of courage, kindliness, and patience, no greater if the possessor of these virtues is in an educated situation, working out far-reaching tasks, than if he be an illiterate nobody, hewing wood and drawing water, just to keep himself alive? Tolstoï's philosophy, deeply enlightening though it certainly is, remains a false abstraction. It savors too much of that Oriental pessimism and nihilism of his, which declares the whole phenomenal world and its facts and their distinctions to be a cunning fraud.

A mere bare fraud is just what our Western common sense will never believe the phenomenal world to be. It admits fully that the inner joys and virtues are the *essential* part of life's business, but it is sure that *some* positive part is also played by the adjuncts of the show. If it is idiotic in romanticism to recognize the heroic only when it sees it labelled and dressed-up in books, it is really just as idiotic to see it only in the dirty boots and sweaty shirt of some one in the fields. It is with us really under every disguise: at Chautauqua; here in your college; in the stock-yards and on the freight-trains; and in the czar of Russia's court. But, instinctively, we make a combination of two things in judging the total significance of a human being. We feel it to be some sort of a product (if such a product only could be calculated) of his inner virtue *and* his outer place, neither singly taken, but both conjoined. If the outer differences had no meaning for life, why indeed should all this immense variety of them exist? They *must* be significant elements of the world as well.

Just test Tolstoï's deification of the mere manual laborer by the facts. This is what Mr. Walter Wyckoff, after working as an unskilled laborer in the demolition of some buildings at West Point, writes of the spiritual condition of the class of men to which he temporarily chose to belong:

"The salient features of our condition are plain enough. We are grown men, and are without a trade. In the labor-market we stand ready to sell to the highest bidder our mere muscular strength for so many hours each day. We are thus in the lowest grade of labor. And, selling our muscular strength in the open market for what it will bring, we sell it under peculiar conditions. It is all the capital that we have. We have no reserve means of subsistence, and cannot, therefore, stand off for a 'reserve price.' We sell under the necessity of satisfying imminent hunger. Broadly speaking, we must sell our labor or starve; and, as hunger is a matter of a few hours, and we have no other way of meeting this need, we must sell at once for what the market offers for our labor.

"Our employer is buying labor in a dear market, and he will certainly get from us as much work as he can at the price. The gang-boss is secured for this purpose, and thoroughly does he know his business. He has sole command of us. He never saw us before, and he will discharge us all when the débris is cleared away. In the meantime he must get from us, if he can, the utmost physical labor which we, individually and collectively, are capable of. If he should drive some of us to exhaustion, and we should not be able to continue at work, he would not be the loser; for the market would soon supply him with others to take our places.

"We are ignorant men, but so much we clearly see that we have sold our labor where we could sell it dearest, and our employer has bought it where he could buy it cheapest. He has paid high, and he must get all the labor that he can; and, by a strong instinct which possesses us, we shall part with as little as we can. From work like ours there seems to us to have been eliminated every element which constitutes the nobility of labor. We feel no personal pride in its progress, and no community of interest with our employer. There is none of the joy of responsibility, none of the sense of achievement, only the dull monotony of grinding toil, with the longing for the signal to quit work, and for our wages at the end.

"And being what we are, the dregs of the labor-market, and

having no certainty of permanent employment, and no organization among ourselves, we must expect to work under the watchful eye of a gang-boss, and be driven, like the wage-slaves that we are, through our tasks.

"All this is to tell us, in effect, that our lives are hard, barren, hopeless lives."

And such hard, barren, hopeless lives, surely, are not lives in which one ought to be willing permanently to remain. And why is this so? Is it because they are so dirty? Well, Nansen grew a great deal dirtier on his polar expedition; and we think none the worse of his life for that. Is it the insensibility? Our soldiers have to grow vastly more insensible, and we extol them to the skies. Is it the poverty? Poverty has been reckoned the crowning beauty of many a heroic career. Is it the slavery to a task, the loss of finer pleasures? Such slavery and loss are of the very essence of the higher fortitude, and are always counted to its credit—read the records of missionary devotion all over the world. It is not any one of these things, then, taken by itself—no, nor all of them together—that make such a life undesirable. A man might in truth live like an unskilled laborer, and do the work of one, and yet count as one of the noblest of God's creatures. Quite possibly there were some such persons in the gang that our author describes; but the current of their souls ran underground; and he was too steeped in the ancestral blindness to discern it.

If there *were* any such morally exceptional individuals, however, what made them different from the rest? It can only have been this—that their souls worked and endured in obedience to some inner *ideal,* while their comrades were not actuated by anything worthy of that name. These ideals of other lives are among those secrets that we can almost never penetrate, although something about the man may often tell us when they are there. In Mr. Wyckoff's own case we know exactly what the self-imposed ideal was. Partly he had stumped himself, as the boys say, to carry through a strenuous achievement; but mainly he wished to enlarge his sympathetic insight into fellow-lives. For this his sweat and toil acquire a certain heroic significance, and make us accord to him exceptional esteem. But it is easy to imagine his fellows with various other ideals. To say nothing of wives and babies, one may have been a convert of the Salvation Army, and had a nightingale singing of expiation and forgiveness in his heart all the while he labored. Or there might have been an apostle like Tolstoï himself, or his compatriot Bondareff, in the gang, voluntarily embracing labor as their religious mission. Class-loyalty was undoubtedly an ideal with many. And who knows how much of that higher manliness of poverty, of which Phillips Brooks has spoken so penetratingly, was or was not present in that gang?

"A rugged, barren land," says Phillips Brooks, "is poverty to live in—a land where I am thankful very often if I can get a berry or a root to eat. But living in it really, letting it bear witness to me of itself, not dishonoring it all the time by judging it after the standard of the other lands, gradually there come out its qualities. Behold! no land like this barren and naked land of poverty could show the moral geology of the world. See how the hard ribs . . . stand out strong and solid. No life like poverty could so get one to the heart of things and make men know their meaning, could so let us feel life and the world with all the soft cushions stripped off and thrown away. . . . Poverty makes men come very near each other, and recognize each other's human hearts; and poverty, highest and best of all, demands and cries out for faith in God. . . . I know how superficial and unfeeling, how like mere mockery, words in praise of poverty may seem. . . . But I am sure that the poor man's dignity and freedom, his self-respect and energy, depend upon his cordial knowledge that his poverty is a true region and kind of life, with its own chances of character, its own springs of happiness and revelations of God. Let him resist the characterlessness which often goes with being poor. Let him insist on respecting the condition where he lives. Let him learn to love it, so that by and by, (if) he grows rich, he shall go out of the low door of the old familiar poverty with a true pang of regret, and with a true honor for the narrow home in which he has lived so long." [4]

The barrenness and ignobleness of the more usual laborer's life consist in the fact that it is moved by no such ideal inner springs. The backache, the long hours, the danger, are patiently endured—for what? To gain a quid of tobacco, a glass of beer, a cup of coffee, a meal, and a bed, and to begin again the next day and shirk as much as one can. This really is why we raise no monument to the laborers in the Subway, even though they be our conscripts, and even though after a fashion our city is indeed based upon their patient hearts and enduring backs and shoulders. And this is why we do raise monuments to our soldiers, whose outward conditions were even brutaller still. The soldiers are supposed to have followed an ideal, and the laborers are supposed to have followed none.

You see, my friends, how the plot now thickens; and how strangely the complexities of this wonderful human nature of ours begin to develop under our hands. We have seen the blindness and deadness to each other which are our natural inheritance; and, in spite of them, we have been led to acknowledge an inner meaning which passeth show, and which may be present in the lives of others where we least descry it. And now we are led to say that such inner meaning can be *complete* and *valid for us also*, only when the inner joy, courage, and endurance are joined with an ideal.

But what, exactly, do we mean by an ideal? Can we give no definite account of such a word?

To a certain extent we can. An ideal, for instance, must be something intellectually conceived, something of which we are not unconscious, if we have it; and it must carry with it that sort of outlook, uplift, and brightness that go with all intellectual facts. Secondly, there must be *novelty* in an ideal —novelty at least for him whom the ideal grasps. Sodden routine is incompatible with ideality, although what is sodden routine for one person may be ideal novelty for another. This shows that there is nothing absolutely ideal: ideals are relative to the lives that entertain them. To keep out of the gutter is for us here no part of consciousness at all, yet for many of our brethren it is the most legitimately engrossing of ideals.

Now, taken nakedly, abstractly, and immediately, you see that mere ideals are the cheapest things in life. Everybody has them in some shape or other, personal or general, sound or mistaken, low or high; and the most worthless sentimentalists and dreamers, drunkards, shirks and verse-makers, who never show a grain of effort, courage, or endurance, possibly have them on the most copious scale. Education, enlarging as it does our horizon and perspective, is a means of multiplying our ideals, of bringing new ones into view. And your college professor, with a starched shirt and spectacles, would, if a stock of ideals were all alone by itself enough to render a life significant, be the most absolutely and deeply significant of men. Tolstoï would be completely blind in despising him for a prig, a pedant and a parody; and all our new insight into the divinity of muscular labor would be altogether off the track of truth.

But such consequences as this, you instinctively feel, are erroneous. The more ideals a man has, the more contemptible, on the whole, do you continue to deem him, if the matter ends there for him, and if none of the laboring man's virtues are called into action on his part—no courage shown, no privations undergone, no dirt or scars contracted in the attempt to get them realized. It is quite obvious that something more than the mere possession of ideals is required to make a life significant in any sense that claims the spectator's admiration. Inner joy, to be sure, it may *have*, with its ideals; but that is its own private sentimental matter. To extort from us, outsiders as we are, with our own ideals to look after, the tribute of our grudging recognition, it must back its ideal visions with what the laborers have, the sterner stuff of manly virtue; it must multiply their sentimental surface by the dimension of the active will, if we are to have *depth*, if we are to have anything cubical and solid in the way of character.

The significance of a human life for communicable and publicly recognizable purposes is thus the offspring of a marriage of two different parents, either of whom alone is barren. The ideals taken by themselves give no reality, the virtues by themselves no novelty. And let the orientalists and pessimists say what they will, the thing of deepest—or, at any rate, of comparatively deepest—significance in life does seem to be its character of *progress*, or that strange union of reality with ideal novelty which it continues from one moment to another to present. To recognize ideal novelty is the task of what we call intelligence. Not every one's intelligence can tell which novelties are ideal. For many the ideal thing will always seem to cling still to the older more familiar good. In this case character, though not significant totally, may be still significant pathetically. So, if we are to choose which is the more essential factor of human character, the fighting virtue or the intellectual breadth, we must side with Tolstoï and choose that simple faithfulness to his light or darkness which any common unintellectual man can show.

But, with all this beating and tacking on my part, I fear you take me to be reaching a confused result. I seem to be just taking things up and dropping them again. First I took up Chautauqua, and dropped that; then Tolstoï and the heroism of common toil, and dropped them; finally, I took up ideals, and seem now almost dropping those. But please observe in what sense it is that I drop them. It is when they pretend *singly* to redeem life from insignificance. Culture and refinement all alone are not enough to do so. Ideal aspirations are not enough, when uncombined with pluck and will. But neither are pluck and will, dogged endurance and insensibility to danger enough, when taken all alone. There must be some sort of fusion, some chemical combination among these principles, for a life objectively and thoroughly significant to result.

Of course, this is a somewhat vague conclusion. But in a question of significance, of worth, like this, conclusions can never be precise. The answer of appreciation, of sentiment, is always a more or a less, a balance struck by sympathy, insight, and good will. But it is an answer, all the same, a real conclusion. And, in the course of getting it, it seems to me that our eyes have been opened to many important things. Some of you are, perhaps, more livingly aware than you were an hour ago of the depths of worth that lie around you, hid in alien lives. And, when you ask how much sympathy you ought to bestow, although the amount is, truly enough, a matter of ideal on your own part, yet in this notion of the combination of ideals with active virtues you have a rough standard for shaping your decision. In any case, your imagination is extended. You divine in the world about you matter for a little more humility on your own part, and tolerance, reverence, and love for others; and you gain a certain inner joyfulness at the increased importance of our common life. Such joyfulness is a religious inspiration and an element of spiritual health, and worth more than large amounts of that sort of technical and accurate information which we professors are supposed to be able to impart.

To show the sort of thing I mean by these words, I will just make one brief practical illustration, and then close.

We are suffering today in America from what is called the labor-question; and, when you go out into the world, you will each and all of you be caught up in its perplexities. I use the brief term labor-question to cover all sorts of anarchistic discontents and socialistic projects, and the conservative resistances which they provoke. So far as this conflict is unhealthy and regrettable—and I think it is so only to a limited extent—the unhealthiness consists solely in the fact that one-half of our fellow-countrymen remain entirely blind to the internal significance of the lives of the other half. They miss the joys and sorrows, they fail to feel the moral virtue, and they do not guess the presence of the intellectual ideals. They are at cross-purposes all along the line, regarding each other as they might regard a set of dangerously gesticulating automata, or, if they seek to get at the inner motivation, making the most horrible mistakes. Often all that the poor man can think of in the rich man is a cowardly greediness for safety, luxury, and effeminacy, and a boundless affectation. What he is, is not a human being, but a pocket-book, a bank-account. And a similar greediness, turned by disappointment into envy, is all that many rich men can see in the state of mind of the dissatisfied poor. And, if the rich man begins to do the sentimental act over the poor man, what senseless blunders does he make, pitying him for just those very duties and those very immunities which, rightly taken, are the condition of his most abiding and characteristic joys! Each, in short, ignores the fact that happiness and unhappiness and significance are a vital mystery; each pins them absolutely on some ridiculous feature of the external situation; and everybody remains outside of everybody else's sight.

Society has, with all this, undoubtedly got to pass toward some newer and better equilibrium, and the distribution of wealth has doubtless slowly got to change: such changes have always happened, and will happen to the end of time. But if, after all that I have said, any of you expect that they will make any *genuine vital difference* on a large scale, to the lives of our descendants, you will have missed the significance of my entire lecture. The solid meaning of life is always the same eternal thing—the marriage, namely, of some unhabitual ideal, however special, with some fidelity, courage, and endurance; with some man's or woman's pains. And, whatever or wherever life may be, there will always be the chance for that marriage to take place.

Fitz-James Stephen wrote many years ago words to this effect more eloquent than any I can speak: "The 'Great Eastern,' or some of her successors," he said, "will perhaps

defy the roll of the Atlantic, and cross the seas without allow-
ing their passengers to feel that they have left the firm land.
The voyage from the cradle to the grave may come to be performed with similar facility. Progress and science may perhaps
enable untold millions to live and die without a care, without
a pang, without an anxiety. They will have a pleasant passage
and plenty of brilliant conversation. They will wonder that
men ever believed at all in clanging fights and blazing towns
and sinking ships and praying hands; and, when they come
to the end of their course, they will go their way, and the
place thereof will know them no more. But it seems unlikely
that they will have such a knowledge of the great ocean on
which they sail, with its storms and wrecks, its currents and
icebergs, its huge waves and mighty winds, as those who
battled with it for years together in the little craft, which, if
they had few other merits, brought those who navigated them
full into the presence of time and eternity, their maker and
themselves, and forced them to have some definite view of
their relations to them and to each other." [5]

In this solid and tridimensional sense, so to call it, those
philosophers are right who contend that the world is a standing thing, with no progress, no real history. The changing
conditions of history touch only the surface of the show. The
altered equilibriums and redistributions only diversify our
opportunities and open chances to us for new ideals. But,
with each new ideal that comes into life, the chance for a life
based on some old ideal will vanish; and he would needs be
a presumptuous calculator who should with confidence say
that the total sum of significances is positively and absolutely
greater at any one epoch than at any other of the world.

I am speaking broadly, I know, and omitting to consider
certain qualifications in which I myself believe. But one can
only make one point in one lecture, and I shall be well content
if I have brought my point home to you this evening in even
a slight degree. *There are compensations:* and no outward
changes of condition in life can keep the nightingale of its
eternal meaning from singing in all sorts of different men's
hearts. That is the main fact to remember. If we could not
only admit it with our lips, but really and truly believe it,
how our convulsive insistencies, how our antipathies and
dreads of each other, would soften down! If the poor and

the rich could look at each other in this way, *sub specie
æternatis,* how gentle would grow their disputes! what tolerance and good humor, what willingness to live and let live,
would come into the world!

THE MORAL EQUIVALENT
OF WAR [1]

The war against war is going to be no holiday excursion or camping party. The military feelings are too deeply grounded to abdicate their place among our ideals until better substitutes are offered than the glory and shame that come to nations as well as to individuals from the ups and downs of politics and the vicissitudes of trade. There is something highly paradoxical in the modern man's relation to war. Ask all our millions, north and south, whether they would vote now (were such a thing possible) to have our war for the Union expunged from history, and the record of a peaceful transition to the present time substituted for that of its marches and battles, and probably hardly a handful of eccentrics would say yes. Those ancestors, those efforts, those memories and legends, are the most ideal part of what we now own together, a sacred spiritual possession worth more than all the blood poured out. Yet ask those same people whether they would be willing in cold blood to start another civil war now to gain another similar possession, and not one man or woman would vote for the proposition. In modern eyes, precious though wars may be, they must not be waged solely for the sake of the ideal harvest. Only when forced upon one, only when an enemy's injustice leaves us no alternative, is a war now thought permissible.

It was not thus in ancient times. The earlier men were hunting men, and to hunt a neighboring tribe, kill the males, loot the village and possess the females, was the most profitable, as well as the most exciting, way of living. Thus were the more martial tribes selected, and in chiefs and people a pure pugnacity and love of glory came to mingle with the more fundamental appetite for plunder.

Modern war is so expensive that we feel trade to be a better avenue to plunder; but modern man inherits all the innate pugnacity and all the love of glory of his ancestors. Showing war's irrationality and horror is of no effect upon him. The horrors make the fascination. War is the *strong* life; it is life *in extremis;* war-taxes are the only ones men never hesitate to pay, as the budgets of all nations show us.

History is a bath of blood. The Iliad is one long recital of how Diomedes and Ajax, Sarpedon and Hector *killed*. No detail of the wounds they made is spared us, and the Greek mind fed upon the story. Greek history is a panorama of jingoism and imperialism—war for war's sake, all the citizens being warriors. It is horrible reading, because of the irrationality of it all—save for the purpose of making "history"— and the history is that of the utter ruin of a civilization in intellectual respects perhaps the highest the earth has ever seen.

Those wars were purely piratical. Pride, gold, women, slaves, excitement, were their only motives. In the Peloponnesian war for example, the Athenians ask the inhabitants of Melos (the island where the "Venus of Milo" was found), hitherto neutral, to own their lordship. The envoys meet, and hold a debate which Thucydides gives in full, and which, for sweet reasonableness of form, would have satisfied Matthew Arnold. "The powerful exact what they can," said the Athenians, "and the weak grant what they must." When the Meleans say that sooner than be slaves they will appeal to the gods, the Athenians reply: "Of the gods we believe and of men we know that, by a law of their nature, wherever they can rule they will. This law was not made by us, and we are not the first to have acted upon it; we did but inherit it, and we know that you and all mankind, if you were as strong as we are, would do as we do. So much for the gods; we have told you why we expect to stand as high in their good opinion as you." Well, the Meleans still refused, and their town was taken. "The Athenians," Thucydides quietly says, "thereupon put to death all who were of military age and made slaves of the women and children. They then colonized the island, sending thither five hundred settlers of their own."

Alexander's career was piracy pure and simple, nothing but an orgy of power and plunder, made romantic by the character of the hero. There was no rational principle in it, and the moment he died his generals and governors attacked one another. The cruelty of those times is incredible. When Rome finally conquered Greece, Paulus Aemilius was told by the Roman Senate to reward his soldiers for their toil by "giving" them the old kingdom of Epirus. They sacked seventy cities and carried off a hundred and fifty thousand inhabitants as slaves. How many they killed I know not; but in Etolia they killed all the senators, five hundred and fifty in number. Brutus was "the noblest Roman of them all," but to reanimate his soldiers on the eve of Philippi he similarly promises to give them the cities of Sparta and Thessalonica to ravage, if they win the fight.

Such was the gory nurse that trained societies to cohesiveness. We inherit the warlike type; and for most of the capacities of heroism that the human race is full of we have to thank this cruel history. Dead men tell no tales, and if there were any tribes of other type than this they have left no survivors. Our ancestors have bred pugnacity into our bone and marrow, and thousands of years of peace won't breed it out of us. The popular imagination fairly fattens on the thought of wars. Let public opinion once reach a certain fighting pitch, and no ruler can withstand it. In the Boer war both governments began with bluff but couldn't stay there, the military tension was too much for them. In 1898 our people had read the word "war" in letters three inches high for three months in every newspaper. The pliant politician McKinley was swept away by their eagerness, and our squalid war with Spain became a necessity.

At the present day, civilized opinion is a curious mental mixture. The military instincts and ideals are as strong as ever, but are confronted by reflective criticisms which sorely curb their ancient freedom. Innumerable writers are showing up the bestial side of military service. Pure loot and mastery seem no longer morally avowable motives, and pretexts must be found for attributing them solely to the enemy. England and we, our army and navy authorities repeat without ceasing, arm solely for "peace," Germany and Japan it is who are bent on loot and glory. "Peace" in military mouths today is a synonym for "war expected." The word has become a pure provocative, and no government wishing peace sincerely should allow it ever to be printed in a newspaper. Every up-to-date dictionary should say that "peace" and "war" mean the same thing, now *in posse*, now *in actu*. It may even reasonably be said that the intensely sharp competitive *preparation* for war by the nations *is the real war*, permanent, unceasing; and that the battles are only a sort of public verification of the mastery gained during the "peace"-interval.

It is plain that on this subject civilized man has developed a sort of double personality. If we take European nations, no legitimate interest of any one of them would seem to justify the tremendous destructions which a war to compass it would necessarily entail. It would seem as though common sense and reason ought to find a way to reach agreement in every conflict of honest interests. I myself think it our bounden duty to believe in such international rationality as possible. But, as things stand, I see how desperately hard it is to bring the peace-party and the war-party together, and I believe that the difficulty is due to certain deficiencies in the program of pacificism which set the militarist imagination strongly, and to a certain extent justifiably, against it. In the whole discussion both sides are on imaginative and sentimental ground. It is but one utopia against another, and everything one says must be abstract and hypothetical. Subject to this criticism and caution, I will try to characterize in abstract strokes the opposite imaginative forces, and point out what to my own very fallible mind seems the best utopian hypothesis, the most promising line of conciliation.

In my remarks, pacificist though I am, I will refuse to speak of the bestial side of the war-*régime* (already done justice to by many writers) and consider only the higher aspects of militaristic sentiment. Patriotism no one thinks discreditable; nor does any one deny that war is the romance of history. But inordinate ambitions are the soul of every patriotism, and the possibility of violent death the soul of all romance. The militarily patriotic and romantic-minded everywhere, and especially the professional military class, refuse to admit for a moment that war may be a transitory phenomenon in social evolution. The notion of a sheep's paradise like that revolts, they say, our higher imagination. Where then would be the steeps of life? If war had ever stopped, we should have to re-invent it, on this view, to redeem life from flat degeneration.

Reflective apologists for war at the present day all take it religiously. It is a sort of sacrament. Its profits are to the vanquished as well as to the victor; and quite apart from any question of profit, it is an absolute good, we are told, for it is human nature at its highest dynamic. Its "horrors" are a cheap price to pay for rescue from the only alternative supposed, of a world of clerks and teachers, of co-educational and zo-ophily, of "consumer's leagues" and "associated charities," of industrialism unlimited, and femininism unabashed. No scorn, no hardness, no valor any more! Fie upon such a cattle-yard of a planet!

So far as the central essence of this feeling goes, no healthy minded person, it seems to me, can help to some degree partaking of it. Militarism is the great preserver of our ideals of hardihood, and human life with no use for hardihood would be contemptible. Without risks or prizes for the darer, history would be insipid indeed; and there is a type of military character which every one feels that the race should never cease to breed, for every one is sensitive to its superiority. The duty is incumbent on mankind, of keeping military characters in stock—of keeping them, if not for use, then as ends in themselves and as pure pieces of perfection—so that Roosevelt's weaklings and mollycoddles may not end by making everything else disappear from the face of nature.

This natural sort of feeling forms, I think, the innermost soul of army-writings. Without any exception known to me, militarist authors take a highly mystical view of their subject, and regard war as a biological or sociological necessity, uncontrolled by ordinary psychological checks and motives. When the time of development is ripe the war must come, reason or no reason, for the justifications pleaded are invariably fictitious. War is, in short, a permanent human *obligation*. General Homer Lea, in his recent book *The Valor of Ignorance*, plants himself squarely on this ground. Readiness for war is for him the essence of nationality, and ability in it the supreme measure of the health of nations.

Nations, General Lea says, are never stationary—they must necessarily expand or shrink, according to their vitality or decrepitude. Japan now is culminating; and by the fatal law in question it is impossible that her statesmen should not long since have entered, with extraordinary foresight, upon a vast policy of conquest—the game in which the first moves were her wars with China and Russia and her treaty with England, and of which the final objective is the capture of the Philippines, the Hawaiian Islands, Alaska, and the whole of our Coast west of the Sierra Passes. This will give Japan what her ineluctable vocation as a state absolute forces her to claim, the possession of the entire Pacific Ocean; and to oppose these deep designs we Americans have, according to our author, nothing but our conceit, our ignorance, our commercialism, our corruption, and our feminism. General Lea makes a minute technical comparison of the military strength which we at present could oppose to the strength of Japan, and concludes that the islands, Alaska, Oregon, and Southern California, would fall almost without resistance, that San Francisco must surrender in a fortnight to a Japanese investment, that in three or four months the war would be over, and our republic, unable to regain what it had heedlessly neglected to protect sufficiently, would then "disintegrate," until perhaps some Cæsar should arise to weld us again into a nation.

A dismal forecast indeed! Yet not unplausible, if the mentality of Japan's statesmen be of the Cæsarian type of which history shows so many examples, and which is all that General Lea seems able to imagine. But there is no reason to think that women can no longer be the mothers of Napoleonic or Alexandrian characters; and if these come in Japan and find their opportunity, just such surprises as *The Valor of Ignorance* paints may lurk in ambush for us. Ignorant as we still are of the innermost recesses of Japanese mentality, we may be foolhardy to disregard such possibilities.

Other militarists are more complex and more moral in their considerations. The *Philosophie des Krieges*, by S. R. Steinmetz is a good example. War, according to this author, is an ordeal instituted by God, who weighs the nations in its balance. It is the essential form of the State, and the only function in which peoples can employ all their powers at once and convergently. No victory is possible save as the resultant of a totality of virtues, no defeat for which some vice or weakness is not responsible. Fidelity, cohesiveness, tenacity, heroism, conscience, education, inventiveness, economy, wealth, physical health and vigor—there isn't a moral or intellectual point of superiority that doesn't tell, when God holds his assizes and hurls the peoples upon one another. *Die Weltgeschichte ist das Weltgericht;* and Dr. Steinmetz does not believe that in the long run chance and luck play any part in apportioning the issues.

The virtues that prevail, it must be noted, are virtues anyhow, superiorities that count in peaceful as well as in military competition; but the strain on them, being infinitely intenser in the latter case, makes war infinitely more searching as a trial. No ordeal is comparable to its winnowings. Its dread hammer is the welder of men into cohesive states, and nowhere but in such states can human nature adequately develop its capacity. The only alternative is "degeneration."

Dr. Steinmetz is a conscientious thinker, and his book, short as it is, takes much into account. Its upshot can, it seems to me, be summed up in Simon Patten's word, that mankind was nursed in pain and fear, and that the transition to a "pleasure-economy" may be fatal to a being wielding no powers of defence against its disintegrative influences. If we speak of the *fear of emancipation from the fear-régime*, we put the whole situation into a single phrase; fear regarding ourselves now taking the place of the ancient fear of the enemy.

Turn the fear over as I will in my mind, it all seems to lead back to two unwillingnesses of the imagination, one æsthetic, and the other moral; unwillingness, first to envisage a future in which army-life, with its many elements of charm, shall be forever impossible, and in which the destinies of peoples shall nevermore be decided quickly, thrillingly, and tragically, by force, but only gradually and insipidly by "evolution"; and, secondly, unwillingness to see the supreme theatre of human strenuousness closed, and the splendid military aptitudes of men doomed to keep always in a state of latency and never show themselves in action. These insistent unwillingnesses, no less than other æsthetic and ethical insistencies, have, it seems to me, to be listened to and respected. One cannot meet them effectively by mere counter-insistency on war's expensiveness and horror. The horror makes the thrill; and when the question is of getting the extremest and supremest out of human nature, talk of expense sounds ignominious. The weakness of so much merely negative criticism is evident—pacificism makes no converts from the military party. The military party denies neither the bestiality nor the horror, nor the expense; it only says that these things tell but half the story. It only says that war is *worth* them;

that, taking human nature as a whole, its wars are its best protection against its weaker and more cowardly self, and that mankind cannot *afford* to adopt a peace-economy.

Pacificists ought to enter more deeply into the æsthetical and ethical point of view of their opponents. Do that first in any controversy, says J. J. Chapman, *then move the point*, and your opponent will follow. So long as anti-militarists propose no substitute for war's disciplinary function, no *moral equivalent* of war, analogous, as one might say, to the mechanical equivalent of heat, so long they fail to realize the full inwardness of the situation. And as a rule they do fail. The duties, penalties, and sanctions pictured in the utopias they paint are all too weak and tame to touch the military-minded. Tolstoï's pacificism is the only exception to this rule, for it is profoundly pessimistic as regards all this world's values, and makes the fear of the Lord furnish the moral spur provided elsewhere by the fear of the enemy. But our socialistic peace-advocates all believe absolutely in this world's values; and instead of the fear of the Lord and the fear of the enemy, the only fear they reckon with is the fear of poverty if one be lazy. This weakness pervades all the socialistic literature with which I am acquainted. Even in Lowes Dickinson's exquisite dialogue, high wages and short hours are the only forces invoked for overcoming man's distaste for repulsive kinds of labor. Meanwhile men at large still live as they always have lived, under a pain-and-fear economy—for those of us who live in an ease-economy are but an island in the stormy ocean —and the whole atmosphere of present-day utopian literature tastes mawkish and dishwatery to people who still keep a sense for life's more bitter flavors. It suggests, in truth, ubiquitous inferiority.

Inferiority is always with us, and merciless scorn of it is the keynote of the military temper. "Dogs, would you live for-ever?" shouted Frederick the Great. "Yes," say our utopians, "let us live forever, and raise our level gradually." The best thing about our "inferiors" today is that they are as tough as nails, and physically and morally almost as insensitive. Utopianism would see them soft and squeamish, while militarism would keep their callousness, but transfigure it into a meritorious characteristic, needed by "the service," and redeemed by that from the suspicion of inferiority. All the qualities of a man acquire dignity when he knows that the service of the collectivity that owns him needs them. If proud of the collectivity, his own pride rises in proportion. No collectivity is like an army for nourishing such pride; but it has to be confessed that the only sentiment which the image of pacific cosmopolitan industrialism is capable of arousing in countless worthy breasts is shame at the idea of belonging to *such* a collectivity. It is obvious that the United States of America as they exist today impress a mind like General Lea's as so much human blubber. Where is the sharpness and precipitousness, the contempt for life, whether one's own, or another's? Where is the savage "yes" and "no," the unconditional duty? Where is the conscription? Where is the blood-tax? Where is anything that one feels honored by belonging to?

Having said thus much in preparation, I will now confess my own utopia. I devoutly believe in the reign of peace and in the gradual advent of some sort of a socialistic equilibrium. The fatalistic view of the war-function is to me nonsense, for I know that war-making is due to definite motives and subject to prudential checks and reasonable criticisms, just like any other form of enterprise. And when whole nations are the armies, and the science of destruction vies in intellectual refinement with the sciences of production, I see that war becomes absurd and impossible from its own monstrosity. Extravagant ambitions will have to be replaced by reasonable claims, and nations must make common cause against them. I see no reason why all this should not apply to yellow as well as to white countries, and I look forward to a future when acts of war shall be formally outlawed as between civilized peoples.

All these beliefs of mine put me squarely into the anti-militarist party. But I do not believe that peace either ought to be or will be permanent on this globe, unless the states pacifically organized preserve some of the old elements of army-discipline. A permanently successful peace-economy cannot be a simple pleasure-economy. In the more or less socialistic future towards which mankind seems drifting we must still subject ourselves collectively to those severities which answer to our real position upon this only partly hospitable globe. We must make new energies and hardihoods continue the manliness to which the military mind so faithfully clings. Martial virtues must be the enduring cement; intrepidity, contempt of softness, surrender of private interest, obedience to command, must still remain the rock upon which states are built—unless, indeed, we wish for dangerous reactions against commonwealths fit only for contempt, and liable to invite attack whenever a centre of crystallization for military-minded enterprise gets formed anywhere in their neighborhood.

The war-party is assuredly right in affirming and reaffirming that the martial virtues, although originally gained by the race through war, are absolute and permanent human goods. Patriotic pride and ambition in their military form are, after all, only specifications of a more general competitive passion. They are its first form, but that is no reason for supposing them to be its last form. Men now are proud of belonging to a conquering nation, and without a murmur they lay down their persons and their wealth, if by so doing they may fend off subjection. But who can be sure that *other aspects of one's country* may not, with time and education and suggestion enough, come to be regarded with similarly effective feelings of pride and shame? Why should men not some day feel that it is worth a blood-tax to belong to a collectivity superior in *any* ideal respect? Why should they not blush with indignant shame if the community that owns them is vile in any way whatsoever? Individuals, daily more numerous, now feel this civic passion. It is only a question of blowing on the spark till the whole population gets incandescent, and on the ruins of the old morals of military honor, a stable system of morals of civic honor builds itself up. What the whole community comes to believe in grasps the individual as in a vise. The war-function has grasped us so far; but constructive interests may some day seem no less imperative, and impose on the individual a hardly lighter burden.

Let me illustrate my idea more concretely. There is nothing to make one indignant in the mere fact that life is hard, that men should toil and suffer pain. The planetary conditions once for all are such, and we can stand it. But that so many men, by mere accidents of birth and opportunity, should have a life of *nothing else* but toil and pain and hardness and inferiority imposed upon them, should have *no* vacation, while others natively no more deserving never get any taste of this campaigning life at all—*this* is capable of arousing indignation in reflective minds. It may end by seeming shameful to all of us that some of us have nothing but campaigning, and others nothing but unmanly ease. If now—and this is my idea— there were, instead of military conscription a conscription of the whole youthful population to form for a certain number of years a part of the army enlisted against *Nature*, the injustice would tend to be evened out, and numerous other goods to the commonwealth would follow. The military ideals of hardihood and discipline would be wrought into the growing fibre of the people; no one would remain blind as the luxurious classes now are blind, to man's relations to the globe he lives on, and to the permanently sour and hard foundations of his higher life. To coal and iron mines, to freight trains, to fishing fleets in December, to dishwashing, clothes-washing, and window-washing, to road-building and tunnel-making, to foundries and stoke-holes, and to the frames of skyscrapers, would our gilded youths be drafted off, according to their choice, to get the childishness knocked out of them, and to come back into society with healthier sympathies and soberer ideas. They would have paid their blood-tax, done their own part in the immemorial human warfare against nature; they would tread the earth more proudly, the women would value them more highly, they would be better fathers and teachers of the following generation.

Such a conscription, with the state of public opinion that would have required it, and the many moral fruits it would bear, would preserve in the midst of a pacific civilization the manly virtues which the military party is so afraid of seeing disappear in peace. We should get toughness without callousness, authority with as little criminal cruelty as possible, and painful work done cheerily because the duty is temporary, and threatens not, as now, to degrade the whole remainder of one's life. I spoke of the "moral equivalent" of war. So far, war has been the only force that can discipline a whole community, and until an equivalent discipline is organized, I believe that war must have its way. But I have no serious doubt that the ordinary prides and shames of social man, once developed to a certain intensity, are capable of organizing such a moral equivalent as I have sketched, or some other just as effective for preserving manliness of type. It is but a question of time, of skilful propagandism, and of opinion-making men seizing historic opportunities.

The martial type of character can be bred without war. Strenuous honor and disinterestedness abound elsewhere. Priests and medical men are in a fashion educated to it, and we should all feel some degree of it imperative if we were conscious of our work as an obligatory service to the state. We should be *owned*, as soldiers are by the army, and our pride would rise accordingly. We could be poor, then, without humiliation, as army officers now are. The only thing needed henceforward is to inflame the civic temper as past history has inflamed the military temper. H. G. Wells, as usual, sees the centre of the situation. "In many ways," he says, "military organization is the most peaceful of activities. When the contemporary man steps from the street, of clamorous insincere advertisement, push, adulteration, underselling and intermittent employment into the barrack-yard, he steps on to a higher social plane, into an atmosphere of service and coöperation and of infinitely more honorable emulations. Here at least men are not flung out of employment to degenerate because there is no immediate work for them to do. They are fed and drilled and trained for better services. Here at least a man is supposed to win promotion by self-forgetfulness and not by self-seeking. And beside the feeble and irregular endowment of research by commercialism, its little short-sighted snatches at profit by innovation and scientific economy, see how remarkable is the steady and rapid development of method and appliances in naval and military affairs! Nothing is more striking than to compare the progress of civil conveniences which has been left almost entirely to the trader, to the progress in military apparatus during the last few decades. The house-appliances of today, for example, are little better than they were fifty years ago. A house of today is still almost as ill-ventilated, badly heated by wasteful fires, clumsily arranged and furnished as the house of 1858. Houses a couple of hundred years old are still satisfactory places of residence, so little have our standards risen. But the rifle or battleship of fifty years ago was beyond all comparison inferior to those we possess; in power, in speed, in convenience alike. No one has a use now for such superannuated things." [3]

Wells adds [4] that he thinks that the conceptions of order and discipline, the tradition of service and devotion, of physical fitness, unstinted exertion, and universal responsibility, which universal military duty is now teaching European nations, will remain a permanent acquisition, when the last ammunition has been used in the fireworks that celebrate the final peace. I believe as he does. It would be simply preposterous if the only force that could work ideals of honor and standards of efficiency into English or American natures should be the fear of being killed by the Germans or Japanese. Great indeed is Fear; but it is not, as our military enthusiasts believe and try to make us believe, the only stimulus known for awakening the higher ranges of men's spiritual energy. The amount of alteration in public opinion which my utopia postulates is vastly less than the difference between the mentality of those black warriors who pursued Stanley's party on the Congo with their cannibal war-cry of "Meat! Meat!" and that of the "general staff" of any civilized nation. History has seen the latter interval bridged over: the former one can be bridged over much more easily.

NOTES

THE PRESENT DILEMMA IN PHILOSOPHY

[1] Morrison I. Swift, *Human Submission,* Part Second, Philadelphia Liberty Press, 1905, pp. 4-10.

WHAT PRAGMATISM MEANS

[1] Translated in the *Revue Philosophique* for January, 1879 (vol. vii).

[2] "Theorie und Praxis," *Zeitsch. des Oesterreichischen Ingenieur u. Architecten-Vereines,* 1905, Nr. 4 u. 6. I find a still more radical pragmatism than Ostwald's in an address by Professor W. S. Franklin: "I think that the sickliest notion of physics, even if a student gets it, is that it is 'the science of masses, molecules, and the ether.' And I think that the healthiest notion, even if a student does not wholly get it, is that physics is the science of the ways of taking hold of bodies and pushing them!" (*Science,* January 2, 1903.)

SOME METAPHYSICAL PROBLEMS PRAGMATICALLY CONSIDERED

[1] *The Foundations of Belief,* p. 30.

THE ONE AND THE MANY

[1] Compare A. Bellanger: *Les concepts de Cause, et l'activité intentionelle de l'Esprit.* Paris, Alcan, 1905, p. 79 ff.

[2] *The Conception of God,* New York, 1897, p. 292.

[3] Compare on the Ultimate, Mr. Schiller's essay "Activity and Substance," in his book entitled *Humanism,* p. 204.

PRAGMATISM AND COMMON SENSE

[1] *The Life of Reason: Reason in Common Sense*, 1905, p. 59.

PRAGMATISM'S CONCEPTION OF TRUTH

[1] A. E. Taylor, *Philosophical Review*, vol. xiv, p. 288.

[2] H. Rickert, *Der Gegenstand der Erkenntniss*, chapter on "Die Urtheilsnothwendigkeit."

[3] I am not forgetting that Professor Rickert long ago gave up the whole notion of truth being founded on agreement with reality. Reality according to him, is whatever agrees with truth, and truth is founded solely on our primal duty. This fantastic flight, together with Mr. Joachim's candid confession of failure in his book *The Nature of Truth*, seems to me to mark the bankruptcy of rationalism when dealing with this subject. Rickert deals with part of the pragmatistic position under the head of what he calls "Relativismus." I can not discuss his text here. Suffice it to say that his argumentation in that chapter is so feeble as to seem almost incredible in so generally able a writer.

PRAGMATISM AND HUMANISM

[1] *Personal Idealism*, p. 60.

[2] Mr. Taylor in his *Elements of Metaphysics* uses this excellent pragmatic definition.

AUTHOR'S PREFACE TO THE MEANING OF TRUTH

[1] But *"verifiability,"* I add, "is as good as verification. For one truth-process completed, there are a million in our lives that function in [the] state of nascency. They lead us towards direct verification; lead us into the surroundings of the object they envisage; and then, if everything runs on harmoniously, we are so sure that verification is possible that we omit it, and are usually justified by all that happens."

[2] *Op. cit.*, p. 75.

[3] It gives me pleasure to welcome Professor Carveth Read into the pragmatistic church, so far as his epistemology goes. See his vigorous book, *The Metaphysics of Nature*, 2d Edition, Appendix A. (London, Black, 1908.) The work *What is Reality?* by Francis Howe Johnson (Boston, 1891), of which I make the acquaintance only while correcting these proofs, contains some striking anticipations of the later pragmatist view. *The Psychology of Thinking*, by

Irving E. Miller (New York, Macmillan Co., 1909), which has just appeared, is one of the most convincing pragmatist documents yet published, tho it does not use the word "pragmatism" at all. While I am making references, I cannot refrain from inserting one to the extraordinarily acute article by H. V. Knox, in the *Quarterly Review* for April, 1909.

THE FUNCTION OF COGNITION

[1] Read before the Aristotelian Society, December 1, 1884, and first published in *Mind*, vol. x (1885). This, and the following articles have received a very slight verbal revision, consisting mostly in the omission of redundancy.

[2] "The Relativity of Knowledge," held in this sense, is, it may be observed in passing, one of the oddest of philosophic superstitions. Whatever facts may be cited in its favor are due to the properties of nerve-tissue, which may be exhausted by too prolonged an excitement. Patients with neuralgias that last unremittingly for days can, however, assure us that the limits of this nerve-law are pretty widely drawn. But if we physically could get a feeling that should last eternally unchanged, what atom of logical or psychological argument is there to prove that it would not be felt as long as it lasted, and felt for just what it is, all that time? The reason for the opposite prejudice seems to be our reluctance to think that so *stupid* a thing as such a feeling would necessarily be, should be allowed to fill eternity with its presence. An interminable acquaintance, leading to no knowledge-*about*—such would be its condition.

[3] See, for example, Green's Introduction to Hume's *Treatise of Human Nature*, p. 36.

[4] If A enters and B exclaims, "Didn't you see my brother on the stairs?" we all hold that A may answer, "I saw him, but didn't know he was your brother;" ignorance of brotherhood not abolishing power to see. But those who, on account of the unrelatedness of the first facts with which we become acquainted, deny them to be "known" to us, ought in consistency to maintain that if A did not perceive the relationship of the man on the stairs to B, it was impossible he should have noticed him at all.

[5] It seems odd to call so important a function accidental, but I do not see how we can mend the matter. Just as, if we start with the reality and ask how it may come to be known, we can only reply by invoking a feeling which shall *reconstruct* it in its own more private fashion; so, if we start with the feeling and ask how it may come to know, we can only reply by invoking a reality which shall *reconstruct* it in its own more public fashion. In either case, however, the datum we start with remains just what it was. One may easily get lost in verbal mysteries about the difference between quality of feeling and feeling of quality, between receiving and

reconstructing the knowledge of a reality. But at the end we must confess that the notion of real cognition involves an unmediated dualism of the knower and the known. See Bowne's *Metaphysics*, New York, 1882, pp. 403-412, and various passages in Lotze, *e.g.*, *Logic* § 308. ["Unmediated" is a bad word to have used. 1909.]

[6] The thoroughgoing objector might, it is true, still return to the charge, and, granting a dream which should completely mirror the real universe, and all the actions dreamed in which should be instantly matched by duplicate actions in this universe, still insist that this is nothing more than harmony, and that it is as far as ever from being made clear whether the dream-world refers to that other world, all of whose details it so closely copies. This objection leads deep into metaphysics. I do not impugn its importance, and justice obliges me to say that but for the teachings of my colleague, Dr. Josiah Royce, I should neither have grasped its full force nor made my own practical and psychological point of view as clear to myself as it is. On this occasion I prefer to stick steadfastly to that point of view; but I hope that Dr. Royce's more fundamental criticism of the function of cognition may ere long see the light. [I referred in this note to Royce's *Religious aspect of philosophy*, then about to be published. This powerful book maintained that the notion of *referring* involved that of an inclusive mind that shall own both the real *q* and the mental *q*, and use the latter expressly as a representative symbol of the former. At the time I could not refute this transcendentalist opinion. Later, largely through the influence of Professor D. S. Miller (see his essay "The Meaning of Truth and Error," in the *Philosophical Review* for 1893, vol. 2, p. 403) I came to see that any definitely experienceable workings would serve as intermediaries quite as well as the absolute mind's intentions would.]

[7] That is, there is no *real* "Ivanhoe," not even the one in Sir Walter Scott's mind as he was writing the story. That one is only the *first* one of the Ivanhoe-solipsisms. It is quite true we can make it the real Ivanhoe if we like, and then say that the other Ivanhoes know it or do not know it, according as they refer to and resemble it or no. This is done by bringing in Sir Walter Scott himself as the author of the real Ivanhoe, and so making a complex object of both. This object, however, is not a story pure and simple. It has dynamic relations with the world common to the experience of all readers. Sir Walter Scott's Ivanhoe got itself printed in volumes which we all can handle, and to any one of which we can refer to see which of our versions be the true one, *i. e.*, the original one of Scott himself. We can see the manuscript; in short we can get back to the Ivanhoe in Scott's mind by many an avenue and channel of this real world of our experience—a thing we can by no means do with either the Ivanhoe or the Rebecca, either the Templar or the Isaac of York, of the story taken simply as such, and detached from the conditions of its production. Everywhere, then, we have the same test: can we pass continuously from two objects

in two minds to a third object which seems to be in *both* minds, because each mind feels every modification imprinted on it by the other? If so, the first two objects named are derivatives, to say the least, from the same third object, and may be held, if they resemble each other, to refer to one and the same reality.

[8] Among such errors are those cases in which our feeling operates on a reality which it does partially resemble, and yet does not intend: as for instance, when I take up your umbrella, meaning to take my own. I cannot be said here either to know your umbrella, or my own, which latter my feeling more completely resembles. I am mistaking them both, misrepresenting their context, etc.

We have spoken in the text as if the critic were necessarily one mind, and the feeling criticised another. But the criticised feeling and its critic may be earlier and later feelings of the same mind, and here it might seem that we could dispense with the notion of operating, to prove that critic and criticised are referring to and meaning to represent the *same*. We think we see our past feelings directly, and know what they refer to without appeal. At the worst, we can always fix the intention of our present feeling and *make* it refer to the same reality to which any one of our past feelings may have referred. So we need no "operating" here, to make sure that the feeling and its critic mean the same real *q*. Well, all the better if this is so! We have covered the more complex and difficult case in our text, and we may let this easier one go. The main thing at present is to stick to practical psychology, and ignore metaphysical difficulties.

One more remark. Our formula contains, it will be observed, nothing to correspond to the great principle of cognition laid down by Professor Ferrier in his *Institutes of Metaphysic* and apparently adopted by all the followers of Fichte, the principle, namely, that for knowledge to be constituted there must be knowledge of the knowing mind along with whatever else is known: not *q*, as we have supposed, but *q plus myself*, must be the least I can know. It is certain that the common sense of mankind never dreams of using any such principle when it tries to discriminate between conscious states that are knowledge and conscious states that are not. So that Ferrier's principle, if it have any relevancy at all, must have relevancy to the metaphysical possibility of consciousness at large, and not to the practically recognized constitution of cognitive consciousness. We may therefore pass it by without further notice here.

[9] Is an incomplete "thought about" that reality, that reality is its "topic," etc.

[10] Though both might terminate in the same thing and be incomplete thoughts "about" it.

[11] The difference between Idealism and Realism is immaterial here. What is said in the text is consistent with either theory. A law by which my percept shall change yours directly is no more mysterious than a law by which it shall first change a physical reality, and

then the reality change yours. In either case you and I seem knit into a continuous world, and not to form a pair of solipsisms.

[12] "There is no distinction of meaning so fine as to consist in anything but a possible difference of practice. . . . It appears, then, that the rule for attaining the [highest] grade of clearness of apprehension is as follows: Consider what effects, which might conceivably have practical bearings, we conceive the object of our conception to have. Then, our conception of these effects is the whole of our conception of the object." Charles S. Peirce: "How to make our Ideas clear," in *Popular Science Monthly*, New York, January, 1878, p. 293.

THE TIGERS IN INDIA

[1] Extracts from a presidential address before the American Psychological Association, published in the *Psychological Review*, vol. ii, p. 105 (1895).

[2] A stone in one field may "fit," we say, a hole in another field. But the relation of "fitting," so long as no one carries the stone to the hole and drops it in, is only one name for the fact that such an act *may* happen. Similarly with the knowing of the tigers here and now. It is only an anticipatory name for a further associative and terminative process that *may* occur.

[3] See Dr. Miller's articles on Truth and Error, and on Content and Function, in the *Philosophical Review*, July, 1893, and Nov., 1895.

[4] What is meant by this is that "the experience" can be referred to either of two great associative systems, that of the experiencer's

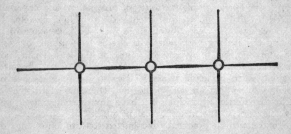

mental history, or that of the experienced facts of the world. Of both of these systems it forms part, and may be regarded, indeed, as one of their points of intersection. One might let a vertical line stand for the mental history; but the same object, O, appears also in the mental history of different persons, represented by the other vertical lines. It thus ceases to be the private property of one experience, and becomes so to speak, a shared or public thing. We can track its outer history in this way, and represent it by the horizontal line. [It is also known representatively at other points of the vertical lines, or intuitively there again, so that the line of its outer history would have to be looped and wandering, but I make it straight for simplicity's sake.] In any case, however, it is the same *stuff* that figures in all the sets of lines.

⁵ [The reader will observe that the text is written from the point of view of *naif* realism or common sense, and avoids raising the idealistic controversy.]

HUMANISM AND TRUTH

¹ Reprinted, with slight verbal revision, from *Mind*, vol. xiii, N. S., p. 457 (October, 1904). A couple of interpolations from another article in *Mind*, "Humanism and truth once more," in vol. xiv, have been made.

² ["Practical" in the sense of *particular*, of course, not in the sense that the consequences may not be *mental* as well as physical.]

³ I know of no "mere" pragmatist, if *mereness* here means, as it seems to, the denial of all concreteness to the pragmatist's thought.

⁴ [I cannot forbear quoting as an illustration of the contrast between humanist and rationalist tempers of mind, in a sphere remote from philosophy, these remarks on the Dreyfus "affaire," written by one who assuredly had never heard of humanism or pragmatism. "Autant que la Révolution," l'Affaire' est désormais une de nos 'origines.' Si elle n'a pas fait ouvrir le gouffre, c'est elle du moins qui a rendu patent et visible le long travail souterrain qui, silencieusement, avait preparé la séparation entre nos deux camps d'aujourd'hui, pour écarter enfin, d'un coup soudain, *la France des traditionalistes (poseurs de principes, chercheurs d'unité, constructeurs de systèmes à priori) et la France éprise du fait positif et de libre examen;*—la France révolutionnaire et romantique si l'on veut, celle qui met très haut l'individu, qui ne veut pas qu'un juste périsse, fût-ce pour sauver la nation, et qui cherche la vérité dans toutes ses parties aussi bien que dans une vue d'ensemble. . . . Duclaux ne pouvait pas concevoir qu'on préferât quelque chose à la vérité. Mais il voyait autour de lui de fort honnêtes gens qui, mettant en balance la vie d'un homme et la raison d'Etat, lui avouaient de quel poids léger ils jugeaient une simple existence individuelle, pour innocente qu'elle fût. *C'etaient des classiques, des gens à qui l'ensemble seul importe.*" *La Vie de Emile Duclaux,* par Mme. Em. D., Laval, 1906, pp. 243, 247-248.]

⁵ Vol. ii, pp. 641 ff.

⁶ [Mental things which are realities of course within the mental world.]

⁷ In an article criticising Pragmatism (as he conceives it) in the *McGill University Quarterly* published at Montreal, for May, 1904.

⁸ This is meant merely to exclude reality of an "unknowable" sort, of which no account in either perceptual or conceptual terms can

be given. It includes of course any amount of empirical reality independent of the knower. Pragmatism is thus "epistemologically" realistic in its account.

AUTHOR'S PREFACE TO THE WILL TO BELIEVE AND OTHER ESSAYS

[1] B. P. Blood: *The Flaw in Supremacy:* Published by the Author, Amsterdam, N. Y., 1853.

THE WILL TO BELIEVE

[1] An Address to the Philosophical Clubs of Yale and Brown Universities. Published in the New World, June, 1896.

[2] Compare the admirable page 310 in S.H. Hodgson's *Time and Space*, London, 1865.

[3] Compare Wilfrid Ward's Essay, "The Wish to Believe," in his *Witnesses to the Unseen*, Macmillan & Co., 1893.

[4] Since belief is measured by action, he who forbids us to believe religion to be true, necessarily also forbids us to act as we should if we did believe it to be true. The whole defence of religious faith hinges upon action. If the action required or inspired by the religious hypothesis is in no way different from that dictated by the naturalistic hypothesis, then religious faith is pure superfluity, better pruned away, and controversy about its legitimacy is a piece of idle trifling, unworthy of serious minds. I myself believe, of course, that the religious hypothesis gives to the world an expression which specifically determines our reactions, and makes them in a large part unlike what they might be on a purely naturalistic scheme of belief.

[5] *Liberty, Equality, Fraternity*, p. 353, 2nd. edition. London, 1874.

THE MORAL PHILOSOPHER AND THE MORAL LIFE

[1] An Address to the Yale Philosophical Club, published in the *International Journal of Ethics*, April, 1891.

[2] *The Principles of Psychology*, New York, H. Holt & Co. 1890.

[3] All this is set forth with great freshness and force in the work of my colleague, Professor Josiah Royce: *The Religious Aspect of Philosophy*. Boston, 1885.

THE GOSPEL OF RELAXATION

[1] Fleming H. Revell Company, New York.

ON A CERTAIN BLINDNESS IN HUMAN BEINGS

[1] "The Lantern-bearers," in the volume entitled *Across the Plains*. Abridged in the quotation.
[2] *The Religious Aspects of Philosophy*, pp. 157-162 (abridged).
[3] De Sénacour: *Obermann*, Lettre XXX.
[4] *The Prelude*, Book III.
[5] *The Prelude*, Book IV.
[6] *Op. cit.*, Boston, Roberts, 1883, pp. 5, 6.
[7] "Crossing Brooklyn's Ferry" (abridged).
[8] "Calamus," Boston, 1897, pp. 41, 42.
[9] *Vita*, lib. 2, chap. iv.
[10] *La Guerre et la Paix*, Paris, 1884, vol. iii. pp. 268, 275, 316.
[11] Quoted by Lotze, *Microcosmus*, English translation, vol. ii, p. 240.
[12] *Op. cit.*, pp. 210-222 (abridged).

WHAT MAKES A LIFE SIGNIFICANT?

[1] This address was composed before the Cuban and Philippine wars. Such outbursts of the passion of mastery are, however, only episodes in social process which in the long run seems everywhere tending toward the Chautauquan ideals.
[2] *My Confession*, X. (condensed).
[3] *Across the Plains:* "Pulvis et Umbra" (abridged).
[4] *Sermons, 5th Series*, New York, 1893, pp. 166, 167.
[5] *Essays by a Barrister*, London, 1862, p. 318.

THE MORAL EQUIVALENT OF WAR

[1] Written for and first published by the Association for International Conciliation (Leaflet No. 27) and also published in *McClure's Magazine*, August, 1910, and *The Popular Science Monthly*, October, 1910.
[2] "Justice and Liberty," N.Y., 1909.
[3] *First and Last Things*, 1908, p. 215.
[4] *Ibid.*, p. 226.

Look for these popular titles from Washington Square Press at your bookseller now

Toni Morrison
THE BLUEST EYE

An unusual, haunting, and profound novel of yearning and despair in black America by the award-winning author of <u>Song of Solomon</u> and <u>Tar Baby</u>.
44720-3 / $2.75 / 160 pp.

John Sayles
UNION DUES

A National Book Award nominee, <u>Union Dues</u> is a novel about the life and love, the corruption and survival of a father and son.
82109-1 / $2.50 / 400 pp.

Wallace Stegner
THE BIG ROCK CANDY MOUNTAIN

The Pulitzer Prize-winning author's first major novel, the story of a drifter who throws everything away in search of a magic land where he can be himself.
82804-5 / $2.75 / 640 pp.

Don DeLillo
END ZONE

A brilliant novel of love, death, and the new gladiators by "the writer Vonnegut, Barth and Pynchon were once oddly and variously taken to be"—<u>Washington Post.</u>
82012-5 / $1.95 / 208 pp.

John Irving
THE HOTEL NEW HAMPSHIRE

The bestselling author of <u>The World According to Garp</u> follows the eccentric Berry family across two continents in this "startlingly original" (<u>Time</u>) novel.
44027-6 / $3.95 / 560 pp.

WSP

WASHINGTON SQUARE PRESS
Published by Pocket Books

Look for these popular titles from Washington Square Press at your bookseller now

Graham Greene
THE END OF THE AFFAIR
"One of the best, most true and moving novels of my time, in anybody's language"—William Faulkner.
44535-9/$2.95/240 pp.

THE HONORARY CONSUL
A compelling tale of political intrigue and heartfelt passion by "the finest living novelist, bar none, in our language"—Harper's.
42881-0/$3.95/320 pp.

ORIENT EXPRESS
A stunning novel of violence and psychological intrigue.
43514-0/$2.75/256 pp.

Joan Didion
PLAY IT AS IT LAYS
At the center of this powerful novel is Maria, a young actress caught off balance by Hollywood, her husband, her hopelessly retarded daughter—and most of all, herself.
43596-5/$2.75/266 pp.

RUN RIVER
An unforgettable novel from one of America's most elegant and brilliant writers.
44258-9/$2.95/256 pp.